David T. Schick
70

me

D0606206

Liberalism and the Moral Life

Liberalism and the Moral Life

EDITED BY

NANCY L. ROSENBLUM

HARVARD UNIVERSITY PRESS
Cambridge, Massachusetts
London, England
1989

Copyright © 1989 by the President and Fellows of Harvard College
All rights reserved
Printed in the United States of America
10 9 8 7 6 5 4 3 2 1

This book is printed on acid-free paper, and its binding materials have been chosen for strength and durability.

Library of Congress Cataloging-in-Publication Data

Liberalism and the moral life / edited by Nancy L. Rosenblum.
    p. cm.
    Bibliography: p.
    Includes index.
    Contents: Introduction / Nancy L. Rosenblum—The liberalism of fear / Judith N. Shklar—Humanist liberalism / Susan Moller Okin—Liberal democracy and the costs of consent / Benjamin R. Barber—Undemocratic education / Amy Gutmann—Civic education in the liberal state / William Galston—Class conflict and constitutionalism in J. S. Mill's thought / Richard Ashcraft—Making sense of moral conflict / Steven Lukes—Liberal dialogue versus a critical theory of discursive legitimation / Seyla Benhabib—Cross purposes: the liberal-communitarian debate / Charles Taylor—Democratic individuality and the meaning of rights / George Kateb—Pluralism and self-defense / Nancy L. Rosenblum—The permanent structure of antiliberal thought / Stephen Holmes.
    ISBN 0-674-53020-9 (alk. paper)
    1. Liberalism—Moral and ethical aspects. 2. Social values. I. Rosenblum, Nancy L., 1947– .
JC571.L5375 1989
320.5'1—dc19   89-30983
                                          CIP

Contents

Liberalism and the Moral Life

Introduction

NANCY L. ROSENBLUM

Like any academic discipline, political theory has its internal dynamic: its dialogue and development, conceptual conflicts, and intellectual common ground. The immediate background to this volume is the ambitious reworking of liberal political thought that began in the 1960s in response to dissatisfaction with classic utilitarianism and to challenges from critics of liberalism on the political left. The most influential of these works in political philosophy is John Rawls's *A Theory of Justice* (1971). For almost twenty years, Rawls and other theorists have worked to broaden liberalism's foundations beyond its conventional basis in Locke, drawing on sophisticated versions of social-choice theory and on the moral and political arguments of Kant and Hume. They have used these resources to reassert the priority of personal liberty—but also to extend liberalism beyond its classical preoccupation with liberty, taking up questions of distributive justice, among others. This renaissance of liberal theory inspired a fresh spate of criticism, mainly from republicans and communitarians who appeal to Aristotle and Hegel and to a recently revived tradition of civic humanism. The latest phase of this discussion has focused on liberalism's relation to moral life, and the authors of the chapters in this book situate themselves on or at the margins of the map of liberalism they are helping to redraw.

Developments within the field of political theory are only part of the picture, however; they take place against the background of external political events. Witnesses to the 1988 United States presidential elections will have little difficulty recalling the political climate when this book was being written; it may have helped to shape the authors' arguments, and it certainly adds to their import. During that campaign, "liberal" was used as a pejorative term. It was identified narrowly with the growth of government and with the welfare state, and welfare-state liberalism has come to be associated with indifference to the moral effects of policies. "Liberalism" has become a negative label signaling a lack of concern for character and moral education, the displacement of parental authority, and the erosion of every vestige of shared values—in particular civic virtue among men and women who see themselves as beneficiaries of government services rather than as responsible citizens.

The identification of liberalism with welfarism is bound to be provocative, certainly to political theorists who are aware that the map of liberalism is liberally dotted with libertarian defenders of free-market arrangements and with civil libertarians mainly concerned with a set of basic rights and the legal institutions that support them. Equating liberalism with egalitarianism is especially jolting because for most of its history liberalism was concerned almost exclusively with questions of personal liberty, privacy, civil rights, and due process. Indeed, liberals have had to defend themselves against socialists and egalitarians for this lapse, and those liberal theorists who argued for greater substantive equality had to fight a hard fight (and still do) against ideological resistance from within as well as without. All this is forgotten in the partisan politics of the day, which in the United States is blatantly, bizarrely, antiliberal. Political theorists writing against a background where liberalism is a term of abuse also know that the main antiliberal catchwords—"community," for example, or "values," or the older "Moral Majority"—are alien to mainstream democratic politics in a way that programs to insure a minimum of social security are not; these have been entrenched in practice and approved by public opinion since the time of Franklin Delano Roosevelt.

Political rhetoric may not help us to chart accurately the field of liberal political thought, but it does provide an incentive to do so. Moreover, it points up a curiosity that needs explaining: at the same time that rhetorical assaults are on the rise in the electoral arena, there is an unmistakable surge of serious reflection on the nature and advantages of liberalism, to which political theorists in America and abroad increasingly turn their attention. Political conditions that make up the deeper background to these essays go some way toward explaining both the openings for partisan attack and the reasons why at another level liberalism is once again compelling.

One development is the continuing decline of the intellectual hold of Marxism, certainly of Marxist utopianism, in both the communist societies of eastern Europe and the industrial democracies of the West. The inadequacies of liberal democratic welfare states seem less severe compared to the desperate productive and distributive failures of many socialist economies, and the equally plain fact that central ownership and planning have not promoted a widespread sense of justice any more than they have produced prosperity. The merits of markets and private ownership (especially if they are considered undogmatically and in the context of concrete difficulties) are important aspects of liberalism's resurgence. The failure of Marxism either to eliminate ethnic and religious pluralism or to accommodate pluralist claims is probably even more important. And there is the unceasing demand for political liberty in states where rights are tenuous and arbitrariness is an everyday experience. In this context, the characteristic strengths of liberal democracy emerge, pointing up the fact that liberalism has survived the century, outliving the transitional historical stage to which it was consigned by Marxist theory and to which it has sometimes seemed doomed by crushing tyrannies of the right as well. The survival of liberalism has insured its intellectual life. Versions of liberal theory proliferate, along with interpretations of their relative suitability for understanding, evaluating, and prescribing for the political world. Our fin de siècle has begun with a veritable "liberalizing" of political thought.

This is not to suggest that every radical alternative to liberalism has been exhausted or found wanting. Critical Theory continues its challenges (as do other more esoteric forms of radicalism); communal and individualist anarchism are untried; feminist objections to liberalism abound. Still, events have helped to reduce the fascination of other doctrines, putting liberal theory and the institutions it supports once again at the center of study; political and intellectual energies have turned there, in Great Britian and France especially.

Since few American political theorists ever stray too far from liberalism, their interest appears less dramatic, but political developments have affected their thinking too. The rise of conservative challenges is the most important. It has resulted in attacks on traditional freedoms of the press in Great Britain and on newer rights to privacy (including the right of women to choose abortion) in the United States; it has meant a falling off of the spirit of toleration let alone respect for differences, and, as we have seen, disparagement if not dismantling of the welfare state. There is a well-documented programmatic division within conservatism today, between social

conservatism and economic libertarianism. And in political philosophy the variations are even more complex. Nothing is more striking
than the rapid increase in strands of thought that may not be avowedly
conservative but that assign priority to responsibility to community
over personal liberty, while rejecting the socialist emphasis on a collectivist economy. Today the premier challenges to liberalism in
political philosophy are Catholic, civic republican, and the communitarianism that champions the particularist claims of groups, families, or "traditions of shared meaning" against neutral principles and
universal rights. This new wave of antiliberalism cannot be ascribed
to the loosening of Marxism's hold on intellectuals, but it is the
beneficiary of the waning of radical thought. As even the New Left
has lost its subversive thrust, the way is clear for civic republicans
and communitarians to represent themselves as the bearers of visions
of a new morality and new society.

The outstanding common characteristic of the present challenge to
liberalism is its moralistic cast, its disdain for what it sees as the moral
purposes and justifications of conventional liberalism. Not all criticisms of liberalism are moral criticisms. Consider the familiar authoritarian attacks on the workings of liberal government: the claim
that liberal democracies are weak and unable to preserve order, or
the claim that the bonds of liberal societies are so loose and anomic
that they are incapable of collective action—especially in war. It is a
peculiarity of antiliberalism today to be moralistic rather than pragmatic. The problem with liberal democracy is that it is not gripping
and fails to mold the moral identity of individuals; the problem with
pluralism is that its tendency toward political compromise is corrupt,
a falling away from shared values and the common good. Obsession
with liberalism's moral failing is nothing new. But this time liberal
theorists are not demoralized by attacks. On the contrary, they have
been inspired to rethink, as the authors of these essays do, whether
and how liberalism allows, supports, inculcates, and preserves a defensible view of moral life.

Current political conditions have had a number of consequences
for political thought. One is that liberalism has emerged as *the* political
theory whose resources are most called upon, most severely tested
and extended, and most aggressively explained and justified. Another
is the proliferation of types of liberalism—not surprising since it has
become something of a residual theory for those disaffected with the
available historical alternatives. Finally, as dissatisfaction focuses increasingly on moral matters, an opening is created for political the-

orists to affirm in the strongest terms the positive connection betweeen liberalism and moral life.

I will try in this introduction to create some order out of the proliferating types of liberalism, the charges of moral failing to which they are peculiarly prone, and the varieties of response political theorists make as they move from defensive postures to positive, recognizably idealistic assertions of the moral claims of liberalism.

Liberalism is a political theory of limited government, providing institutional guarantees for personal liberty. It is clear enough what liberalism opposed in the past and must stand opposed to still: political absolutism and arbitrariness, and an array of officially sanctioned obstacles to the free exercise of religion, speech, and association. It protects at least some forms of private property and prohibits certain uses of wealth in public and private life. Although the boundary liberal theorists have drawn between public and private spheres is shifting and the content of rights is regularly redefined, its central political thesis—the need to defend individuals and groups against the oppressive demands and intrusions of authority—is plain. In contrast, liberalism's positive promise, especially its moral purposes and justifications, is more elusive. In part this is the result of the fact that liberalism has two faces.

One face of liberalism reflects moral idealism. Natural or individual rights and the personal liberty they prescribe had their origin in boldly articulated ideals. Enlightenment was one, and not a cold intellectual rationality but a beneficent reason that could produce real, humane consequences. Condorcet's liberalism, with its exquisitely detailed picture of moral progress, epitomizes this ideal, reminding us that liberalism has had an affinity to utopianism. Infinite perfectability, the hope of a radically transformed world, is not a necessary part of its moral idealism, however. Liberalism has also been seen as inseparable from security for religious faith as an essential element of moral life and for the realization of divinely sanctioned rights. And it has been seen as inseparable from the affirmation of secular moral purposes by autonomous individuals—keeping in mind that the heart of this vision is not an arid, circular argument for autonomy for its own sake but reasoned assent to substantive moral obligations. The relationship between liberalism and these various ideals has been conceived variously, too: as reflection, support, condition, or political embodiment. Constitutional government and personal and political rights are the political conditions most compatible with an undisturbed moral life, on one view. On a stronger view, they are necessary political conditions for the exercise of certain moral capacities that simply do not come into play at all in the absence of pluralism and personal freedom. And for some theorists, liberalism is more than just enabling; it has its own distinctive moral purposes and accompanying virtues, which justify its theory of government, give its institutions an educational character, and impose on those who enjoy liberty an obligation to enlightenment, or self-realization, or affirmation of respect for the dignity of others.

The other face of liberalism is resolutely turned away from moral idealism toward a sober political modus vivendi. It designs public laws and institutions that can be administered by a nation of devils and demands that public officials remain indifferent toward the pursuits of private life and to character so long as men and women are reasonably law-abiding. It recommends due process and equal protection as neutral, universally desirable defenses against official arbitrariness and abuse. And where diverse and rival interests and opinions (and moral justifications) are inescapable, liberalism prescribes a framework of institutions and procedures to break the violence of faction, as James Madison instructed, by bringing them into the frame of government. The alternatives to a pluralist modus vivendi must be avoided: separatist movements, or majority or minority tyranny, or civil war among communities each bound by a singular moral purpose. This deliberate distancing of government, and of justifications for government action, from official recognition of a view of the good life is not always based on moral skepticism. It may rest on the commonsense political skepticism born of historical experience. Time, which Thomas Paine thought makes more converts than reason, makes self-protection against the accumulation of power imperative, whatever its current form. There is nothing minimalist about modus-vivendi liberalism. The demands of impartiality are onerous; the institutional guarantees of due process and representation are complex; ultimately, this liberalism depends upon men and women having a keen psychological and historical sensibility.

Both idealist and modus-vivendi liberalism provoke charges of moral failing, and it is useful to designate two categories of criticism corresponding to the two faces of liberalism. The charge leveled mainly at liberal idealism assails the adequacy of its substantive ideals, or, alternatively, the offensiveness of its presumed indifference toward an aspect of moral life that liberalism, by privatizing it, seems to depreciate or neglect. The second type of charge, leveled mainly at modus-vivendi liberalism, is hypocrisy. It says that liberalism will-fully misrepresents its norms and institutions as uncontroversial, ex-aggerating its claim to inclusiveness and impartiality.

Those who accuse liberalism of moral failing often acknowledge that it rests on and promotes some moral vision for public and private life, but judge its values deficient, even depraved. Liberal virtues are really vices (greed, uncontrolled selfishness generally, intellectual hu-bris). Or signs of pathology (impartiality is a weird and abnormal sort of self-distancing). Or, critics charge that the inevitable conse-quence of liberal values is viciousness; for example, tolerance of a plurality of views of the good life weakens the duties and consolations of religion and invites abominable license. Liberalism's substantive values have often been described as bourgeois values, deficient because private ownership of most forms of property is itself morally unjus-tifiable, or because its inevitable accompaniment is conflict or obsta-cles to the self-realization of workers, or because the moral habits associated with the acquisition and preservation of property—making and abiding by contracts, for example—are intolerably cold and empty. Of course, it is also the case that what critics see as the absence of a specifically political or civic virtue is by itself a fatal lack, a terrible personal and collective deprivation that indicates the absence of a moral life in common and of virtues such as honor, loyalty, and courage.

Liberalism is perennially prone to these attacks, for one reason above all. Every version of liberal theory draws a boundary between public and private life. As a result it is vulnerable to the claim that some form of virtuous conduct has been assigned wrongly, or left out of consideration altogether. What belongs to public life has been erroneously privatized (ownership of productive forces, religious in-spiration, even personal identity itself, which is properly seen as con-stituted by citizenship). And what belongs to private life has been allowed to infiltrate and corrupt the public sphere (selfish economic interests, rigid contractual relations, scientific models of thinking). Liberalism is exposed to this attack on two fronts. Contemporary political theorists seize the opportunity to chart a creative, often so-ciologically sensitive, account of what is contained on either side of the public-private divide and the way in which this divide serves moral life.

Hypocrisy makes up the second line of attack, directed chiefly against modus-vivendi liberalism. It claims that liberal claims to gov-ernment impartiality are false, as are representations of reasons, rights, and benefits as universal. The array of arguments along these lines is familiar. Pluralist politics operates to the advantage of some groups over others; "pure tolerance" cuts against unpopular opinions and subversive ideas; impartiality itself is a partial and characteristically masculine norm that eclipses the distinctive moral attitudes and inclinations of women; the preference for so-called neutral goods such as material comfort or security is prejudicial to rival goods such as asceticism or heroic adventurism. Charges of self-delusion or blindness to the practical consequences of allegedly neutral principles are only slightly less hostile variations on this theme. That the division between public and private life, intended or not, inherently traps and exploits women is a familiar argument. Another is the claim that the unintended result of legalism and legalistic moralities is to create an adversarial culture; to elbow out a more expansive and empathic ethic of caring or reciprocity; to make it impossible to enjoy a community that is beautiful to its members for its particularities rather than its universalism.

We have come to expect the whole gamut of charges of moral deficiency and hypocrisy from antiliberals armed with a single, unified view of the good life and good society, who argue for some official orthodoxy and invite political authorities to promote, preserve, and enforce it—from Marxists and other socialists, fascists, authoritarians, some nationalists, religious fundamentalists, civic republicans, and feminist critics of patriarchy. And until recently, we have come to expect that the main line of defense by liberals will be grimly defensive. Indebted in both argument and tenor to Isaiah Berlin's "Two Concepts of Liberty," this response defines liberalism in terms of its commitment to a last protective frontier, a sacrosanct private realm immune from government interference and control. The expected moral justification for limited government and negative liberty is taken from Berlin as well: the idea that as much as possible men and women be left alone follows from the belief that there is a plurality of ultimate ends and that it is impossible to reconcile these incommensurable values.

This book reflects important changes that have emerged in the last several years. Today accusations about the moral failings of liberalism frequently come from North American political theorists who do not identify themselves with historic antiliberalism of the left or right and who do not advance a comprehensive moral agenda of their own. In "The Permanent Structure of Antiliberal Thought," Stephen Holmes describes the main outlines of nineteenth- and twentieth-century antiliberalism and points out the peculiar position of contemporary critics. They employ a set of arguments well known to those versed in the long history of European antiliberalism; their charges are not new. And they resort to a recurrent set of fallacies and distortions, which Holmes catalogues and dissects. At the same time, they tend to dissociate themselves from the anticipated political framework of left and right in a way Holmes finds disturbing. Some of the most vehement charges of liberalism's moral failing are leveled by political theorists whose opposition to liberal institutions may be qualified and who do not always part company with liberals on matters of policy, but who are reluctant to explain just when and why they do. It is clear that they are frankly repulsed by what they see as liberalism's lack of moral inspiration. They want moral uplift, and they want to find it in political theory. Yet they neither propose orthodox Marxist, democratic, or rightist alternatives nor resurrect the old idealism of revolutionary liberalism—rationality, enlightenment, progress, and autonomy.

In a parallel development, liberalism's defenders have assumed a new stance, too. They do not meet contemporary charges of moral deficiency by recapitulating the traditional argument for a sacrosanct private sphere, assigning all longings for moral life there. Nor do they found their defenses as much as before on moral skepticism or the possibility of discovering and applying neutral principles. Instead, political theorists are responding to the latest challenges with newly formulated visions of the moral life consistent with and supported by a liberal theory of government. They invent fresh arguments for individualism and its moral status. They consider whether there are distinctively liberal virtues and practices that are publicly recognized and constitute a moral life in common. Openings to arguments for moral education are seized. Increased notice is taken of the concrete social and institutional contexts, both actual and possible, for developing moral habits and expressing moral values. Theorists are also rethinking the nature of neutrality in public life, sharpening their definitions, identifying its objectives and limits, pointing out those opinions and institutions that are simply incompatible with liberalism. Even arguments for modus-vivendi liberalism are respirated.

While a schematic overview cannot do justice to these developments in liberal thought, it can help to highlight what is new. The sequence of essays in the book is thematic, but I have chosen to depart from that order here in the hope of creating some order of a different kind. I want to suggest that these essays represent three main approaches to the question of liberalism's relation to moral life. One approach responds directly to liberalism's critics: it asserts that even if their description of liberalism is accurate, their assessment is wrong. The argument is that liberalism contains moral resources overlooked by its critics (and sometimes by liberals themselves) and that these resources can be reclaimed and failings corrected. Another approach actively infuses liberalism with a new moral idealism. It is resonant of the world-transforming hopes of revolutionary liberalism, but it is soberly nonutopian in its attention to the evidence of inspiration and moral life in everyday practices. The third approach defends the idea of neutrality in public life, while acknowledging its limits and insisting that there are other justifications for neutrality besides moral indifference or moral skepticism.

One response of the first type accepts the criticism that liberalism has failed to realize its own moral ideals, without accepting that this failure is logical or inevitable. It reclaims these ideals and insists that liberalism has the resources to repair its failings. Most often the faith that must be kept is with universalism. Indeed, the history of liberal political thought in western Europe and America is a history of thinkers extending—sometimes reluctantly, sometimes willingly—moral assumptions and institutional protections to new groups. Liberal theorists attend to internal inconsistencies in accounts of who counts as rational or autonomous, and who should be admitted to democratic dialogue and deliberation. They recognize failures in affording individuals equal protection and the way substantive inequalities (among them unequal access to education or health care, employment or income) affect the worth of nominally universal rights.

In "Humanist Liberalism," Susan Okin carries on this work of inclusion from a feminist perspective. She shows that contemporary liberal theorists persist in developing arguments that have the appearance of universality but that on inspection exclude women; gender-neutral language is not a sure sign that gender is taken seriously. In particular, the ideal of autonomy conceals unacknowledged assumptions about moral self-development in the context of the family, whose structure has been historically unjust. Okin also shows that it is not a simple matter to include women; theoretically as well as practically, making universalism real requires changes in liberalism, among them recasting the separation of personal and public life. Yet she believes that if only we would attend to them, liberalism contains conceptual resources uniquely equipped to enable us to recognize the way government reinforces the gendered division of labor within the family, systematically imposing constraints on women, inhibiting their liberty and opportunities for individuality. And suitably recast but not erased, liberalism's notion of separate public and private spheres can relieve the oppression of women, while respecting privacy and individual differences.

In "Liberal Democracy and the Costs of Consent," Benjamin Barber sets himself a different task of reparation. He argues that although the idea of original consent had important liberating consequences, and the idea of periodic consent opened liberalism out to representative government, the thrust of consent is essentially resistant and reactive. Barber accepts the criticism that liberalism is negative, but he believes negativity can be turned around. He appeals to neglected aspects of liberal democratic thought that support active political participation in a way that preoccupation with consent does not. And he looks to participation for more than just self-protection. Liberal democracy, he argues, points beyond self-defense without going all the way to coercive unity; he calls this latent ideal "harmony."

Seyla Benhabib focuses on another element: the notion of liberalism as a political culture of public dialogue. In "Liberal Dialogue Versus a Critical Theory of Discursive Legitimation," she argues that liberal theorists often impose unjustifiable restraints on the content and scope of public dialogue, which inhibit its full potential as a way of legitimizing institutions and relations of power. She is especially critical of the tacit assumption that people know in advance of discussion what their moral positions are—an assumption that allows liberal theorists to exclude some differences and disagreements from public discussion in advance, designating them moral, religious, or aesthetic. This is an unjustifiable retreat to pragmatic reasoning, she argues, designed to insure peace more than normative justification. Moreover, exclusion and restraint are self-defeating, since it is only through dialogue that we come to understand the meaning issues have for us. Benhabib draws attention to the way oppression has been recognized and lifted only when social movements are able to move issues from private to public light and redefine them as matters of public policy: work conditions, civil rights, women's issues. Critical theory, she argues, supports liberalism's emphasis on proceduralism and dialogue in particular by showing that procedures are not purely formal, as some antiliberals charge, but replete with content and themselves subject to reflection and change. At the same time, critical theory stands as a severe challenge and corrective to the weakness of liberal models insofar as they have lost sight of dialogue's transforming possibility. Her "discourse model" offers a frankly utopian family of arguments for social practices embodying the principle of "egalitarian reciprocity."

Another approach of the first type also begins with the very elements of liberalism that critics call morally deficient. The chief business here, however, is less extension and inclusion than redescription. Critics misunderstand what they see, and liberal theorists redescribe the very features under attack in a way that is transforming. Judith Shklar does this in "The Liberalism of Fear," which pushes a familiar line of argument—the viciousness of the known political alternatives—in a new direction. The standard version of this defense concedes that liberalism is a morally truncated theory, prudent rather than inspired, but claims that assigning limited purposes to limited government is a lesser evil, just as liberalism's characteristic practices are lesser evils (acquisitiveness is less dangerous than solicitousness for the souls of others, or hunger for military glory). Shklar is unwilling to make this concession. She turns the tables on assailants of modus-vivendi liberalism. Liberalism is uniquely able to avoid the worst evils inflicted by governments because it is inspired by genuine moral insight into what is the worst. A coherent account of cruelty as an absolute political summum malum sustains the theory of limited government, she argues. Shklar rehabilitates liberalism's preoccupation with public cruelty and the official infliction of pain. From what some have called a modest (even degraded) attachment to "mere life" and to a political modus vivendi, she elicits a strong and universal moral foundation for self-protective liberalism.

Redescription is the approach I take in a chapter that tries to recover and reassess the pluralist face of liberalism. Individualist and communitarian critics of liberalism converge in their aversion to materialist individualism and to what they describe as a cold, fragmented, and unexpressive public life. Their recommended alternatives are respirited Emersonian individualism or the strong grip of civic community. In "Pluralism and Self-Defense," I argue that although these attacks on liberalism succeed in capturing a common experience of "romantic" aversion, they disregard the element of liberalism that provides an antidote to these discontents: pluralism—the existence of a complex social structure of groups and spheres, which disperses power and among which men and women can shift involvements. Diagnoses of liberalism that start out from either side of the individualist-communitarian dichotomy result in false pictures of pathology and in faulty prescriptions because they fail to recognize the mediating, transforming experience of pluralism. I review the political advantages of pluralism, but my argument focuses on shifting involvements among diverse groups and spheres as the condition and material for self-development. Pluralism makes exuberant Humboldtian promises of the self-realization of "beautiful souls" conceivable. More modestly, it is a resource for an elementary kind of self-defense, a protection against dreaded identification with one role and confinement to one place; against finitude, exhaustion, satiation, and ennui; against the frustration of familiar longings for individuality and self-expression that comes from too much "embeddedness" and "belonging." Ignoring pluralism is particularly costly, given the propensity of contemporary theorists to tie political arguments (especially arguments for community) to theories of the self. If we are to adopt the notion of the "constituted self" as a way of thinking about moral personality, then political theorists should take notice of the multiplicity of contexts in which self-formation actually goes on, and the way coherence can be drawn from differentiation.

Approaches of the first kind extend, reclaim, and redescribe familiar resources from within liberalism to meet contemporary challenges. In approaches of the second kind, political theorists respond to accusations of moral failing by actively infusing liberalism with a new, positive idealism. Their efforts have historical antecedents, but instead of turning to classical liberal ideals of enlightenment, natural rights, or autonomy, which may be stale or made vulnerable from misuse, political theorists tap fresh historical and philosophical resources. In "Democratic Individuality and the Meaning of Rights," George Kateb not only defends individualism against communitarian critics who fail to see it in all its fullness, but respirits it entirely. He speaks of the "idealism of individualism," dissociating it from narrow possessive individualism, showing its dependence on a broader tradition of individual rights, but ultimately attaching it to the inspired American individualism of Emerson, Thoreau, and Whitman. Liberal rights-based individualism provides the indispensable cultural setting for what Kateb calls "democratic individuality." The procedures and processes of rights-based individualism instruct citizens that government depends on their sufferance, educating them out of inferiority and docility, inviting them to demand recognition, mandating toleration. And "the mere absence of oppression and degradation is sweet." But for Kateb, individualism of rights exists for the sake of a still richer democratic individuality, which is its completion and perfection, and which aspires to still greater expressiveness, resistance, and responsiveness.

Kateb is not the only theorist to articulate a new idealism, or to marshall evidence that ideals are recognized and realized, even if imperfectly, in everyday thought and practice. Reconstructing possibilities for moral life within liberal democracy and attending to living instances where it is expressed also characterize Charles Taylor's chapter, "Cross-Purposes: The Liberal–Communitarian Debate"—though the infusion of moral idealism he performs is at the other end of the spectrum from Kateb's "democratic individuality."

Taylor charges political theorists with insensitivity to the fact that choice of an ontological position (the choice between atomism and holism) does not necessarily entail a choice of moral norms and public policies. Ontology and advocacy are distinct, he argues, and their relation is complex; atomism and holism structure the field of political possibilities without pointing directly to individualist or communitarian recommendations. Confusion about these issues has restricted our understanding of the range of options which it is meaningful to advocate. There have been not only atomist individualists and holist collectivists, Taylor reminds us, but also atomist collectivists and holist individualists who recognize that human agents are socially embedded but prize liberty and individual differences. He goes on to illustrate what is gained by unlinking ontology and advocacy. Atomistic ontology sees the common good as a convergence of individual goods, he argues, and excludes an understanding of an "immediate" common good whose good is that we share—the kind of common good that animates patriotism. Thus, the atomistic ontology he says is commonly adopted by liberal theorists inhibits them from recognizing patriotism where it exists. Taylor intends not only to defend the view that democratic society needs some commonly recognized definition of the good life but also to point to its presence within the liberal framework of American political life. Outrage at the crimes of Watergate was generated by a species of patriotic identification that is defined by commitment to certain "American" ideals, among them rule of law. Thus, a holist ontology can sensitize us to the fact that procedural liberalism rests on internalized discipline and that motivation for this discipline comes from republican solidarity. A procedural liberal can be a holist.

The third starting point for evaluating and countering charges of liberalism's moral deficiency is reconsideration of what is meant and demanded by neutrality. Political theorists approach the matter from a number of directions. The tools of analytic philosophy are employed to distinguish nondiscrimination and impartiality from neutrality and to show that even as a conceptual matter, neutrality in a designated range of disputes need not and should not be translated into an impossibly extensive neutrality with regard to every conflict of interest and opinion. Historically minded theorists point out that liberalism arose amid specific conflicts, principally wars of religion, so that from its inception liberalism did not pretend to be neutral among all characters or values. The view that state action could not be justified by appeals to some exclusive idea of the good life had its origin in actual disputes, in intractable political predicaments rather than in moral indifference, complacence, or naive disregard of the difficulties and costs of neutrality.

In "Class Conflict and Constitutionalism in J. S. Mill's Thought," Richard Ashcraft gives a genetic account of Mill's efforts to comprehend and resolve class conflict within the traditional liberal apparatus of constitutionalism and impartiality. Ashcraft describes how Mill's growing preoccupation with the clash of class interests corresponded to his increasingly sociological approach to political thought. It led him to change his thinking about the public-private divide and to admit socioeconomic matters into public life, and it led him to reject the thought that the market is an impartial mechanism for determining wages. At the same time, Ashcraft shows, Mill rejected the practicability of having government officials act either as neutral arbiters of opposing class interests or as agents of justice. Though he came to believe that justice supported some sort of cooperative socialism, Mill did not propose that government should impose justice so long as the claims of capital and labor rested on rival standards of equity. His claims for representative government were in the end and of necessity more modest. By bringing these conflicts of interest and principle into public life, antagonism will work to avoid social stagnation, and participatory institutions will be a force against stultifying bureaucratization.

One recurrent problem political theorists address in this connection is the tendency of liberalism's critics to carelessly identify neutrality with amorality or moral indifference. In "Making Sense of Moral Conflict," Steven Lukes discusses the connection between liberalism and moral pluralism. He argues against philosophers who say that moral conflict is more apparent than real, reducing it to a matter of ignorance or error, logical inconsistency or the failure to recognize the appropriate cultural contexts of relativist claims. Lukes insists that not only a plurality of morals but also the experience of moral conflict is a prevailing feature of modern life. He creates a typology of moral conflict: diversity, incompatibility, and incommensurability—each more intractable than the one preceding. He goes on to use this typology to indicate the several respects in which a comprehensive, all-embracing moral view is impossible. Taking moral conflict seriously lends support to a pluralist defense of liberal government, while answering the charge that such a defense is morally "anemic." If we take moral conflict seriously we understand that pluralist arguments for liberalism need not reflect moral indifference, moral skepticism, or value relativism.

Other political theorists are concerned with correcting the mistaken notion that neutrality is the sole liberal imperative and with demonstrating its limits. Certainly private life is supposed to be a scene of privileged particularist attachments and obligations. Impartiality and respect for others in public life are experienced as a rigorous discipline precisely because liberty encourages special affections and identifications and the felt obligations arising from them. Standing back from your own particular opinions describes only one kind of agency; it is demanded of people only sometimes; and even then the capacity to set aside certain considerations deemed politically unjustifiable is achieved only with the greatest discipline. This discipline is internalized as a result of deliberately fostered social practices and forms one aspect of moral personality.

Liberal political thought is not committed to maximizing personal freedom at the expense of every other consideration. At the extreme, neutrality would mean treating repressive practices as irrepressible and dismantling public institutions and practices that promote certain virtues or moral attitudes (all practices, in practice). Instead, as Amy Gutmann suggests, liberal theorists try to identify a bundle of virtues compatible with a certain range of competing conceptions of human flourishing.

Amy Gutmann and William Galston explore the limits of neutrality as it applies to education. They agree that civic education is necessary and possible, rejecting the stereotype of liberal education as the presentation of neutral facts and tools for choice. They recognize that inculcating certain virtues and habits will certainly come up against the conflicting moral views of some parents and should triumph over them. Where the authors differ is on what conception of a good liberal society provides the pattern and justification for civic education. In "Undemocratic Education," Gutmann presents an ideal of democratic

deliberation and a corresponding theory of education aimed at enabling citizens to participate in decisions and democratic society to
reproduce itself. She would build in protections against discrimination
and repression, but where disagreements persist about the relative
value of freedom and cultivated virtue, democracy decides. This idea
of civic education explains why children of religious fundamentalist
parents should not be exempted from readings in secular texts their
parents disapprove: neutrality in the service of personal freedom is
not the sole imperative, Gutmann argues; it does not extend this far.
William Galston gives less weight to participation and democratic
deliberation in his essay, "Civic Education in the Liberal State." Representative democracy is the basic feature of liberal society, he argues,
so pedagogy aims at a somewhat different set of virtues, among them
the ability to recognize and appreciate the place of specific excellences
and kinds of expertise in public life. He too thinks that liberal democracy requires tolerance and civic deliberation, but denies that
either one depends on educating children to evaluate ways of life
different from their parents'. Tolerance and deliberation are compatible with unshakable personal commitment to a way of life, so long
as it accepts certain minimal civic commitments. For Galston, liberty
entails the right to live unexamined as well as examined lives.

The chapters in this volume share several notable features. The
authors are less concerned to marshal authoritative arguments from
classic texts than to create arguments that address contemporary concerns; they use historical examples mainly to correct current errors
(such as the conflation of liberalism and modernity). A second common feature is the considerable amount of attention paid to concrete
institutions, social conditions, and actual practices. The authors demonstrate the tendency of contemporary political theory to open out
to the findings of social science, to ethnography and psychology. But
the most important common ground is a commitment to acknowledge and address the full range of positions on moral life that live
within and at the margins of liberalism. As a result, this book embodies at least one aspect of the moral life of liberalism: the imperative
to argue and persuade that follows from pluralism and respect for
differences.

· I ·

Varieties of Liberalism Today

The Liberalism of Fear

JUDITH N. SHKLAR

Before we can begin to analyze any specific form of liberalism we must surely state as clearly as possible what the word means. For in the course of so many years of ideological conflict it seems to have lost its identity completely. Overuse and overextension have rendered it so amorphous that it can now serve as an all-purpose word, whether of abuse or praise. To bring a modest degree of order into this state of confusion we might begin by insisting that liberalism refers to a political doctrine, not a philosophy of life such as has traditionally been provided by various forms of revealed religion and other comprehensive *Weltanschauungen*. Liberalism has only one overriding aim: to secure the political conditions that are necessary for the exercise of personal freedom.

Every adult should be able to make as many effective decisions without fear or favor about as many aspects of her or his life as is compatible with the like freedom of every other adult. That belief is the original and only defensible meaning of liberalism. It is a political notion, because the fear and favor that have always inhibited freedom are overwhelmingly generated by governments, both formal and informal. And while the sources of social oppression are indeed numerous, none has the deadly effect of those who, as the agents of the modern state, have unique resources of physical might and persuasion at their disposal.

Apart from prohibiting interference with the freedom of others, liberalism does not have any particular positive doctrines about how people are to conduct their lives or what personal choices they are to make. It is not, as so many of its critics claim, synonymous with modernity. Not that the latter is a crystal clear historical concept. Generally it does not refer to simply everything that has happened since the Renaissance, but to a mixture of natural science, technology, industrialization, skepticism, loss of religious orthodoxy, disenchantment, nihilism, and atomistic individualism. This is far from being a complete list, but it covers the main characteristics of modernity as it is perceived by those who believe that the word stands for centuries of despair and that liberalism is its most characteristic political manifestation.

It is by no means necessary to engage in disputes about the quality of the historiography or factual validity of this sort of discourse in general, but for the student of political theory at least one point must be noted. That is that liberalism has been very rare both in theory and in practice in the last two hundred odd years, especially when we recall that the European world is not the only inhabited part of the globe. No one could ever have described the governments of eastern Europe as liberal at any time, though a few briefly made a feeble effort in that direction after the First World War. In central Europe it has been instituted only after the Second World War, and then it was imposed by the victors in a war that we forget at our peril. Anyone who thinks that fascism in one guise or another is dead and gone ought to think again. In France liberalism under the three Republics flickered on and off and is only now reasonably secure, though it is still seriously challenged. In Britain it has enjoyed its longest political success, but not in the vast areas, including Ireland, that England ruled until recently. Finally, let us not forget that the United States was not a liberal state until after the Civil War, and even then often in name only. In short, to speak of a liberal era is not to refer to anything that actually happened, except possibly by comparison to what came after 1914.

The state of political thought was no more liberal than that of the reigning governments, especially in the years after the French Revolution. And we should not forget the deeply illiberal prerevolutionary republican tradition of which John Pocock has reminded us so forcefully. It is in any case difficult to find a vast flow of liberal ideology in the midst of the Catholic authoritarianism, romantic corporatist nostalgia, nationalism, racism, proslavery, social Darwinism, imperialism, militarism, fascism, and most types of socialism which dominated the battle of political ideas in the last century. There was a current of liberal thought throughout the period, but it was hardly the dominant intellectual voice. In the world beyond Europe it was not heard at all. It was powerful in the United States only if black people are not counted as members of its society.

Why then, given the actual complexity of the intellectual history of the past centuries, is there so much easy generalizing about modernity and its alleged liberalism? The reason is simple enough: liberalism is a latecomer, since it has its origins in post-Reformation Europe. Its origins are in the terrible tension within Christianity between the demands of creedal orthodoxy and those of charity, between faith and morality. The cruelties of the religious wars had the effect of turning many Christians away from the public policies of the churches to a morality that saw toleration as an expression of Christian charity. One thinks of Sebastien Castellion among Calvinists, for example.[1] Others, torn by conflicting spiritual impulses, became skeptics who put cruelty and fanaticism at the very head of the human vices; Montaigne is the most notable among them. In either case the individual, whether the bearer of a sacred conscience or the potential victim of cruelty, is to be protected against the incursions of public oppression.

Later, when the bond between conscience and God is severed, the inviolability of personal decisions in matters of faith, knowledge, and morality is still defended on the original grounds that we owe it to each other as a matter of mutual respect, that a forced belief is in itself false and that the threats and bribes used to enforce conformity are inherently demeaning. To insist that individuals must make their own choices about the most important matter in their lives—their religious beliefs—without interference from public authority, is to go very far indeed toward liberalism. It is, I think, the core of its historical development, but it would be wrong to think of principled toleration as equivalent to political liberalism. Limited and responsible government may be implicit in the claim for personal autonomy, but without an explicit political commitment to such institutions, liberalism is still doctrinally incomplete. Montaigne was surely tolerant and humanitarian but he was no liberal. The distance between him and Locke is correspondingly great. Nevertheless, liberalism's deepest grounding is in place from the first, in the conviction of the earliest defenders of toleration, born in horror, that cruelty is an absolute evil, an offense against God or humanity. It is out of that tradition that the political liberalism of fear arose and continues amid the terror of our time to have relevance.[2]

There are of course many types of liberalism that remain committed to the primacy of conscience, whether in its Protestant or Kantian versions. There is Jeffersonian liberalism of rights, which has other foundations; and the Emersonian quest for self-development has its own liberal political expression. Liberalism does not in principle have to depend on specific religious or philosophical systems of thought. It does not have to choose among them as long as they do not reject toleration, which is why Hobbes is not the father of liberalism. No theory that gives public authorities the unconditional right to impose beliefs and even a vocabulary as they may see fit upon the citizenry can be described as even remotely liberal. Of all the cases made against liberalism, the most bizarre is that liberals are really indifferent, if not openly hostile, to personal freedom. This may follow from the peculiar identification of *Leviathan* as the very archetype of liberal philosophy, but it is a truly gross misrepresentation which simply assures that any social contract theory, however authoritarian its intentions, and any anti-Catholic polemic add up to liberalism.[3]

The convoluted genealogy of liberalism that insists on seeing its origins in a theory of absolutism is not in itself interesting. More common is a sort of free association of ideas that perceives a danger to traditional revealed religion in toleration and hence assumes that liberalism is of necessity atheistic, agnostic, relativistic, and nihilistic. This catalogue of accusations is worth mentioning, because it is commonplace and because it is easily and usefully refuted. The original mistake is the failure to distinguish psychological affinities from logical consequences. As a result, these critics cannot grasp that the liberalism of fear as a strictly political theory is not necessarily linked to any one religious or scientific doctrine, though it is psychologically more compatible with some rather than with others. It must reject only those political doctrines that do not recognize any difference between the spheres of the personal and the public. Because of the primacy of toleration as the irreducible limit on public agents, liberals must always draw such a line. This is not historically a permanent or unalterable boundary, but it does require that every public policy be considered with this separation in mind and be consciously defended as meeting its most severe current standard.

The important point for liberalism is not so much where the line is drawn, as that it be drawn, and that it must under no circumstances be ignored or forgotten. The limits of coercion begin, though they do not end, with a prohibition upon invading the private realm, which originally was a matter of religious faith, but which has changed and will go on changing as objects of belief and the sense of privacy alter in response to the technological and military character of governments and the productive relationships that prevail. It is a shifting line, but not an erasable one, and it leaves liberals free to espouse a very large range of philosophical and religious beliefs.

The liberalism of fear is thus not necessarily tied to either skepticism or to the pursuit of the natural sciences. There is, however, a real psychological connection between them. Skepticism is inclined toward toleration, since in its doubts it cannot choose among the competing beliefs that swirl around it, so often in murderous rage. Whether the skeptic seeks personal tranquility in retreat or tries to calm the warring factions around her, she must prefer a government that does nothing to increase the prevailing levels of fanaticism and dogmatism. To that extent there is a natural affinity between the liberal and the skeptic. Madison's discussion in the *Federalist* of how to end sectarian and similar factional conflicts through freedom is the perfect example of the fit between skepticism and liberal politics.[4] Nevertheless, a society of believers who choose never to resort to the use of the agencies of government to further their particular faith is imaginable, though not usual.

The intellectual flexibility of skepticism is psychologically more adapted to liberalism, but it is not a necessary element of its politics. A society governed by extremely oppressive skeptics can be easily imagined if, for example, they were to follow Nietzsche's political notions energetically. That is also true of the natural sciences. These tend to flourish most in freedom, quite unlike the fine arts and literature in this respect, but it is not impossible to imagine a science-friendly dictatorship. The publicity and the high standards of evidence, as well as the critical cast of mind which the natural sciences ideally require, again may suggest a psychological bond between the inner life of science and liberal politics. That is, however, far from being necessarily or even normally the case. There are many thoroughly illiberal scientists, in fact. The alliance between science and liberalism was one of convenience at first, as both had much to fear from the onslaughts of religion. With this shared enemy of censorship and persecution in abeyance, the identity of attitudes tended to fade. Science and liberalism were not born together; the former is far older. Nothing, however, can erase the chief difference between the two. The natural sciences live to change, while liberalism does not have to take any particular view of tradition.

To the extent that the European past was utterly hostile to freedom and that the most ancient of Indo-European traditions is the caste society, liberals must reject particular traditions. No society that still has traces of the old tripartite division of humanity into those who pray, those who fight, and those who labor can be liberal.[5] To turn one's back on some or even most traditions does not, however, mean that one must forego all tradition as a matter of intellectual honesty. Liberalism need not decide among traditions that are not hostile to its aspirations, nor does it have to regard the claims of any traditions inherently false, simply because it does not meet scientific standards of rational proof. It all depends on the content and tendencies of the tradition. Clearly representative government is impregnated with traditions in Britain and in the United States. The habits of voluntarism depend on a variety of traditions. These are surely more than merely compatible with liberalism.

Intellectual modesty does not imply that the liberalism of fear has no content, only that it is entirely nonutopian. In that respect it may well be what Emerson called a party of memory rather than a party of hope.[6] And indeed there are other types of liberalism that differ from it sharply in this respect. First of all there is the liberalism of natural rights which looks to the constant fulfillment of an ideal preestablished normative order, be it nature's or God's, whose principles have to be realized in the lives of individual citizens through public guarantees. It is God's will that we preserve ourselves, and it is our own and society's duty to see that we are protected in our lives, liberties, and property and all that pertains to them. To that end we have a duty to establish protective public agencies and the right to demand that they provide us with opportunities to make claims against each and all.

If we take rights seriously we must see to it that principles such as those of *The Declaration of Independence* be made effective in every aspect of our public life. If the agencies of government have a single primary function it is to see to it that the rights of individuals be realized, because our integrity as God's or nature's creations requires it. Conceivably one might argue that a perfect or optimal society would be composed solely of rights claiming citizens. In all cases, therefore, the liberalism of natural rights regards politics as a matter of citizens who actively pursue their own legally secured ends in accordance with a higher law. The paradigm of politics is the tribunal in which fair rules and decisions are made to satisfy the greatest possible number of demands made by individual citizens against one another individually, and against the government and other socially powerful institutions. The liberalism of natural rights envisages a just society composed of politically sturdy citizens, each able and willing to stand up for himself and others.

Equally given to hope is the liberalism of personal development. Freedom, it argues, is necessary for personal as well as social progress. We cannot make the best of our potentialities unless we are free to do so. And morality is impossible unless we have an opportunity to choose our courses of action. Nor can we benefit from education unless our minds are free to accept and reject what we are told and to read and hear the greatest variety of opposing opinions. Morality and knowledge can develop only in a free and open society. There is even reason to hope that institutions of learning will eventually replace politics and government. It would not be unfair to say that these two forms of liberalism have their spokesmen in Locke and John Stuart Mill respectively, and they are of course perfectly genuine expressions of liberal doctrine. It must be said, however, that neither one of these two patron saints of liberalism had a strongly developed historical memory, and it is on this faculty of the human mind that the liberalism of fear draws most heavily.

The most immediate memory is at present the history of the world since 1914. In Europe and North America torture had gradually been eliminated from the practices of government, and there was hope that it might eventually disappear everywhere. With the intelligence and loyalty requirements of the national warfare states that quickly developed with the outbreak of hostilities, torture returned and has flourished on a colossal scale ever since.[7] We say "never again," but somewhere someone is being tortured right now, and acute fear has again become the most common form of social control. To this the horror of modern warfare must be added as a reminder. The liberalism of fear is a response to these undeniable actualities, and it therefore concentrates on damage control.

Given the inevitability of that inequality of military, police, and persuasive power which is called government, there is evidently always much to be afraid of. And one may, thus, be less inclined to celebrate the blessings of liberty than to consider the dangers of tyranny and war that threaten it. For this liberalism the basic units of political life are not discursive and reflecting persons, nor friends and enemies, nor patriotic soldier-citizens, nor energetic litigants, but the weak and the powerful. And the freedom it wishes to secure is freedom from the abuse of power and intimidation of the defenseless that this difference invites. This apprehension should not be mistaken for the obsessive ideologies which concentrate solely on the notion of totalitarianism. This is a shorthand for only the extremity of institutionalized violence and almost implies that anything less radically destructive need not concern us at all.

The liberalism of fear, on the contrary, regards abuses of public powers in all regimes with equal trepidation. It worries about the excesses of official agents at every level of government, and it assumes that these are apt to burden the poor and weak most heavily. The history of the poor compared to that of the various elites makes that obvious enough. The assumption, amply justified by every page of political history, is that some agents of government will behave lawlessly and brutally in small or big ways most of the time unless they are prevented from doing so.

The liberalism inspired by these considerations does resemble Isaiah Berlin's negative liberty, but it is not exactly the same. Berlin's negative liberty of "not being forced" and its later version of "open doors" is kept conceptually pure and separate from "the conditions of liberty," that is, the social and political institutions that make personal freedom possible. That is entirely necessary if negative liberty is to be fully distinguished from what Berlin calls "positive liberty," which is the freedom of one's higher from one's lower self. It cannot be denied, moreover, that this very clear demarcation of negative liberty is the best means of avoiding the slippery slope that can lead us to its threatening opposite.

Nevertheless, there is much to be said for not separating negative liberty from the conditions that are at least necessary to make it possible at all. Limited government and the control of unequally divided political power constitute the minimal condition without which freedom is unimaginable in any politically organized society. It is not a sufficient condition, but it is a necessary prerequisite. No door is open in a political order in which public and private intimidation prevail, and it requires a complex system of institutions to avoid that. If negative freedom is to have any political significance at all, it must specify at least some of the institutional characteristics of a relatively free regime. Socially that also means a dispersion of power among a plurality of politically empowered groups, pluralism, in short, as well as the elimination of such forms and degrees of social inequality as expose people to oppressive practices. Otherwise the "open doors" are a metaphor—and not, politically, a very illuminating one at that.

Moreover, there is no particular reason to accept the moral theory on which Berlin's negative freedom rests. This is the belief that there are several inherently incompatible moralities among which we must choose, but which cannot be reconciled by reference to a common criterion—paganism and Christianity being the two most obvious examples.[8] Whatever the truth of this metapolitical assumption may be, liberalism can do without it. The liberalism of fear in fact does not rest on a theory of moral pluralism. It does not, to be sure, offer a *summum bonum* toward which all political agents should strive, but it certainly does begin with a *summum malum,* which all of us know and would avoid if only we could. That evil is cruelty and the fear it inspires, and the very fear of fear itself. To that extent the liberalism of fear makes a universal and especially a cosmopolitan claim, as it historically always has done.

What is meant by cruelty here? It is the deliberate infliction of physical, and secondarily emotional, pain upon a weaker person or group by stronger ones in order to achieve some end, tangible or intangible, of the latter. It is not sadism, though sadistic individuals may flock to occupy positions of power that permit them to indulge their urges. But public cruelty is not an occasional personal inclination. It is made possible by differences in public power, and it is almost always built into the system of coercion upon which all governments have to rely to fulfill their essential functions. A minimal level of fear is implied in any system of law, and the liberalism of fear does not dream of an end of public, coercive government. The fear it does want to prevent is that which is created by arbitrary, unexpected, unnecessary, and unlicensed acts of force and by habitual and pervasive acts of cruelty and torture performed by military, paramilitary, and police agents in any regime.

Of fear it can be said without qualification that it is universal as it is physiological. It is a mental as well as a physical reaction, and it is common to animals as well as to human beings. To be alive is to be afraid, and much to our advantage in many cases, since alarm often preserves us from danger. The fear we fear is of pain inflicted by others to kill and maim us, not the natural and healthy fear that merely warns us of avoidable pain. And, when we think politically, we are afraid not only for ourselves but for our fellow citizens as well. We fear a society of fearful people.

Systematic fear is the condition that makes freedom impossible, and it is aroused by the expectation of institutionalized cruelty as by nothing else. However, it is fair to say that what I have called "putting cruelty first" is not a sufficient basis for political liberalism. It is simply a first principle, an act of moral intuition based on ample observation, on which liberalism can be built, especially at present. Because the fear of systematic cruelty is so universal, moral claims based on its prohibition have an immediate appeal and can gain recognition without much argument. But one cannot rest on this or any other naturalistic fallacy. Liberals can begin with cruelty as the primary evil only if they go beyond their well-grounded assumption that almost all people fear it and would evade it if they could. If the prohibition of cruelty can be universalized and recognized as a necessary condition of the dignity of persons, then it can become a principle of political morality. This could also be achieved by asking whether the prohibition would benefit the vast majority of human beings in meeting their known needs and wants. Kantians and a utilitarian could accept one of these tests, and liberalism need not choose between them.

What liberalism requires is the possibility of making the evil of cruelty and fear the basic norm of its political practices and prescriptions. The only exception to the rule of avoidance is the prevention of greater cruelties. That is why any government must use the threat of punishment, though liberalism looks upon this as an unavoidable evil, to be controlled in its scope and modified by legally enforced rules of fairness, so that arbitrariness not be added to the minimum of fear required for law enforcement. That this formulation owes something to Kant's philosophy of law is evident, but the liberalism of fear does not rest on his or any other moral philosophy in its entirety.[9] It must in fact remain eclectic.

What the liberalism of fear owes to Locke is also obvious: that the governments of this world with their overwhelming power to kill, maim, indoctrinate, and make war are not to be trusted unconditionally ("lions"), and that any confidence that we might develop in their agents must rest firmly on deep suspicion. Locke was not, and neither should his heirs be, in favor of weak governments that cannot frame or carry out public policies and decisions made in conformity to requirements of publicity, deliberation, and fair procedures. What is to be feared is every extralegal, secret, and unauthorized act by public agents or their deputies. And to prevent such conduct requires a constant division and subdivision of political power. The importance of voluntary associations from this perspective is not the satisfaction that their members may derive from joining in cooperative endeavors, but their ability to become significant units of social power and influence that can check, or at least alter, the assertions of other organized agents, both voluntary and governmental.

The separation of the public from the private is evidently far from stable here, as I already noted, especially if one does not ignore, as the liberalism of fear certainly does not, the power of such basically public organizations as corporate business enterprises. These of course owe their entire character and power to the laws, and they are not public in name only. To consider them in the same terms as the local mom and pop store is unworthy of serious social discourse. Nevertheless, it should be remembered that the reasons we speak of property as private in many cases is that it is meant to be left to the discretion of individual owners as a matter of public policy and law, precisely because this is an indispensable and excellent way of limiting the long arm of government and of dividing social power, as well as of securing the independence of individuals. Nothing gives a person greater social resources than legally guaranteed proprietorship. It cannot be unlimited, because it is the creature of the law in the first place, and also because it serves a public purpose—the dispersion of power.

Where the instruments of coercion are at hand, whether it be through the use of economic power, chiefly to hire, pay, fire, and determine prices, or military might in its various manifestations, it is the task of a liberal citizenry to see that not one official or unofficial agent can intimidate anyone, except through the use of well-understood and accepted legal procedures. And that even then the agents of coercion should always be on the defensive and limited to proportionate and necessary actions that can be excused only as a response to threats of more severe cruelty and fear from private criminals.

It might well seem that the liberalism of fear is radically consequentialist in its concentration on the avoidance of foreseeable evils. As a guide to political practices that is the case, but it must avoid any tendency to offer ethical instructions in general. No form of liberalism has any business telling the citizenry to pursue happiness or even to define that wholly elusive condition. It is for each one of us to seek it or reject it in favor of duty or salvation or passivity, for example. Liberalism must restrict itself to politics and to proposals to restrain potential abusers of power in order to lift the burden of fear and favor from the shoulders of adult women and men, who can then conduct their lives in accordance with their own beliefs and preferences, as long as they do not prevent others from doing so as well.

There are several well-known objections to the liberalism of fear. It will be called "reductionist," because it is first and foremost based on the physical suffering and fears of ordinary human beings, rather than on moral or ideological aspirations. Liberalism does not collapse politics into administration, economics, or psychology, so it is not reductive in this sense. But as it is based on common and immediate experiences, it offends those who identify politics with mankind's most noble aspirations. What is to be regarded as noble is, to be sure, highly contestable.

To call the liberalism of fear a lowering of one's sights implies that emotions are inferior to ideas and especially to political causes. It may be noble to pursue ideological ambitions or risk one's life for a "cause," but it is not at all noble to kill another human being in pursuit of one's own "causes." "Causes," however spiritual they may be, are not self-justifying, and they are not all equally edifying. And even the most appealing are nothing but instruments of torture or craven excuses for it, when they are forced upon others by threats and bribes. We would do far less harm if we learned to accept each other as sentient beings, whatever else we may be, and to understand that physical well-being and toleration are not simply inferior to the other aims that each one of us may choose to pursue.

There is absolutely nothing elevated in death and dying. Even if that were the case, it is not the task of public authority to encourage, promote, and enforce them, as they still do. Self-sacrifice may stir our admiration, but it is not, by definition, a political duty, but an act of supererogation which falls outside the realm of politics. There is nothing "reductive" about building a political order on the avoidance of fear and cruelty unless one begins with a contempt for physical experience. The consequences of political spirituality are, moreover, far less elevating than it might seem. Politically it has usually served as an excuse for orgies of destruction. Need one remind anyone of that truly ennobling cry: "Viva la muerte!"—and the regime it ushered in?

A related objection to the liberalism of fear is that it replaces genuine human reason with "instrumental rationality."[10] The meaning of the former is usually left unclear, but as a rule it is not a version of Platonic idealism. "Instrumental rationality" refers to political practices that pursue only efficiency or means-ends calculations, without any questioning of the rationality or other possible worth of their aims or outcomes. Since the liberalism of fear has very clear aims—the reduction of fear and cruelty—that sort of argument appears to be quite irrelevant.

More telling is the notion that "instrumental reasoning" places all its confidence in procedures, without adequate attention to the rationality of the conduct and discourse of those who participate in and follow them. It trusts the mechanisms for creating consent and ensuring fairness, without any attention to the character of the individual citizens or to that of the society as a whole. Even if a pluralistic political system under the rule of law were to yield a free and relatively peaceful society, it would not be genuinely rational, and not at all ethical, unless it also educated its citizens to a genuine level of political understanding and with it the capacity to be masters of their collective life. This is supposed to be "substantially" rational in a way that the liberalism of fear, with its attention to procedures and outcomes, is not. But in fact the argument is not about rationality at all, but about expectations of radical social change and of utopian aspirations. The accusation of "instrumentality," if it means anything at all, amounts to a disdain for those who do not want to pay the price of utopian ventures, least of all those invented by other people. It refuses to take risks at the expense of others in pursuit of any ideal, however rational.

It cannot be denied that the experience of politics according to fair procedures and the rule of law do indirectly educate the citizens, even though that is not their overt purpose, which is purely political. The habits of patience, self-restraint, respect for the claims of others, and caution constitute forms of social discipline that are not only wholly compatible with personal freedom, but encourage socially and personally valuable characteristics.[11] This, it should be emphasized, does not imply that the liberal state can ever have an educative government that aims at creating specific kinds of character and enforces its own beliefs. It can never be didactic in intent in that exclusive and inherently authoritarian way. Liberalism, as we saw, began precisely in order to oppose the educative state. However, no system of government, no system of legal procedures, and no system of public education is without psychological effect, and liberalism has no reason at all to apologize for the inclinations and habits that procedural fairness and responsible government are likely to encourage.

If citizens are to act individually and in associations, especially in a democracy, to protest and block any sign of governmental illegality and abuse, they must have a fair share of moral courage, self-reliance, and stubbornness to assert themselves effectively. To foster well-informed and self-directed adults must be the aim of every effort to educate the citizens of a liberal society. There is a very clear account of what a perfect liberal would look like more or less. It is to be found in Kant's *Doctrine of Virtue,* which gives us a very detailed account of the disposition of a person who respects other people without condescension, arrogance, humility, or fear. He or she does not insult others with lies or cruelty, both of which mar one's own character no less than they injure one's victims. Liberal politics depend for their success on the efforts of such people, but it is not the task of liberal politics to foster them simply as models of human perfection. All it can claim is that if we want to promote political freedom, then this is appropriate behavior.

This liberal prescription for citizenship, it is now often argued, is both a very unhistorical and an ethnocentric view that makes quite unwarranted claims for universality. That it arose at a given time and place is, after all, inevitable, but the relativist now argues that the liberalism of fear would not be welcomed by most of those who live under their traditional customs, even if these are as cruel and oppressive as the Indian caste system.[12] To judge inherited habits by standards that purport to be general, even though they are alien to a people, is said to be an arrogant imposition of false as well as partial principles. For there are no generally valid social prohibitions or rules, and the task of the social critic is at most to articulate socially immanent values. All this is not nearly as self-evident as the relativistic defenders of local customs would have us believe.

Unless and until we can offer the injured and insulted victims of most of the world's traditional as well as revolutionary governments a genuine and practicable alternative to their present condition, we have no way of knowing whether they really enjoy their chains. There is very little evidence that they do. The Chinese did not really like Mao's reign any more than we would, in spite of their political and cultural distance from us. The absolute relativism, not merely cultural but psychological, that rejects the liberalism of fear as both too "Western" and too abstract is too complacent and too ready to forget the horrors of our world to be credible. It is deeply illiberal, not only in its submission to tradition as an ideal, but in its dogmatic identification of every local practice with deeply shared local human aspirations. To step outside these customs is not, as the relativist claims, particularly insolent and intrusive. Only the challenge from nowhere and the claims of universal humanity and rational argument cast in general terms can be put to the test of general scrutiny and public criticism.[13]

The unspoken and sanctified practices that prevail within every tribal border can never be openly analyzed or appraised, for they are by definition already permanently settled within the communal consciousness. Unless there is an open and public review of all the practical alternatives, especially of the new and alien, there can be no responsible choices and no way of controlling the authorities that claim to be the voice of the people and its spirit. The arrogance of the prophet and the bard who pronounce the embedded norms is far greater than that of any deontologist. For they profess not only to reveal a hidden popular soul, but to do so in a manner that is not subject to extratribal review. That orgies of xenophobia just might lie in the wake of these claims of hermeneutical primacy is also not without historical example. The history of nationalism is not encouraging. But even at its best, ethnic relativism can say little about fear and cruelty, except that they are commonplace everywhere.[14] War also, though not perhaps in its present nuclear possibilities, has always existed. Are we to defend it on that ground? Actually, the most reliable test for what cruelties are to be endured at any place and any time is to ask the likeliest victims, the least powerful persons, at any given moment and under controlled conditions. Until that is done there is no reason not to assume that the liberalism of fear has much to offer to the victims of political tyranny.

These considerations should be recalled especially now, as the liberalism of fear is liable also to being charged with lacking an adequate theory of "the self." The probability of widely divergent selves is obviously one of the basic assumptions of any liberal doctrine. For political purposes liberalism does not have to assume anything about human nature except that people, apart from similar physical and psychological structures, differ in their personalities to a very marked degree. At a superficial level we must assume that some people will be encumbered with group traditions that they cherish, while others may only want to escape from their social origins and ascriptive bonds. These socially very important aspects of human experience are, like most acquired characteristics, extremely diverse and subject to change. Social learning is a great part of our character, though the sum of all our roles may not add up to a complete "self." For political purposes it is not this irreducible "self" or the peculiar character that we acquire in the course of our education that matter, but only the fact that many different "selves" should be free to interact politically.

To those American political theorists who long for either more communal or more expansively individualistic personalities, I now offer a reminder that these are the concerns of an exceptionally privileged liberal society, and that until the institutions of primary freedom are in place these longings cannot even arise. Indeed the extent to which both the communitarian and the romantic take free public institutions for granted is a tribute to the United States, but not to their sense of history.[15] Too great a part of past and present political experience is neglected when we ignore the annual reports of Amnesty International and of contemporary warfare. It used to be the mark of liberalism that it was cosmopolitan and that an insult to the life and liberty of a member of any race or group in any part of the world was of genuine concern. It may be a revolting paradox that the very success of liberalism in some countries has atrophied the political empathies of their citizens. That appears to be one cost of taking freedom for granted, but it may not be the only one.

Liberalism does not have to enter into speculations about what the potentialities of this or that "self" may be, but it does have to take into account the actual political conditions under which people live, in order to act here and now to prevent known and real dangers. A concern for human freedom cannot stop with the satisfactions of one's own society or clan. We must therefore be suspicious of ideologies of solidarity, precisely because they are so attractive to those who find liberalism emotionally unsatisfying, and who have gone on in our century to create oppressive and cruel regimes of unparalleled horror. The assumption that these offer something wholesome to the atomized citizen may or may not be true, but the political consequences are not, on the historical record, open to much doubt. To seek emotional and personal development in the bosom of a community or in romantic self-expression is a choice open to citizens in liberal societies. Both, however, are apolitical impulses and wholly self-oriented, which at best distract us from the main task of politics when they are presented as political doctrines, and at worst can, under unfortunate circumstances, seriously damage liberal practices. For although both appear only to be redrawing the boundaries between the personal and the public, which is a perfectly normal political practice, it cannot be said that either one has a serious sense of the implications of the proposed shifts in either direction.[16]

It might well seem that the liberalism of fear is very close to anarchism. That is not true, because liberals have always been aware of the degree of informal coercion and educative social pressures that even the most ardent anarchist theorists have suggested as acceptable substitutes for law.[17] Moreover, even if the theories of anarchism were less flawed, the actualities of countries in which law and government have broken down is not encouraging. Does anyone want to live in Beirut? The original first principle of liberalism, the rule of law, remains perfectly intact, and it is not an anarchistic doctrine. There is no reason at all to abandon it. It is the prime instrument to restrain governments. The potentialities of persecution have kept pace with technological advances; we have as much to fear from the instruments of torture and persecution as ever. One half of the Bill of Rights is about fair trials and the protection of the accused in criminal trials. For it is in court that the citizen meets the might of the state, and it is not an equal contest. Without well-defined procedures, honest judges, opportunities for counsel and for appeals, no one has a chance. Nor should we allow more acts to be criminalized than is necessary for our mutual safety. Finally, nothing speaks better for a liberal state than legal efforts to compensate the victims of crime rather than merely to punish the criminal for having violated the law. For he did injure, terrify, and abuse a human being first and foremost.

It is at this point that the liberalism of fear adopts a strong defense of equal rights and their legal protection. It cannot base itself upon the notion of rights as fundamental and given, but it does see them as just those licenses and empowerments that citizens must have in order to preserve their freedom and to protect themselves against abuse. The institutions of a pluralist order with multiple centers of power and institutionalized rights is merely a description of a liberal political society. It is also of necessity a democratic one, because without enough equality of power to protect and assert one's rights, freedom is but a hope. Without the institutions of representative democracy and an accessible, fair, and independent judiciary open to appeals, and in the absence of a multiplicity of politically active groups, liberalism is in jeopardy. It is the entire purpose of the liberalism of fear to prevent that outcome. It is therefore fair to say that liberalism is monogamously, faithfully, and permanently married to democracy—but it is a marriage of convenience.

To account for the necessity of freedom in general, references to particular institutions and ideologies are not enough. One must put cruelty first and understand the fear of fear and recognize them everywhere. Unrestrained "punishing" and denials of the most basic means of survival by governments, near and far from us, should incline us to look with critical attention to the practices of all agents of all governments and to the threats of war here and everywhere.

If I sound like Caesare Beccaria, or some other refugee from the eighteenth century, it may well be that I have read the sort of reports they read about the ways of governments. The foreign news in the

New York Times suffice, as do its accounts of the prevalence of racism, xenophobia, and systematic governmental brutality here and everywhere. I cannot see how any political theorist or politically alert citizen can possibly ignore them and fail to protest against them. Once we do that, we have moved toward the liberalism of fear, and away from the more exhilarating but less urgent forms of liberal thought.

Humanist Liberalism

SUSAN MOLLER OKIN

Compared with some other academic disciplines, contemporary political theory is in one significant respect in the Dark Ages. Literary theory and, to a lesser extent, history have both risen to the challenge and incorporated many of the insights of more than a decade of feminist scholarship. But most political theorists have yet to take gender—by which I mean the social institutionalization of sexual difference—seriously. This challenge will have to be taken up and responded to before any political theory can be rightly regarded as "humanist."

Liberalism has been constructed around distinctions between the public realm, which includes politics, and the private, which includes personal and domestic life. The world of wage-work and the marketplace is sometimes included in the public sphere (and contrasted with the domestic), but sometimes it is placed in the private (and contrasted with the state or governmental). The main purpose of these distinctions, since their seventeenth-century origins, has been to promote individual security and freedom and to restrain the arm of governments. However, as feminist scholars have by now amply demonstrated, in traditional liberal thought the distinction between the public and the domestic realms rests on the assumption that men inhabit both, easily moving from one to the other, but that women inhabit only the realm of family life, where they are properly subordinate to their husbands. Thus, women were long denied most of the crucial political and legal rights defended by liberals.[1] The "autonomous individuals" of whom liberal theorists wrote before the twentieth century—with the notable exception of John Stuart Mill—

were male heads of households. Liberalism's past is deeply and, for the most part unambiguously, patriarchal.

Contemporary liberal theorists often write with far greater ambiguity. Often, though by no means always, they employ gender-neutral language, such as "men and women," "he or she," "persons," or "the self." More often than not, however, this usage is highly misleading, since its supposed gender neutrality is false. At worst, it is ludicrous. It serves only to disguise the fact that contemporary liberalism has *not* yet taken up the challenge of converting a theory that was built on both the separation of public from private and the confinement of women to family life into a theory that can be about all of us as participants in public as well as private life.[2] In conjunction with their false gender neutrality, contemporary liberal theorists typically ignore the family. They fail to analyze its politics or to consider the justice or injustice of its structure and its practices. At the same time, however, they assume its existence somewhere outside of the scope of their theories. With gender and the family ignored but assumed, most liberalism is still clearly patriarchal. The question is whether and how we can replace this patriarchal liberalism with a political theory of humanist liberalism.

But why liberalism? Some feminists have concluded that any reconciliation of liberalism with feminism is impossible, that the demands of feminism expose unresolvable contradictions in liberalism.[3] I endorse fundamental principles of liberalism, despite its difficulties, for reasons shared by some of the other contributors to this book. Not the least of these is that we live in an age of a great plurality of beliefs, preferred ways of life, conceptions of the good. Liberalism in many ways takes this fact of modern life seriously.[4] It values the individuality that is promoted and preserved by the respect for personal preferences and for the need for privacy; it promotes the opportunity of persons to live their own lives and to seek out their own conceptions of the good; and it is well aware of the dangers that can result from the imposition of supposed "community values." I also believe—and here I break ranks with some of the other contributors to this volume—that these aims of liberalism are much more likely to be achieved in a society considerably more egalitarian than the oligarchical-democratic hybrid that the United States is today. A liberalism that is founded on the plurality of beliefs, modes of life, and attachments, and that aims to maximize persons' opportunities to live a good life as they wish is not only *compatible* with a significant degree of socialization of the means of production and redistribution of wealth—indeed it *requires* it.[5]

In certain respects the challenges of feminists who endorse the fundamental aims of liberalism are parallel to some of the challenges that liberals with leftist sympathies present to more traditional versions of liberalism. Just as the left disputes the liberal definition of politics that has drawn a firm line between state and society and claims that "the economic is political," so feminists challenge the traditional liberal dichotomy between public and private that divides the personal and domestic from the rest of life. As I shall argue here, if liberalism is to include all of us, women and men, it must address the challenge presented by the claim that "the personal is political."

Challenges of Feminist Theory

Feminist theorists have made a number of arguments that bear on current disputes in mainstream political thought. They argue that claims that the subjects of classic liberal theory are autonomous, basically equal, unattached rational individuals—in Hobbes's words "men as if but even now sprung out of the earth . . . like mushrooms"[6]—rest on the often unstated *assumption* of women's unpaid reproductive and domestic work, their dependence and subordination within the family, and their exclusion from most spheres of life. With women's status left ambiguous and the family assumed but not discussed, contemporary liberal theory has yet to take account of the fact that men are not mushrooms. It pays remarkably little attention to how we *become* the adults who form the subject matter of political theories. This deficit is of particular importance when we concern ourselves with issues of gender. For feminist scholars have shown how the characteristics required of men and women in societies structured by gender are reproduced, not only through the more obvious devices of sex-role socialization, but largely through the maintenance of female parenting. The characteristics that we develop as we become women or men, Nancy Chodorow has argued, are largely a result of the fact that children of both sexes are raised primarily by women.[7] Liberal theorists who take such arguments seriously cannot continue to regard the structure and practices of family life as separate from and irrelevant to "the political."

Feminists have challenged the liberal distinction between the public realm and the private life of the family in several other ways. The aim of the theoretical dichotomy has been, allegedly, to sustain the protection of private life from intervention by the state. By its non-intervention, the state is supposed to maintain its neutrality with regard to what goes on within the private sphere. Feminism challenges this claim. First, the liberal state *has* regulated and controlled the family, in innumerable ways, and in such ways as to reinforce patriarchy. For hundreds of years in Britain and the United States, the Common Law notion of coverture deprived women of legal person-hood upon marriage. The state enforced the rights of husbands to their wives' property and persons and made it virtually impossible for women to divorce or even to live separately from their husbands. Until very recently it reinforced the patriarchal structure of marriage by denying women rights routinely exercised by men in the spheres of work, marketplace, and politics, on the grounds that the exercise of such rights would interfere with women's performance of their domestic responsibilities.[8] This history of inequality between the sexes is of continued significance. We cannot fully comprehend, much less change, the gender structure of our present society without constant reference to the practices and traditions of its past.[9]

Even since the major aspects of legal coverture and most obvious instances of legal sex discrimination have been abolished, however, the state cannot be perceived as neutral in relation to family life. It still regulates such crucial family issues as marriage, divorce, and child custody. As feminist scholarship has made clear, the current divorce laws and practices of American courts place women and children at a considerable social and economic disadvantage, and I have argued elsewhere that this fact affects the conditions of ongoing family life, reinforcing male dominance.[10] Women, whether or not they also work for pay, continue to perform far more of the unpaid labor of families than men.[11] It is equally clear that this has a considerable effect on their success and security in the world of wage-work, on their capacity to be economically self-supporting, and thence on their bargaining power within the family.

Thus, the still heavily gendered structure of family life affects the relative positions of men and women in the "public" world outside, which in turn reverberate within the family. "Public" and "private" life are inextricably intertwined, not only for women as individuals, but for women as an entire "sex-class." This fact was graphically illustrated by two articles that appeared recently on subsequent days on the front page of the *New York Times*.[12] One was about a tiny and highly paid elite among women—those who work as lawyers for the top law firms in the United States. If these women become mothers and spend any time at all with their children, they find themselves off the partnership track and instead, with no prospects of advancement in the profession, on the "mommy track." "Nine to five" is decidedly "part-time work," in the ethos of these firms. One mother reports that, in spite of her twelve-hour workdays and frequent working weekends, she has no chance of making partner. The article ignores the fact that these women's children also have fathers, or that most of the men working for the top firms also have children, except to report that male lawyers who take parental leave are seen as "wimp-like." The division of labor within the family, even in these cases, where the women are extremely well qualified, successful, and potentially influential, seems to be taken for granted.

The next day's *Times* reports on a case of major significance for abortion rights, decided by a Federal Appeals Court in Minnesota. The all-male panel of judges ruled seven to three that the state may require women under eighteen years who wish to obtain an abortion to notify *both* parents (even in cases of divorce, separation, or desertion) or get special approval from a state judge. The significance of the second article is amplified when it is read in juxtaposition with the other. For the first shows us how those who rise to the top in the highly politically influential profession of law are among those in our society who have had the least experience of all of raising children.[13] They would therefore seem to be those least well-informed to make *any* decisions about abortion, and especially such decisions involving relations between teenage girls and their parents. Here we find a systematically built-in absence of mothers (and, presumably, of "wimp-like" participating fathers too) from high-level political decisions concerning some of the most vulnerable persons in our society—women who become pregnant while still in their teens, and their children. It is not hard to discern the interconnections of the supposedly separate public and private domains here.

Public life is far less distinct from personal and domestic life for women than for men. Their experience in each radically affects their possibilities in the other. The claim that the two spheres are separate is premised upon, but does not recognize, both a material and a psychological division of labor between the sexes. Since wage and salaried work, as well as other social institutions such as schools, are still structured as if the worker has a wife at home to take care of the children and perform other domestic responsibilities, it is not surprising that mothers, and especially single mothers, have a difficult time when they try to manage both. Institutions such as workplaces and schools, courts and legislatures, are still to a large extent built on the old assumption that "someone" is home to take care of children, the sick, the disabled, and anyone else who might need to be taken care of. Now that many workers *are* also that someone, either as a joint, a sole, or a primary parent, they (mostly women) are finding it much less easy to move from one sphere to the other and back in the way that the "liberal individual" is supposed to be able to do. It is neither by chance nor because of some innate defectiveness that full-time working women earn (after some recent improvement) 70 percent of the wages of full-time working men, or that women are still virtually absent from positions of great political power. Nor is it puzzling that, of married couples with children, only 27 percent of the women, compared with 77 percent of the men, have full-time year-round jobs.[14] Compounding the situation of women's economic dependence on men, half of all women who work full-time earn less than $20,000 per year. Underlying all these public inequalities is the continuing unequal division of the unpaid labor of the family, especially its childcare and other nurturing responsibilities. In turn, the inequalities between the sexes in the public sphere, by limiting women's influence and underrepresenting their perspectives, serve in a multitude of ways to allow public policy and the economy to reinforce the inequalities of the private sphere.

As well as these serious practical difficulties, the division of labor within most families raises psychological barriers against women in all other spheres. In liberal democratic politics, as well as in many workplace situations, speech and argument are often recognized as crucial components of full participation. Michael Walzer, for example, writes: "Democracy is—*the political way* of allocating power . . . What counts is argument among the citizens. Democracy puts a premium on speech, persuasive argument, rhetorical skill. Ideally, the citizen who makes the most persuasive argument . . . gets his way."[15] Yet women are often handicapped, deprived of any authority in their speech. Kathleen Jones's recent Foucaultian analysis diagnoses the problem as not "that women have not learned how to be in authority," but rather "that authority currently is conceptualized so that female voices are excluded from it."[16] Women's private and public personae are inextricably linked in the minds of many men, a problem exacerbated by the fact that we are so often represented in token numbers. Sometimes women in the public sphere are just ignored, not seen or heard. Sometimes we are seen and heard only insofar as we make ourselves seem as much as possible like men. Sometimes we are sexually harassed and demeaned at work, as many women are at home. And sometimes what we say is silenced or distorted because we get projected onto us the personae of particular important females in the intrapsychic lives of men.[17] All these handicaps, the baggage that women carry with them from the sexual division of labor at home into all the other spheres of life, certainly do not make it easy for us to make the transition back and forth. Thus, because of the past and present division of labor at home, for women the public and the private are in many ways not separate, distinct realms at all.

Finally, feminists have pointed out that, in many respects, the liberal ideal of nonintervention of the state into the realm of family life serves to reinforce actual inequalities within that realm. In earlier versions of liberalism it was quite clear that privacy rights of families meant the rights of male heads of households to regulate their families as they thought fit. Thus, for example, Locke, who drew a clear distinction between paternal and political power, gives, as an example of the things that no one would consider interfering with, a man's right to marry off his daughter. He does not consider whether a daughter might herself have an interest, and therefore a right of privacy to choose her own husband.[18]

Until very recently, Supreme Court decisions resting on a presumed constitutional right of family privacy roughly followed this model, and many still do; they asserted the rights of families to make decisions regulating their members. But in recent years, and particularly since the feminist and children's rights movements emerged in the 1960s, the courts have begun to recognize that in the domain of family life, as they had already recognized in the realm of work, nonintervention by the state in effect affirms the power of the physically or economically stronger. Thus they have recently also defended new, sometimes conflicting, claims to privacy, which are perhaps better labeled individual privacy within the family than family privacy. They have sometimes argued that the Constitution protects the rights of individual family members, even against the wishes of more powerful members or the collective decision of the family as a whole. Thus, for example, the rights of married women or of minors to seek abortions, though initially derived from the precedent of the right of family privacy, may be more reasonably viewed as individual rights, and sometimes constitute rights against families. These ongoing and still much disputed changes in perceptions of rights to privacy have brought into the light of day a fundamental problem that must be solved in the transition from patriarchal to humanist liberalism.[19]

These are some of the central feminist critiques of liberalism and its theory. Most mainstream political theory, however, proceeds regardless of these arguments and discoveries.

Gender and the Family in the Liberal-Communitarian Debate

The central debate in Anglo-American political theory during the 1980s has been between defenders of liberalism and its communitarian critics. There is a ghostly element to this debate, since communitarians have so far failed to come up with even the outlines of a theory of their own. Nevertheless, their criticisms of liberalism have attracted much attention and have put liberal theorists on the defensive. By examining some of the assumptions, arguments, and conclusions set forth by those on both sides of this debate, I shall point out some problems that result from the continuing neglect of feminist theory, and particularly of its critiques of the public-domestic dichotomy. Whether they rely on it heavily, argue as if it is of little significance at all, or at times seem aware and at other times equally unaware of the political nature and relevance of so-called "private" institutions, none of them seems either to give it much *thought,* or to be aware of the significant objections to the liberal version of the dichotomy that have been expressd by feminist theorists.

John Rawls's *A Theory of Justice,* published before much of the new scholarship on gender had appeared, continues the ambiguities and omissions of modern liberalism about both gender and the distinction between public and domestic life. Rawls states clearly at the outset that his theory of justice is to apply to "the basic structure of society," by which he means "the political constitution and the principal economic and social arrangements." These are basic because "taken together as one scheme, [they] define men's rights and duties and influence their life prospects, what they can expect to be and how well they can hope to do. The basic structure is the primary subject of justice because its effects are so profound and present from the start."[20]

Rawls's conception of the basic structure clearly transcends the state-society version of the public-private distinction, since it includes markets and property arrangements as well as the distribution of political rights and legally protected liberties. Thus, the theory is not confined to political justice, narrowly understood. It is equally clear, in its initial formulation, that the basic structure transcends the public-domestic version of the distinction. For Rawls includes "the monogamous family" as a basic institution to which the principles of social justice must apply. While perhaps surprising in the light of the history of liberal thought, this seems unavoidable, given his own criteria for inclusion in the basic structure. It would be difficult to deny that different family structures and distributions of rights and duties within families affect men's "life prospects, what they can expect to be and how well they can hope to do"—and even more difficult of course to deny their effects on the life prospects of women.

Despite this promising beginning, Rawls's theory as a whole does not depart from the liberal tradition's failure to perceive the family as a political institution, to which principles of justice should apply. The family is to a large extent ignored, though assumed, in the rest of the theory. It is addressed specifically only in three contexts: as a barrier to equal opportunity; as the mechanism to resolve issues of justice between generations; and as the initial setting in which individuals begin to develop a sense of justice.[21] Rawls is unique among contemporary theorists of justice in his attention to the family as the first school of moral development. In this context, he *assumes* that the family "in some form" is a just institution.[22] However, in contrast to his discussions of the other institutions that form the basic structure, he does not examine alternative forms of family life in the light of his principles of justice. Indeed, the assumption that the parties in the original position who arrive at the principles of justice are "heads of families" makes it impossible for the theory to include consideration of justice *within* the family. In spite of its enormous effect on the differentials in political power, economic position, and life opportunities between men and women, the division of labor within the family is never mentioned.

Thus, while in his initial definition of the basic structure Rawls appears to contest both versions of the public-private distinction, and also needs a just family to make his theory of moral development convincing, he does not depart from the traditional liberal stance on the public-domestic dichotomy. He *assumes* domestic or family life, but pays no attention to its prevalent gendered division of labor, nor to distributions of power, responsibilities, privileges, and so on within it. Moreover, this stance is typical of contemporary theorists of justice. They persist, despite the wealth of feminist challenges, in their refusal to discuss the family, much less to recognize it as a political institution of primary importance. Recent theories of justice that pay even less attention to the issues of family justice than Rawls's include Bruce Ackerman's *Social Justice in the Liberal State,* Ronald Dworkin's *Taking Rights Seriously,* William Galston's *Justice and the Human Good,* and Robert Nozick's *Anarchy, State and Utopia.*[23] Michael Walzer's theory of justice is exceptional in this regard but, as I have argued elsewhere, the conclusion that emanates from his discussion of the family—that its gender structure is unjust—does not sit easily with his emphasis on shared meanings as the foundations for justice.[24] Though the feminist arguments already discussed have demonstrated the interconnections between the gender structure inside and outside the family, and have shown how crucial the assignment of primary parenting to women is both in making men and women what they are and in determining their respective opportunities in life, the impact of these arguments has yet to be felt in mainstream liberal theory. Indeed, as I shall argue later, one of the recent defenses that liberals have proposed against communitarian critique involves a reemphasis on and a rereification of the public-private distinction.

The communitarian critics of liberalism have by and large compounded liberal theory's blindness to the facts of gender and neglect of the family as a politically relevant institution. The more conservative, nostalgic communitarians have, either implicitly or explicitly, fallen back on an ahistorical idealization of the traditional family. In Alasdair MacIntyre's nostalgic communitarianism, the idealization of traditional family forms and the acceptance of gender are largely implicit. In *After Virtue* his turning back to the Aristotelian tradition of the virtues without regard for Aristotle's exclusion of women from not only politics but the entire "good life" provides a clue to his neglect of the political significance of gender. So does his reading of Jane Austen as a celebrant rather than an ironic critic of late-eighteenth-century domestic life. At another point MacIntyre gives, with no apparent consciousness of its sexism, a list of the characters "we" need as the models around which to shape our lives as narratives. The only female characters in the list are a wicked stepmother and a suckling wolf.[25]

MacIntyre's reliance on the rationality of traditions of the virtues that have assumed and extolled variants of gender structure highly oppressive of women is continued into his most recent book. Though he briefly addresses feminist criticism of Aristotle, his response is quite inadequate. For he refers us to Plato, without mentioning the fact that Plato's integration of the guardian women into public life depends upon the abolition of the family, which hardly seems a satisfactory solution for one who identifies himself at the beginning of the book as an Augustinian Christian and at the end as a Thomist.[26] In attempting to develop a theory of justice founded upon adjudicating among the rationality of certain traditions—"that which runs from Homer to Aristotle and later passes through Arab and Jewish writers to Albertus Magnus and Aquinas; that which is transmitted from the Bible through Augustine to Aquinas; and that which carries the Scottish moral tradition from Calvinist Aristotelianism to its encounter with Hume"—MacIntyre continues to ignore the fact that all these traditions assumed and justified the subordination and dependence of women in the family and their exclusion from full participation in nondomestic life.[27] Traditions such as these have been major ideological tools in sustaining the continued inequality of the sexes. But MacIntyre is still largely ignoring feminist political theory and its critiques of the traditions on which he relies for historically grounded rationality in political and moral thinking.

In the case of Michael Sandel's nostalgic communitarianism, most attention has been paid to his critique of the Rawlsian self as disembodied and unencumbered, and his insistence that the self be understood as constituted at least in part by its attachments, convictions, and conceptions of the good. It is remarkable that in making this case he pays no attention to the earliest and most fundamental respect in which our "selves" *are* constituted, in the gender-structured families of a gender-structured society.[28] Despite his rejection of the "disembodied self," he fails to notice that embodied selves have different kinds of bodies, and that in all societies up to and including the present the sexual differences between them have been imbued with enormous social significance.

Far less noticed than his concept of the self has been Sandel's unreflective idealization of the family and denial of *any* meaningful distinction between public and personal life. Early in his critique, Sandel attacks Rawls's claim that justice is the first virtue of social institutions. This claim depends on Rawls's assertion that "a human society is characterized by the circumstances of justice," by which he means conditions of moderate scarcity and different conceptions of the good (together leading to conflicting claims about the resources available), and human imperfection in powers of reasoning and judgment.[29] The primacy of justice, Sandel acknowledges, is a "deep and powerful . . . claim," which, taken together with some related assertions, "if they can be defended, provides an impressive foundation, at once moral and epistemological, for certain liberal doctrines."[30] He sets out to show that they *cannot* be defended, since Rawls's claim that human society is characterized by the circumstances of justice is unfounded.

Sandel argues that the case for the primacy of justice is undermined by the existence of numerous social groupings, best exemplified by the family, in which the circumstances of justice do not predominate. He argues that in such "intimate or solidaristic associations . . . the values and aims of the participants coincide closely enough that the circumstances of justice prevail to a relatively small degree."[31] This claim depends heavily upon acceptance of Hume's idealized picture of family life, and in particular on his depiction of marriage as an institution in which "the cement of friendship is so strong as to abolish all divisions of possessions."[32] Sandel plucks this vision out of context to employ it in a modern argument, without any apparent concern that "the family" might not be the same now as in the eighteenth century. He seems quite unaware of the mythical nature or of the ideological purposes of such appeals to the "enlarged affections" and unity of the family, which were employed in Hume's day and later to justify the common law doctrine of coverture. This is a clear case of reification of "the family" and failure to pay attention to the historical and ideological dimensions of assertions about it. Sandel's blurring of distinctions between relations among citizens and relations among intimates seems to depend upon an idealization of both. But if we are realistic about the family and see it as a basic social institution that should at least meet, even though it may often surpass, the standards of justice, Sandel's case against the primacy of justice crumbles.

In Charles Larmore's recent defense of Rawlsian liberalism he is skeptical of Sandel's complete fusion of personal with political life, which he sees as a somewhat naive romanticism.[33] However, he falls into the opposite error, in his own reliance on simple, clear-cut, and ahistorical distinctions between the political and the personal, the public and the private. This occurs in the course of his defense of liberalism against Sandel's rejection of the "disembodied self."

In my view, there are other, quite plausible counterarguments. One is that "what is central to the liberal view is not that we can *perceive* a self prior to its ends, but that we understand ourselves to be prior to our ends, *in the sense that no end or goal is exempt from possible re-examination*."[34] We do not, after all, except in a metaphorical sense, think of someone who has converted to Catholicism, or who has left the Communist Party, despite the depth of such commitments, as having a different *self.* An alternative rebuttal might stress that there is nothing objectionable about conceiving of a person as able and willing to abstract from his or her characteristics, circumstances, and conception of the good *for the purposes of formulating principles of justice,* while being to a greater or less extent identified with them in day to day life. But Larmore does not consider such counterarguments. Instead he endorses Sandel's view that "we should not let ourselves be bullied by Kantians into thinking that our deepest self-understandings must lie prior to any vision of the good life, which may be embodied in a form of life shared with others."[35]

In order to defend liberalism against Sandel's refutation of the Kantian ideal of the person, Larmore turns to what he terms modus-vivendi liberalism, which he finds first in Locke's and Bayle's arguments for toleration, then in Hume's theory of justice. In this version of liberalism, the ideal of the neutrality of the state is seen as a response to the generally accepted fact of modern times, that reasonable people have competing conceptions of the good life.[36] As I stated earlier, I have no disagreement with the importance of this fact for liberal theory. However, Larmore argues that this approach, which he finds side by side with the Kantian approach in *A Theory of Justice* and of central importance in Rawls's recent writings, is crucially dependent on the "significant and liberating separation" of the public and political from the private. According to this approach, the liberal claim of neutrality, or the priority of the right over the good, is a political and not a personal ideal.[37] With this part of the argument I do disagree, on the grounds that it rests on a misleadingly clear and unrealistic dichotomy.

Larmore asserts that in claiming that neutrality among competing and controversial conceptions of the good is an essential political stance in a liberal state, one is not committed, as communitarians have claimed, to a personal stance of detachment from or neutrality toward competing conceptions of the good. He, like others, regards marriage and the family as exemplifying the nonpolitical, the personal and private. He says that, within the liberal ideal of political neutrality: "Marriage, for example, will . . . be, for legal purposes, a contractual relation between persons of utterly separate identities, who may thus also divorce; obviously the lived reality of a marriage can be a more mutually entwining bond than this. *Such constitutive ties are not for a liberal, however, politically or legally relevant.*"[38] Significantly, Rawls too indicates directly in a recent article that families belong with private associations like churches, universities, clubs, and relations between individuals that are outside of the realm of the political, where the principles of justice are to apply and the "political virtues" are appropriate.[39] This stance is in keeping with the neglect of familial justice in *A Theory of Justice,* but, as I have suggested, it is inconsistent both with Rawls's own explanation of why the basic structure is basic, and with the demands of his theory of moral development.

As feminist challenges to the political-personal dichotomy make clear, there are serious problems with the vision of the "lived reality" of marriage as politically or legally irrelevant and, by extension, with this renewed heavy reliance on the dichotomy as a whole. Both those who struggled to change all the laws that kept women oppressed in marriage and those who fought to retain them were intensely aware of the political and legal relevance of the terms and conditions of marriage.[40] Moreover, we are still left with a gendered family and social structure in which full and equal political and economic participation is incompatible with the family responsibilities that are still very largely borne by women. Within such a social structure it is by no means easy to see how, or indeed whether, the state can maintain neutrality on the subject of gender in policies having to do with family life, especially divorce.[41]

This is so because marriage is not only normally "a more mutually entwining bond" than is suggested by its legal structure; it is also likely, in a gender-structured society, to involve relations of dependence and power. Typically, given the division of labor between the sexes, the once "utterly separate identity" of a woman is more seriously affected by being a wife and particularly by motherhood than is the separate identity of a man by being a husband and father. The law must take *some* stance in regard to this fact. Either, recognizing the inequalities liable to be created or at least exacerbated by marriage, the law will try to prevent them and, where they occur, take account of them (as divorce law used to, at least in principle); or else the law will ignore them, both refusing to intervene in domestic disputes and regarding divorcing parties, even after long traditional marriages, as equal individuals. There is good reason for us to think that the second approach, though it may seem more neutral, is *far less neutral* in the context of a gendered society than the first. The lived reality of marriage is, clearly, more than its legal structure. But because this reality is so deeply affected by its legal structure, as well as by many other facets of "the political," it is no easy task for a liberal state to remain neutral in the face of deep disagreements about gender, and therefore about what constitutes "the good" in marital relations. The demands of neutrality in this case, unlike the case of friendship, cannot be met by simple nonintervention. As feminists have argued, though "the personal" is not identical with "the political," many aspects of the personal are undeniably political.

Conclusion

Can there be a humanist liberalism? The theoretical underpinnings of such a liberalism must focus heavily on private as well as public life. We can have a liberalism that fully includes women only if we can devise a theoretical basis for public policies that, recognizing the family as a fundamental political institution, extends standards of justice to life within it. There are undoubtedly many public policies that could considerably help people to share parenting responsibilities, and in many cases improve the current situation of children, without even raising issues of privacy. The provision of subsidized, first-rate, small-scale day care is one. Making parental leave and flexible wage-working hours mandatory for employers are others.[42] The practical, political problem here is whether such things can be achieved as long as those in power are overwhelmingly men who continue to benefit from the division of labor in the family that, in many cases, has helped them to achieve the power they have. Can we hope to change the world outside the household without changing *its* division of labor first? And, if not, how is this to be achieved?

Any solution that is to be consistent with the basic principles of liberalism must respect the fact that, in our society at present, gender is a hotly disputed issue. Since the liberal state must, in Larmore's words, "remain neutral toward disputed and controversial ideals of the good life," it cannot simply dictate and enforce the abolition of gender. But neither may it favor gender, or even *allow* gendered practices that make women and children vulnerable. If it is to be neutral on this crucial issue, family law must clearly provide for alternative conceptions of marriage. By doing so, it can ensure that citizens live their domestic lives in conditions of equality—that they either share the unpaid and the paid work, and the concomitant time, leisure, and opportunities or enter into enforceable contracts ensuring that any division of labor between the sexes that is agreed to does not involve economic dependence or the jeopardizing of the long-term chances of either partner to participate fully in life in the realm of work or politics. Because of the inextricable connections between the family and its political and legal context, a liberalism that aspires to be humanist must apply its standards of justice to the most private of our attachments.

THREE

Liberal Democracy and the Costs of Consent

BENJAMIN R. BARBER

In its erratic, often glorious, political history since 1688, liberalism has forged many alliances: with rationalism and with empiricism, with revolution and with bureaucracy, with enlightenment and with romanticism, and with laissez-faire economics and with nationalism. But no alliance has served it better than the one it established with democracy. For, by itself, liberalism was a struggle for emancipation from religious and political absolutism that exacted costs liberal principles could not contend with. In establishing the solitary individual as the model citizen, liberalism shortchanged ideas of citizenship and community, and contrived a fictional self so unencumbered by situation and context as to be useful only in challenging the very idea of the political.[1] In emphasizing freedom as the absence of all governmental restraints, it impeded the march of popular sovereignty. In combating higher ecclesiastic and secular authority, it attenuated the capacity of religion and tradition to sustain and integrate.

As Tocqueville noticed, societies organized around the anarchic blessings of freedom are more rather than less in need of the unifying blessings of religion.[2] Yet liberalism's virtues—the wall between church and state, the toleration of conflicting confessions, the acknowledgement of uncertainty, even skepticism, in public thinking—could only further undermine the religious principles whose consolation it needed. Liberalism created a safe haven for individuals and their property, but a poor environment for collective self-government. As liberals were quick to remonstrate, if traditional authoritarian governments endangered the rights and freedoms of individuals, the tyranny of "legitimate" majorities founded on popular sovereignty could be still more onerous. Equality obviously might be an entailment of the idea of the common liberty of individuals, but in its political form (rectification, redistribution, government intervention, social justice) it endangered liberty understood as being left alone. Even friends of democracy such as William Connolly worry that democracy "contains danger" and that it is a danger that "resides within the ideal itself."[3]

The pure liberal state was in fact an oxymoronic conundrum. Anarchy—the absence of all government—was liberalism's purest expression, to be found in principles like the ones inhering in Robert Nozick's minimalist Protective Association, or in the Watchdog State (the state as arbitrator, umpire, regulator or free market rule-keeper).[4] In this pure sense Hobbes—who is sometimes construed as a liberal by virtue of the instrumentalism with which he makes absolute authority prudentially serve absolute liberty—is no liberal at all.[5]

Of course there has never been an actual state constituted by pure liberal principles. From the start, liberalism forged (at times, was thrown into) a working relationship with democracy, which seemed to share so many of its goals (the welfare and freedom, differently understood, of the individual), even as it created problems for their realization.

Western liberal states are in fact all liberal democracies, combining principles of individual liberty with principles of collective self-government and egalitarianism. And, as a matter of practice, such states have done comparatively well, both by liberty, property, and individualism, on the one hand, and by equality, justice, and self-government, on the other. Many observers would attribute their success precisely to their hybrid form.

Yet in England and North America, the mix has been less than judicious, the balance less then dialectical. Although liberalism has benefited from democracy, it has rarely acknowledged the benefits and has generally treated democratic practices (if not also democratic ideas) as perilous. Rather then permitting democracy to complement liberty, liberty has been given lexical priority over all other principles. Even the manner in which the central problem of politics in the West is formulated is liberal (this is Rousseau's version of that formulation): how to find a form of association that defends and protects the person and goods of each individual, by means of which each one, uniting with all, nonetheless obeys himself alone and remains as free as before.[6] This assumes the priority of the individual and his freedom over the community and its rights, and makes the accommodation of the individual, regarded as an a priori, the task of the community, regarded as an artificial contrivance.[7]

The priority of the "liberal" in liberal democracy has rendered it vulnerable to modernity's most devastating political pathology: deracination. The impact of the Enlightenment on religion and the impact of epistemological skepticism and post-Enlightenment science on nature and natural law have left modern women and men to live in an era after virture, after God, after nature, an era offering neither comfort nor certainty. Freedom has been won by a ruthless severing of ties ("all that is solid melts into air," wrote Marx) and an uprooting of human nature from its foundations in the natural, the historical, and the divine.[8]

The specific pathologies that have been occasioned by deracination need little comment, for they are by now a very old story. Yet they still are frequently overlooked by those who champion liberalism's defensive properties as a protector of individuals against communities gone awry and states run amok.[9] Indeed, it is arguable that the forces that created the greatest pressures on the liberty of individuals in the twentieth century are, at least in part, the consequences of deracination, social anarchy, and rampant individualism—the consequence not of too much democracy and too little liberalism but of too little democracy and too much liberalism. Fascism in Germany was preceded by the Weimar Republic's wan liberalism; and the authoritarian personality would seem to be at least in part the product of deracination.[10]

I believe that liberal democracy has been given an insufficiently dialectical reading in modern political theory, as a result in large part of the theorists' reliance on the notion of consent as the crucial bridge between the individual and the community (between liberty and justice and between right and utility). The doctrine of consent was originally intended to give obedience a justification rooted in the interests of individuals rather than in the authority of states (in the rights of the ruled rather than the rights of rulers) and did not necessarily entail democratic arrangements. But it also created principled grounds for democracy by making all political legitimacy a function of popular will. The consent device skewed the relationship toward liberal individualism from the outset, however. It deprived liberals of the comforts of democracy as they tried to accommodate the communities produced by individuals (whom they recognized as such) with the individuals produced by communities (which they refused to recognize).

Unlike pure liberalism of the Nozickean variety, in which the individual stands as the sole measure of right, liberal democracy claims both to unite individuals with the community and to preserve individual liberty in the face of community—leaving men "as free as they were before" (Rousseau's formulation). In Sandel's language, it aspires to mediate the extremes of the "radically situated self" (presumably the collectivist conception) and the "radically disembodied subject" (the libertarian conception).[11] Moreover, it seeks a bridge that does not depend on some foundationalist conception either of right or the good. Liberal democrats are not unmitigated voluntarists, but per force they eschew traditional foundationalism of the kind that makes politics depend entirely upon ideas derived from grounds independent of and anterior to the political. The liberal democrat prizes justice but believes justice without consent is a form of heteronomy incompatible with the moral responsibility of the individual. Consent becomes the crucial link: for Locke, for example, what men will consent to in the state of nature binds them henceforward; for Rawls, what men will consent to in a hypothetical original position, before they know the actual identities they will assume in society, binds them to the rules they will live by in society.[12]

By consenting to the substantive rules to which he will subordinate his will, the liberal individual obeys without compromising his freedom. The conception of democracy that emerges from contract—that is to say, from consent theory—does provide some security for liberty and rights, by rooting them in a voluntarism that is immune from the immediacy of popular will. The arbitrary whimsy (the subjectivism) of pure voluntarism is avoided without embracing discredited forms of metaphysical foundationalism.

Consent plays a central role in all liberal theory, but it is differently construed in Hobbes, in Locke, in Nozick, and in Rawls. As consent changes the forms it takes, liberal democracy changes its colors. Yet in every form it permits liberal ideas to take precedence over democratic ideas. Moving from the weakest to the strongest, three primary forms of consent can be discerned: we may understand them as original consent, periodic consent, and perpetual consent. The first, in which individuals offer consent once in the form of a covenant that obliges them henceforward to obey whatever rules the civil society they have thus created may promulgate, is original consent or the doctrine of the social contract. Original consent embraces both the form where individuals agree to procedures by which rules are made (social contract constitutionalism), without consenting to the actual rules, as well as the form where individuals agree in advance to the actual rules, as with Rawls. The second major form taken by consent theory, calling for a kind of ongoing commitment to the contract, engages individuals in periodic rehearsals of consent, most often through the election of representatives. This form is periodic consent or the doctrine of representative government. It employs elections not merely to assure the accountability of representative governors but also to elicit periodic fidelity from citizens whose commitments might otherwise weaken. The third, and strongest, form requires consent to each and every collective act (each law, contract, bargain, encroachment, and so on). It approaches the spirit of pure liberalism, where government exists and acts exclusively at the pleasure of each individual with whom it interacts. This is perpetual consent, or the market doctrine of libertarianism (a stone's throw from what I earlier called "pure liberalism").[13]

In terms of the hypothetical politics they produce, the three regimes that emerge from these three forms of consent look very different. Social-contract theorists may be satisfied with highly authoritarian and illiberal regimes that are still legitimate by liberal standards because they are authorized by an original contract to which all subjects initially give their consent (if only tacitly). One thinks of Hobbes or Hamilton. Advocates of representative government, such as Locke, require that citizens reaffirm their government and thus their civic commitment from time to time by periodically reauthorizing the governors (who are only trustees of their electors). Libertarians are fierce and constant consenters who demand perpetual vigilance by individuals for whom every new social act is a potential encroachment.

Social-contract theorists take a tacit and relatively passive view of the role of consent—once suffices for all time—raising issues of compliance (covenants without the sword, free riders, and so on); advocates of representation take the middle ground, enhancing the autonomous activity of citizens as individuals while limiting their common power to the act of selecting rulers, but otherwise discouraging ongoing self-rule; and libertarians make consent a cudgel with which they beat the very idea of collective governmental activity into senselessness.

However different they are in theory, all three versions of consent theory merge in the practice of Western governments, almost all of which are "mixed" regimes with respect to original, periodic, and perpetual consent. Indeed the pluralism of such governments arises in part out of jurisdictional quarrels between these conflicting forms of consent—as when the Supreme Court intervenes in the name of original consent (the integrity of the Constitution, representing the original voice of the people) to overrule elected officials operating in the name of periodic consent (they represent the citizens who have elected them to office) in order to uphold the complaint of a private citizen who has challenged the government in the name of his own liberty (embodying the principle of perpetual consent). These mixed liberal democratic regimes share certain fundamental weaknesses that take us to the heart of the problem—with consent as the liberal linchpin.

Perhaps most disconcerting among the defects of liberalism that arise out of its dependence on consent is the reactivity—and thus the negativity—consent imparts to liberal politics. Politics become purely defensive; the model political act is resistance to encroachment on a private sphere defined by the autonomous and solitary person. And while the radically isolated individual may originate a purely logical priority, the ideal individual's sphere of activity in the real world seems always to be expanding, as the domain of the person is enlarged by outward pushing liberties and rights, and then enlarged still more by that extension of the person and its liberties liberals call property— ownership of things as an entailment of self-ownership.[14] The ultimate battle cry of the liberal is "Don't cross this line!" The political slogan always reads "Don't walk on my turf!" Liberalism is a politics of negativity, which enthrones not simply the individual but the individual defined by his perimeters, his parapets, and his entrenched solitude. Politics is at best a matter of "Let's make a deal," where the stakes are exclusively private ("What will it take to get you to honor my liberty?").

Politics understood as reactive negativity and the denial of every commonality other than that of aggregated individuality reduces the role of will to one of obstinate resistance. Hence it obstructs common willing—what Rousseau called general willing—where communities essay to disclose common purposes or discover common ground through the political interaction of active wills. The very idea of sovereignty, construed as the paramountcy of a common will, cannot exist in a setting defined by the primacy of the right of the individual to unlimited resistance (that resistance being seen as a property of essential—and hence rightful—human nature). Politics becomes a matter of "not doing" rather than of "doing," and the individual becomes sovereign, always trumping the community.

Historically the focus on resistance had powerful political uses in emancipating individuals from feudal authority. The priority of the individual was an artificial device, which (although everywhere contradicted by the real life dependency of individuals on hierarchical social structures) helped to free men from bondage. The fiction preceded the reality: in fact, the fiction created the reality, for it was meant not as a defense of preexisting individuals against encroaching authority, but a justification for the forging of individuals from socially constructed subjects. The point was not to legitimize natural individuals, but to legitimize individuation in the face of "natural" (historical and traditional) collectivism. The "natural" man was merely a hypothetical contrivance whose wholly rhetorical significance was not to be mistaken for the kind of anthropological conjectures that would in time be favored by the romantics (noble savages and all that).[15]

The useful fiction of the independent person soon hardened into a supposed reality of naturally autonomous men, and this new and contrived "reality" became the basis for denying both the historical legitimacy of unfree commonality (feudalism, ancient slavery, traditional tyranny) and thus the future possibility of a free commonality. Abstract personhood, so fruitful as an emancipatory hypothesis, subverted ideas of democratic community and democratic cooperation in its inevitable reification. We have traditionally worried about the consequences of the reification of the collectivity or the state. I am suggesting that we might also have some reason to worry about the political consequences of the reification of the individual—an idealized abstraction given a concrete incarnation if ever there was one. Individuals, merely separate in the hypothesis, became competitive and adversarial in the anthropologized version where they were confounded with bargainers in the new capitalist economy and predators in the dawning age of imperialism. And where every individual faces every other individual not merely as distinct but as an adversary, where possessiveness and aggressiveness are primary and highly prized social traits, where the Other is seen first as an antagonist and last (if at all) as a neighbor, where suspicion of encroachment is the chief political motive, there can be no politics of cooperation. Nor is a viable conception of a public sector or a common good likely to emerge. Crippled from the outset by the very framework that made it liberating, liberalism needed democracy. It had to have a politics to complement its antipolitics. Yet it was averse to the democratic ideas that provided it with that politics.

The tensions have persisted. Anxious witnesses to our century's statist and collectivist depredations may understandably perceive in the resisting negativity of pure liberalism our best defense against every form of unfreedom. Judith Shklar reminds us how often some noble common purpose has been employed to hurt vulnerable bodies, as if their animal fragility made them ignoble.[16] But it is also true that twentieth-century collectivism is in part a consequence of the failure of liberalism to offer a healthy politics of community. There is a deep yearning, well known to liberals, for a more supple and intersubjective identity than that offered by the hollow shell of legal personhood; when it is not satisfied by some safe, democratic form of mutualism, the door is wide open to unsafe, totalitarian forms of mutualism. By construing politics exclusively in terms of reaction, liberals limit it to resisting Others (or the political incarnation of Others, the state)—an antipolitical act at best—or to acquiescing to them—politics understood as compliance, agreeing to but not doing. Even Robert Nozick's self-interested anarchist busybodies, perpetually examining potential bilateral exchanges with others for signs of encroachment, are limited to a political vocabulary of "OK, I'll buy it" or "No deal!" In these one-shot yea/nay situations, the role of common deliberation, general willing, and public judgment is negligible. There is little room for anything resembling public space—except for those who seize it for their own private purposes.

Indeed, for liberals, public space has an exclusively prudential feel (that space ceded to government which permits government to enforce the integrity of private boundaries) and is not intended to convey a rich sense of publicness or commonwealth or *res publica*. Contrary to historical reality, where public space was the condition of the emergence of individuals, it exists in liberal theory only as a concession reluctantly proffered by individuals pursuing self-preservation or self-aggrandizement. It is at best the domain of prudence where individuals strike public bargains (like the Social Contract) in the pursuit of private interests. Even in Hobbes's authoritarian version, every act of the omnipotent, irresistible sovereign finds its ultimate justification in the original authority of those self-interested authors of the contract who are struggling to avoid lives which, in the state of nature where liberty is theoretically uncompromised, are solitary, poor, nasty, brutish, and short.[17] American pluralist theory does not advance much beyond Hobbes in this regard, since the Madisonian formula is distrustful of democracy and places its faith in dividing power (and interest) against itself so as to safeguard liberty from its putative governmental protectors. Madison emulates Locke in worrying more about the peril to liberty presented by the sovereign Lion than about the small mischiefs polecats and foxes might do to their common liberties. In general, liberals deploy a political language drawn from the menagerie, reenforcing with metaphor their essentially adversarial (what could later be called Darwinian) conception of the social relations of their fictive "persons."

To be sure the language of consent is in principle an attempt at bridging the liberty of liberalism and the demos of democracy, but the foregoing survey of what consent actually entails suggests that it does little to bring individual and commons into equilibrium. Its final result is the dogmatic justification of the priority of liberty (liberty understood as the absence of all external—read public—constraint),[18] and thus the priority—even in Rawls—of right over utility, of the liberty of the abstract individual over the needs of community-created citizens.[19]

For some time critics of the skewed liberal version of liberal democracy have been urging an alternative formulation, one centering on participation rather than consent. My own elaboration of the theory and practice of "strong democracy" is intended to help conceptualize this alternative view.[20] Participation turns out to provide a much more dialectical account of the relation between individuals and the community than consent can possibly hope to. It offers a framework for institutions that safeguards the liberty of individuals without alienating them from public space—since their liberty is constructed in and with respect to that public space.

Taking participation seriously does not reverse the priority of individual and community (which would produce some form of totalist collectivism) but strikes a genuine balance between the two.[21] To do so acknowledges the interdependence of individuals on one another and on the communities from which they derived sustenance for their identities and their (socially constructed) rights, and thus makes of morally autonomous citizens the aim rather than the premise of liberal democratic politics.

Participation is less a way of linking previously or "naturally" autonomous persons to an artificial and sovereign collectivity than it is of characterizing and legitimizing the provisional autonomy that real men and women living under conditions of actual dependency can elicit from the social milieus in which they are embedded. Participation is a form of belonging in which active agency is transferred from the whole to the parts, which, however, possess a capacity for effective action by virtue of their membership in the whole.

The hypothetical act by which the community based on the consent of "naturally free" individuals is formed must be: "Let's make a state we all obey, in return for which it will protect us from each other [Hobbes] and from itself [the prudent Locke]." The hypothetical act by which the community based on participation is formed is "Let's take this collectivity into which we were all born and to which, willy-nilly, we all are bound and legitimize it by subjecting it to our common will." Where with consent, the archetypical political act is *resistance against or acquiescence to encroachment,* with participation, the archetypical political act is *disclosing and legitimizing common ground,* or *willing common action in the absence of common ground.* In a word, it is collaboration rather than antagonism, learning to live with conflict rather than constructing a geometry and vector physics of conflict.[22]

Underlying the model of participation is a conception of the person radically distinctive from the one underlying the model of consent.[23] The liberal person is a fixed being with an identity arising out of theoretically constructed interests made legitimate by the heightened language of rights. Liberal rights are in fact individual interests posturing as moral claims. (This is an oddity, in that moral claims presuppose a moral-social environment in which claims have meaning—the point T. H. Green makes in his work.)[24] The force of this conception lies precisely in the fixity and immutability of interests, which define the natural and unchanging social monads who constitute liberal persons.

The participating citizen, however, is a being with a mutable nature, whose evolution is in part a function of its social habitat. It is this very talent for self-transformation that enables the citizen thus conceived to engage in the process of individuation: not merely to engage in bargaining and exchange over fixed and permanent interests but to modify the notion of what those interests actually are. Participation entails change—a faculty for self-transformation—for the community as well as for the participating member. The bachelor who becomes a spouse is not a bachelor who has made a bargain, but someone who has given up the identity and interests appropriate to bachelorhood and assumed the identity and interests of someone participating in a life partnership. Spousehood supplants bachelorhood as a point of view, so that the spouse ceases to think or act like a bachelor. A spouse who in turn becomes a parent is not a spouse who has cut a deal with pushy and self-preoccupied (that is, infantile!) newcomers who were not parties to the original marital contract. He is someone who has given up the identity of spouse in favor of an identity that includes the interests and concerns of children. In moving from bachelor to parent, the man and the woman are transformed by the relations they enter into, even as, by virtue of their participation, they transform the character of the community they belong to. The compass of their sympathies enlarge; their capacity to identify the concerns of a growing "neighborhood" as *their* concerns alters their own sense of identity.

Participatory citizenship is an extension of the same principles to strangers. The moves from parent to neighbor, from neighbor to townsperson, from townsperson to citizen of the United States, all have the same potential of self-transformation, when the link to the community is participatory and not merely consensual. As the sphere of identification grows, identity undergoes a change. The office of citizen is not just a role assumed momentarily by the individual; it is a mantle that settles over the shoulders and in time becomes an organic epidermis of the skin on which it rests. The state is a neighborhood of strangers. It cannot deal with its constituents through the intimate roles of friendship or kinship because they are strangers; yet it need not treat them as adversaries, one to the other, because they are also neighbors.

If the individuals who participate are changelings whose consciousness grows (or can potentially grow) as the sphere of their activity enlarges, then their activity when they participate is far more demanding—more engaging, more enthralling, more disquieting—than their activity when they merely consent, when they act exclusively to resist or to acquiesce. Participation entails constant activity, ceaseless willing, and endless interaction with other participants in quest of common grounds for common living. The one-time contract offends the idea of participation, which demands with Jefferson that principles be constantly remembered, deliberated, reembraced, even reinvented, if they are to earn their legitimacy among the living.[25] Nor is the sometime contract called representation an adequate surrogate for civic participation. For while the election of representatives requires some periodic activity from citizens, it is a political act whose purpose is to terminate political action for all but the elected delegates. It achieves accountability by alienating responsibility, and leaves elected politicians as the only real citizens of the state.[26]

The perpetual consent demanded by libertarians would on first inspection seem better to approximate the vigorous civic activity associated with participation, and the libertarian is certainly a busy fellow as he rushes to and fro, defending his perimeters against the endless encroachments of his hungry neighbors. But not only is his activity limited to fight/flight reactions (yea/nay judgments on potential encroachments), whatever he does lacks public import of any kind. Public relations become private relations, and commonality is reduced to a series of trustless bilateral exchanges.

This liberal vision calls to mind a kind of Brownian motion by agitated human molecules that results in random movement with no consistent or patterned (that is, public) character. On the other hand, participation is by its very nature public activity whose aim is to produce publicity or public-mindedness. Participation is participating in public discourse (finding discourse that is public) and participating in public action (action possible only when actors act together) in the name of creating public things (*res publica*). The language of consent is *me* language: "*I* agree" or "*I* disagree." The language of participation is *we* language: "Can *we*?" or "Is that good for *us*?"

The libertarian damns the contractarian for being satisfied with a single act of willed compliance and then sitting in torpor for eternity. How can a man speak but once and then remain forever mute? The libertarian knows he must sing on, and so, on and on he sings (on and on and on and on). But chirping away from his solitary branch against the din of rival birds he produces only cacophony.

Noise is of course a concomitant of democratic politics, and the citizen has nothing to fear from a little high decibel cacophony. But the aim is harmony: the discovery of a common voice. Not unity, not voices disciplined into unison, but musical harmony in its technical meaning. Liberals grow particularly anxious at what they believe is a democratic penchant for consensus and unity. William Connolly, for example, insists that democracy must be limited by ambiguity and open to discord.[27] He might recall, however, that in music, harmony is not a matter of a single voice but of several voices, of distinct notes, which complement and support one another, creating not the ennui of unison but a pleasing plurality. Harmony is not monism, and the consensus reached by democratic deliberation and action has nothing in common with the unity imposed by the collectivist demagogue armed with a plebiscite.

Democratic politics need not be limited by ambiguity because it embraces and teaches us how to live with ambiguity. It is precisely about common decisionmaking in the face of ambiguity and uncertainty. (Certain knowledge would transform politics into an exercise in expertise and promote a Platonic government of the most knowledgeable.) It is precisely where we cannot know for sure that we must act democratically. In the best of circumstances we may achieve a harmony within our civic communities that preserves our hard-won individuality but permits us to support and complement the individuality of other participants. In those rare moments where inevitable cacophony is transformed briefly into harmony (but not totalitarian unity), participation achieves its greatest civic victory, realizing an egalitarian community that accommodates individuals without destroying their individuality—an achievement which, though perhaps beyond the liberal imagination, is deeply satisfying to the liberal spirit.

These images, I know, are redolent of a kind of democratic idealism that is worrisome to liberals, whose chief political concern remains the abuse of individual bodies (and spirits, but bodies first of all) by illegitimate power. But the possibility of harmony is a byproduct of participatory politics: a remarkable achievement when accomplished, but not essential to the argument on behalf of participation. For, as I have suggested, participatory politics is in the first instance simply a more realistic way of understanding the actual relationship that obtains between individual and community, as well as a more dialectical way of envisioning how that relationship (which by nature is one of dependency) can be made legitimate (just). In fact, it is the most prudent defense liberty can deploy in an era uprooted from foundations in religion, history, or tradition.

In a world after virtue, where the foundational certainties of God and Nature have gone the way of metaphysics, and where men and women are compelled to live together and find both mediators for their conflicts and a forge for their commonality, liberal democracy in the participatory mode may be humankind's safest form of politics. The individual is a paltry vessel when torn apart from within by doubt and vacillation. Liberty rings hollow to women and men whose lives lack purpose and meaning: it is then only the right to do everything in a world where one has no idea of what to do. In emancipating us from authority, liberalism separated us from one another. Resistance was a powerful instrument in taking on popes and kings and their ex cathedra arguments, but when the very idea of God withers and when, freed from arbitrary authority, women and men grow desperate for almost any authority at all, resistance ceases to be a useful political tool. To the creature trapped within the fortress, the impregnable redoubt may come to feel like a prison. Liberals, ever wary, still preach "Defend yourselves! The enemy is everywhere!" And, to be sure, wherever there are policies, policemen, and power, there lurk potential enemies of liberty. Yet the price we pay for this vigilance is also to see enemies where there are only neighbors, antagonism where there may be cooperation. In safeguarding our separate bodies, we neglect the body politic; in expressing our dignity as individuals, we fail to dignify our sociability and give it a safe form of expression. The alternative to legitimate community is not natural liberty but illegitimate community. The alternative to democratic politics is not the absence of all politics but undemocratic politics. An unhealthy polity is not an occasion for a righteous return to prepolitical individuality: it is the occasion for the destruction of individuality tout court.

Our human strength lies in our capacity for community. Abandoned by God and nature, we must depend on each other; yet we are saddled with a residual politics of emancipation that forbids us mutual consolation or cooperation. In the long freedom wars liberalism won a thousand important battles, securing first the individual and his rights, and then the rights of others long excluded from liberty's fruits. But the costs of victory are now being paid: the price of liberal reliance on contract and consent has been the impoverishment of its politics. The argument for participation is thus not idealistic but brutally realistic. It is how liberals can safely pay the piper— who, one way or the other, *will* be paid.

A more dialectically balanced liberal democracy employing the language and institutions of participation can respond to modernity's losses by reenforcing the individual from within and by offering artificial membership in new contrived communities of common will from without. Participation subjects standards, whose roots in natural or metaphysical foundations have withered, to the voluntary and common conventions of a democratic polity, permitting artifice to achieve what nature no longer can. And if artifice is to be safe, it is clear, it must be democratic: the subject of common deliberation and decision. Participation greets the loss of certainty with neither cynicism nor despair but with a novel epistemology of political judgment: concrete processes by which our convictions can be measured by something firmer than private prejudice in a world where cognitive certainty is no longer vouchsafed us.[28]

If we are to learn to live with what Clifford Geertz has called the vertigo of relativism, participatory democracy can be an instructive teacher. It offers hope without making foolish promises. It proffers not a civic religion but a civic life that binds without enslaving, that ties together the frayed pieces left behind by the unraveling of religion. It instructs us to look to common invention for the social sustenance we once derived from tradition.

Participatory democracy cannot replace the loss of foundations that is modernity's legacy, but it promises a certain prudence in place of mores, tradition, and history. It is a politics of modest hope in a world of despair. And, liberal skepticism notwithstanding, liberty remains today what it has always been: the hope we fling into the teeth of sovereign necessity to make a small space for human will and for the virtue will enjoins.

· II ·

Education and the Moral Life

Undemocratic Education

AMY GUTMANN

In the seventeenth century, when Locke wrote *Some Thoughts Concerning Education,* the English word "to educate" was a synonym for "to govern." The identification has ceased to be apparent not only in our language but also in our political theory. I have made a modest effort to revive the identification in political theory, which began with Plato's *Republic,* a treatise on undemocratic education, the education necessary not for democratic citizens but for members of a family state, a state that aims to establish a constitutive relation between individual and social good based on knowledge.[1]

The identification of education and governance is total in *The Republic.* Governance *is* education in Plato's family state. A few philosophers educate and rule not just children but other adults. The few rule by virtue of knowledge, not by virtue of having first been ruled. And they rule not so the many might rule in turn, but so everyone can live the good life, as authoritatively understood and instituted by philosophers.[2]

We can appreciate Plato's harmonizing of private and public good without accepting it as a legitimate political project. In *The Republic* Socrates tells Glaucon that "it's better for all to be ruled by what is divine and prudent, especially when one has it as his own within himself; but, if not, *set over one from outside,* so that insofar as possible all will be alike and friends, piloted by the same thing."[3] Children must not be set free until the right regime—the "divine and prudent" one—is established within their souls. But who holds the key to the right regime? Not the Socrates who boasts of being the only Athenian wise enough to know his own ignorance.

But Plato's Socrates imagines that there may be someone wiser even than he, someone who has left the cave and seen the light, someone who therefore knows the right regime for all souls. To create a family state the philosopher must return to the cave, become "king," and wipe the social slate clean by exiling "all those in the city who happen to be older than ten; and taking over their children . . . rear them—far away from those dispositions they now have from their parents."[4] Socrates himself recoils from the idea on behalf of his imaginary philosopher-king, suggesting that he "won't be willing to mind the political things . . . unless some divine chance coincidentally comes to pass."[5]

Those of us who do not imagine our souls in such good order also recoil on behalf of those disorderly souls whom Socrates' philosopher-king would order. Our recoil is not self-serving. Even if there were someone wiser than Socrates in our midst, she still could not claim the right to order the souls of all citizens. Just as an unexamined life is not worth living, so too a good life must be one that a person recognizes as such, lived from the inside, according to one's own best lights. The neo-Platonic quest for "the one best system"[6] denies this insight of individualism. Even if Plato were right about the objectively good life, political philosophy would still have to look past *The Republic* for a politically legitimate way of associating private and public good, through governing.

We need not look far past Plato's family state to find a political alternative. One suggested in the *Crito* and resurrected by Rousseau in the *Government of Poland* is a non-Platonic family state. When the laws and the constitution of Athens speak to Socrates of his duty to obey, they claim not that they are right, but that they have a right to rule him just as parents have a right to rule a child. ("Did we not give you life in the first place? Was it not through us that your father married your mother and begot you? Since you have been born and brought up and educated, can you deny, in the first place, that you were our child and servant, both you and your ancestors?")[7] This argument proves insufficient for Socrates. It would also obligate him to a highly repressive regime, one lacking those freedoms that he subsequently cites as reason to obey the Athenian jury's verdict. Because citizens are not children, the force of a state's claim to sovereignty over citizens is more suspect than parental claims to sovereignty over their children.

Parental claims to sovereignty are suspect enough. Children are not, as Charles Fried suggests, merely extensions of their parents' personalities anymore than they are creatures constituted by a state.[8]

It is one thing to recognize the authority of parents to educate their children as members of a family, and quite another to claim that parental authority may serve as a shield against exposing children to ways of life or thinking that offend their parents. The state of families—a state that cedes parents sovereignty over the education of their children—mistakenly conflates the welfare of children with the freedom of parents when it assumes that the former is best defined or secured by the latter. Just as a substantial realm of parental authority is essential to both the freedom of adults and the welfare of children as members of families, so too is a substantial realm of political authority essential to both the future freedom of children and their welfare as citizens. Because children are members of both families and states, the educational authority of parents and polities has to be partial to be justified. The reconciliation of public and private good suggested by the state of families is no more acceptable than that of the family state. Whereas the family state reconciles private and public good by denying the private realm any independent moral status, the state of families denies the public realm any moral independence and any hold on our identities.

The appeal of the state of individuals, the liberal state as it is loosely called, may stem from the fact that it recognizes claims of both realms, without attempting to subsume or constitute one by the other.[9] Its reconciliation of public and private good may therefore seem more reasonable. The state of individuals enforces only those laws, subsidizes only those goods, and professes only those doctrines that are neutral among conceptions of the good life. The state's principled neutrality aims to maximize the freedom of individuals to pursue their diverse conceptions of the private good. The state of individuals does not claim to rest upon a neutral doctrine, as some of its critics suppose. It aspires to neutrality among conceptions of the private good. And precisely for this reason, it champions a conception of the public good: the public good consists of maximizing the freedom of citizens to pursue their diverse conceptions of the private good. An advocate of the state of individuals might paraphrase John Stuart Mill: all attempts by the state to bias the conclusions of its citizens, including its children, on disputed subjects are evil, as are all unnecessary restrictions on their choices.[10] This is a credo of neutrality for the sake of opportunity and choice.

Of course all educators must limit children's choices, but only for the sake of developing their capacity for rational choice or for the sake of cultural coherence. American schoolchildren are taught English not by choice but by cultural determination. This cultural determination legitimately limits the range of their future choices, even if it does not uniquely determine whom they become. The limitations on learning language and literature are legitimated by the need for "cultural coherence." But this need does not justify "adult pretensions to moral superiority."[11]

The horticultural imagery so prevalent in Plato—pruning and weeding children's desires, carefully shaping their character—has no place in this liberal theory of education. "We have no right to look upon future citizens as if we were master gardeners who can tell the difference between a pernicious weed and a beautiful flower."[12] But we do have a right, even a duty, to shape the character and bias the choices of children for the sake of cultural coherence. Education in the state of individuals builds on our cultural but not our moral biases. We educate children to be Americans who are free to choose, but we do not bias their choices (or shape their character) for the sake of moral goodness. We educate rational shoppers but not good people or virtuous citizens.

Why say that parents and teachers should be free to guide children's choices for the sake of cultural coherence but not for the sake of cultivating good character or choosing a morally good life? Because no one has a right to act according to the belief that his or her conception of the good life is better than anyone else's.[13] This premise, which grounds the state of individuals, is as shaky as the premise underlying the family state, that the objectively correct conception of the good ought to govern everyone's life. After all, sometimes the claim on the part of parents and teachers that they know the difference between morally good and bad, or better and worse, is not a pretension to moral superiority, but a reflection of their greater moral understanding. Honesty is better than deceitfulness, industriousness better than sloth, insight better than insensitivity, kindness better than cruelty—and not just because honest, industrious, insightful, and kind people have more freedom of choice. They may have less, precisely because they are constrained by these virtues. We nonetheless value these virtues because there is more to a good life and to a good society than freedom.

The resistance to recognizing the legitimacy of education for civic virtue stems, I suspect, from formulating our educational options as a dichotomy. Either we must educate children so that they are free to choose among the widest range of lives because freedom of choice is the paramount good, or we must educate children so that they will choose *the* life that is best because a rightly ordered soul is the paramount good. Let children define their own identity or define it for them. Give children liberty or give them virtue. This is a morally false choice. Cultivating character and intellect through education constrains children's future choices, but it does not uniquely determine them. There need be nothing illegitimate about such constraints, although some surely are illegitimate.

The question is not whether to maximize freedom or to inculcate virtue, but how to combine freedom with virtue. Which freedoms and what virtues? We must focus not just on the future freedom of children but also on the present freedom of parents, not just on the virtues necessary for a good life but also on those necessary for a just society. Alternatively, we may integrate the virtues necessary to constitute a good society into those necessary for a good life. The result of one important integration is a bundle of virtues tied together by a Lockean notion of "rational liberty."[14] Rationality informs liberty of what is necessary to live well in a morally good society; it does not simply serve as a means of satisfying individual desires. A necessary (but of course not sufficient) condition of living well in a society where people differ in their moral convictions is effective teaching of the liberal virtue of toleration. A more distinctively democratic virtue that a good society must also teach effectively is mutual respect for reasonable differences of moral opinion. Mutual respect demands more than the attitude of live and let live; it requires willingness and ability to accord due intellectual and moral regard to reasonable points of view that we cannot ourselves accept as correct. In the political realm, toleration is a precondition for peaceful competition and pragmatic compromise; mutual respect is a precondition for democratic deliberation and moral compromise. Education in both virtues supports rational liberty in a liberal democracy.

Yet another liberal way of appreciating the need to combine freedom with virtue is to question whether the many virtues valued by a liberal society can be ordered by one and only one overarching conception of individual flourishing. William Galston's account of competing conceptions of individual flourishing suggests that there is no singularly correct conception. There seems instead to be a plurality of reasonable conceptions of the good life, which converge in defending a group of individual virtues. Galston concludes that the best liberal polity is "a community that encourages all of these overlapping but distinct conceptions of individual excellence and that provides an arena within which each may be realized, in part through struggle against the others."[15] Two of the most appropriate arenas for the struggle are democratic politics and education. The liberty polity at its best must be substantially democratic.

This democratic understanding of liberalism does not resolve but at least it comprehends the problem of associating individual freedom and civic virtue in the United States today. Citizens of a religiously and ethnically diverse society disagree on the relative value of freedom and virtue; we disagree on the nature of a good life and good character. And no political philosophy can authoritatively resolve all our disagreements—not only because no one is smart enough to comprehend a comprehensive good, but because no mortal, no matter how wise, can legitimately impose the good life on people who cannot live that life from the inside. Nor can anyone legitimately impose liberal neutrality on people who value virtue as well as freedom. We stand at a philosophical and political impasse unless we can defend another alternative.

The most defensible alternative is democratic in a frankly liberal or Deweyan sense. First, it does not tyrannize over common sense, either by subsuming individual freedom into social (or familial) good or by reducing social justice or civic virtue to individual freedom.[16] Second, it provides principled criticism of any educational authority that tries to tyrannize over children, whether by depriving them of an education adequate to citizenship or by repressing reasonable challenges to popular ideas. Third, it supports educational institutions that are conducive to democratic deliberation, institutions that make a democratic virtue out of our inevitable disagreements over educational problems. The virtue, too simply stated, is that we can publicly debate educational problems in a way much more likely to increase our understanding of education and each other than if we were to leave the management of schools, as Kant suggested, "to depend entirely upon the judgment of the most enlightened experts."[17] The policies that result from our democratic deliberations will not always be the right ones, but they will be more enlightened—by the values and concerns of the many communities that constitute a democracy—than those that would have been made by unaccountable experts.

But this alternative understanding is incomplete. The threat of repression and discrimination remains. Democratic processes can be used to destroy democratic education. They can be used to undermine the intellectual foundations of future democratic deliberations by repressing unpopular ways of thinking or excluding some future citizens from an education adequate for participating in democratic politics.

A democratic society must not be constrained to legislate what the wisest parent or philosopher wants for a child, but it must be constrained not to legislate policies that render democracy repressive or discriminatory. A democratic theory of education recognizes the importance of empowering citizens to make educational policy and also of constraining their choices to those policies that are nonrepressive and nondiscriminatory, so as to preserve the intellectual and social foundations of democracy. Democracy must be understood not merely (or primarily) as a *process* of majority rule, but rather as an *ideal* of a society whose adult members are, and continue to be, equipped by their education and authorized by political structure to share in ruling. A democratic society should educate all educable children to be capable of participating in collectively shaping their society.

Democracy makes no claim to being a noncontroversial standard. Not all societies or all citizens in our society—let alone all philosophers—are committed to democracy. Those that are not are stuck at the impasse I characterized earlier. They assert their commitment to civic virtue or to individual freedom at the expense of denying the legitimacy of the other value. The practical consequence of this thinking is that basic freedoms are sacrificed to communal virtue or freedom is expanded so far as to forego the virtues essential to a just society.

The legitimating claim of democracy is not that it will be accepted by all citizens—no political philosophy can sensibly claim such a Panglossian future. Its legitimating claim is one of political morality: a state of democratic education is minimally objectionable insofar as it leaves maximum room for citizens deliberately to shape their society, not in their own image but in an image that they can legitimately identify with their informed, moral choices. "Conscious social reproduction" is the ideal of democratic education. Democratic citizens support a set of educational and political practices of which the following can be said: These are the practices and authorities to which we, acting collectively as a society, have consciously agreed.

For a society to reproduce itself consciously, it must be nonrepressive. It must not restrict rational consideration of different ways of life. Instead it must cultivate the kind of character and the kind of intellect that enables people to choose rationally (some would say "autonomously") among different ways of life. The democratic principle of nonrepression prevents the state, and any group within it, from using education unnecessarily to restrict rational deliberation of differing conceptions of good lives and societies. It also requires the state to cultivate the capacity for rational deliberation. Nonrepression is not a principle of purely negative freedom. It secures freedom from interference only to the extent that it forbids using education to restrict rational deliberation or consideration of different ways of life. Nonrepression is therefore compatible with—indeed it requires—the use of education to inculcate those character traits, such as honesty, religious toleration, and mutual respect for persons, that serve as foundations for rational deliberation of differing ways of life.

Nonrepression is not neutral among all ways of life. It is justified as a means by which to guide the cultivation of rational deliberation among citizens. Although nonrepression often sets practical limits on democratic authority, its defense derives from the primary value of democratic education. Because conscious social reproduction is the ideal of democratic education—and democracy—communities must be prevented from using education to stifle rational deliberation of competing conceptions of good lives and good societies.

For a society, rather than some segment of it, to reproduce itself, it must be nondiscriminatory. Everyone must be educated. Nondiscrimination extends the logic of nonrepression, since states and families can be selectively repressive by excluding entire groups of children from schooling or by denying them an education conducive to rational deliberation. Repression has commonly taken the more passive form of discrimination in education against racial minorities, girls, and other disfavored groups of children. Its effect often is to repress, at least temporarily, the capacity and even the desire of these groups to participate in politics or to assert their own preferences in private life. Nondiscrimination is the distributional complement to nonrepression.

In its most general application to education, the principle of nondiscrimination prevents the state, and all groups within it, from denying anyone an educational good on grounds irrelevant to the legitimate social purpose of that good. Applied to the education needed to prepare children for future citizenship, the nondiscrimination principle becomes a principle of nonexclusion. No educable child may be excluded from an education adequate to participate in democratic politics.

For a society to be reproductive, it must institute practices of democratic deliberation and decisionmaking for its adult citizens (and for children to the extent necessary for cultivating the capacities of democratic deliberation). To shape their society, citizens and their representatives engage in collective deliberations and decisionmaking at different levels of government. They need not replicate their current practices, and they must not do so in the many instances where those practices are repressive or discriminatory. Reproduction never requires replication. Nonrepression and nondiscrimination often do not permit it.

Like the family state, a democratic state tries to teach virtue—what might best be called liberal democratic virtues, the virtues that are necessary for a flourishing liberal democracy. These virtues include veracity, nonviolence, religious toleration, mutual respect for reasonable differences of opinion, the ability to deliberate and therefore to participate in conscious social reproduction.

Like the state of families, a democratic state secures a degree of parental authority over education, resisting the strong communitarian view that children are creatures of the state. Within the family, parents are free to foster in children deep convictions to particular ways of life. But by educating children also as future citizens, the democratic state resists the view that parents are the ultimate authorities of their children's education, that they may invoke their parental rights—or their right to religious freedom—to prevent schools from exposing their children to ways of life or thinking that challenge their personal commitments.

Like the state of individuals, a democratic state defends a degree of professional authority over education—for the sake not of neutrality but of rational deliberation among differing ways of life. The democratic commitment to teaching rational deliberation rests on a rejection of the view, embraced by the state of individuals, that no way of life is better than any other. One purpose of teaching rational deliberation—as opposed to skepticism toward any ultimate values, or deference to authority—is to foster in future citizens the ability to defend their personal and political commitments, and revise those that are indefensible. Although a democratic state permits adults to live unexamined lives as well as examined one, it does not support education that is neutral between these two options nor does it claim that the two ways of life are equally good. Democratic education cannot be neutral between these two options and still educate citizens (or public officials) who are capable of exercising good political judgment.

If this understanding of democratic education is correct, then the ideal of democratic education lies at the core of a commitment to democracy. The ideal of democracy is often said to be collective self-determination. But there is no "collective self" to be determined. There are just so many individual selves that must find a fair way of sharing the goods of a society together. It would be dangerous, as critics often charge, to assume that the democratic state constitutes the collective self of a society and that its policies define the best interests of its individual members.

We do not need this metaphysical assumption, however, to defend an ideal closely related to that of collective self-determination—an ideal of citizens sharing in deliberate determination of the future shape of their society. If democratic society is the "self" that citizens determine, it is a self that does not define their best interests. There remain independent standards for defining the best interests of individuals and reasons for thinking that individuals, rather then collectivities, are generally the best judges of their own interests. To avoid the misleading metaphysical connotations of the concept of collective self-determination, we might better understand the democratic ideal as that of conscious social reproduction, the same ideal that guides democratic education.

The convergence of democratic ideals is not coincidental. Democratic education supplies the foundations upon which a democratic society can secure the civil and political freedoms of its adult citizens without placing their welfare or its very survival at great risk. In the absence of democratic education, risks—perhaps even great risks—will still be worth taking for the sake of respecting the actual preferences of citizens, but democracy depends on democratic education for its full moral and political strength.

The dependency is reciprocal. Without democratic government the best education to which a society could aspire might be similar to that practiced for thirteen centuries in Imperial China, where a centralized state supported schools and designed a thorough system of examinations that determined access on highly meritocratic grounds to all state offices. When working at its best, the Chinese educational system stimulated considerable social mobility and supported a widespread belief in what one scholar describes as an "academic Horatio Alger myth."[18] Although highly meritocratic, such a nondemocratic state usurps control of what rightly belongs to citizens: decisions concerning how the character and consciousness of future citizens take shape outside the home. In usurping democratic authority, the state also eliminates the strongest political rationale for democratic education: teaching the virtues of democratic deliberation for the sake of future citizenship. Democratic education follows at the same time as it reinforces our commitment to democracy.

"You cannot be a ruler unless you have first been ruled. You must become a ruler after you have been ruled." These twin maxims, not Platonic but Aristotelian in origin, are at the root of a democratic understanding of both politics and education. Better still, the seventeenth-century English locution: "You cannot govern unless you have first been governed. You must govern after you have been governed." This is a democratic understanding of politics and education: being governed and governing in turn, where governing includes the nurturing of children by parents, their formal instruction by professionals, the structuring of public instruction by public officials accountable to citizens, and the shaping of culture by both private and public authorities.

There are many ways that this democratic understanding, more fully elaborated, could make a difference in the way Americans think about and practice education. I would like to consider two examples— one in the realm of lower education and the other in the realm of high culture—of how the ideal of democratic education offers an alternative to practices of undemocratic education.

In October 1986 a federal district court ruled that the public schools of Hawkins County, Tennessee, must exempt the children of a group of fundamentalist Christian parents from basic reading classes. Those classes assigned Holt, Rinehart & Winston texts, texts that had been unanimously approved by the Hawkins County Board of Education on recommendation of their textbook selection committee. The content of the series offended the religious views of these parents, who had joined together as Citizens Organized for Better Schools (COBS) and unsuccessfully petitioned the School Board to have their children taught from unoffensive texts. The parents objected to, among other things: a story depicting a young boy "having fun" while cooking, on grounds that it "denigrates the differences between the sexes" that the Bible endorses; a story entitled "A Visit to Mars," on grounds that it encourages children to use their imaginations in ways imcompatible with fundamentalist faith; a story entitled "Hunchback Madonna," which describes the religious and social practices of an Indian settlement in New Mexico, on grounds that it teaches Catholicism; and an excerpt from Anne Frank's *Diary of a Young Girl,* on grounds that it suggests that nonorthodox belief in God is better than no belief at all. The principal and school board refused to exempt the children from using the Holt, Rinehart readers. The parents took the school district to court.

District Court Judge Thomas Hull found nothing wrong with the textbooks and said so. Yet he concluded that the children must be exempted from reading the series, and from their reading classes, because, in his words, "Plaintiffs [the parents] sincerely believe that the affirmation of these philosophical viewpoints is repulsive to their Christian faith, so repulsive that they must not allow their children to be exposed to the Holt series. This is their religious belief. They have drawn a line, 'and it is not for us to say that the line they drew was an unreasonable one.' "[19]

Why is it not for us to say?

—Not because the parents of those children should have ultimate authority over their education. If that were the case, it would not be for us (or Judge Hull) to say that they must be educated at all. Yet Judge Hull ruled that the children take standardized tests in reading rather than read standardized texts. If standardized tests are justified, then there must be something that all children should learn independently of what their parents want them to learn.

—Not because democratic education is compatible with the Christian fundamentalist view that forbids exposure to knowledge about religions, cultures, and convictions that differ from their own, on grounds that such knowledge corrupts the soul. The parents claimed that their children would be corrupted by exposure to beliefs and values that contradict their own religious views without a statement that the other views are incorrect and that their views are the correct ones. Democratic education is surely incompatible with this fundamentalist view of knowledge and morality.

—Not because democratic education rests on a conception of the good society that threatens the fundamentalist view of a good life and must defer to fundamentalism for the sake of neutrality. Any defensible political understanding of education depends on some conception of a good society, and every conception worth defending threatens some conception (or conceptions) of a good life. It is a sad fact of democracy in the United States that some citizens still hold religious beliefs that reject teaching children the democratic values of mutual respect (for reasonable differences of opinion) and rational deliberation (among differing ways of life). But their rejection of democratic values does not constitute a criticism of democracy any more than the rejection by a committed misogynist of the rights of women constitutes a critique of feminism. Both the parents and the misogynist of course have a right to voice their opinions. But the crucial questions to be addressed by a political theory in each controversy is which set of values (or virtues) must a democratic state defend and which should it criticize?

Another argument sometimes offered in defense of the claims of fundamentalist parents is that democratic education consists solely of teaching certain facts, not certain values or virtues, to future citizens. This position is superficially similar to John Stuart Mill's conclusion that the state should limit its educational authority to public examinations "confined to facts and positive science exclusively."[20] But if this is what we should say about public education, it cannot be because knowing facts is more crucial to a good life or good citizenship than being virtuous. Nor can it be because facts are neutral, while values are not. Might it be because citizens can more easily agree on a body of facts than on a set of values or virtues to be taught to all children? Perhaps the argument was soundly prudential when Mill made it, but its premise is very shaky today. The political controversies that have raged in recent years over the biases of testing and the claims of creationism against evolution reveal how controversial the teaching and testing of facts can be. But it is no more nor less controversial than the teaching (or not teaching) of civic virtue. If we wish political authorities to avoid political controversy above all else, our only alternative is to advocate repression, in its most thoroughgoing and insidious form.

There is no defensible political understanding of education that is not tied to some conception of a good society, and there is no conception that is not controversial. So which one should we defend? Judge Hull hinted at a conception of liberal neutrality: Secular texts must not be imposed on fundamentalist children because they are not neutral among all competing conceptions of the good life. The Holt readers surely are not neutral between fundamentalist Christianity and democratic humanism. Nor, as Judge Hull recognized, could any readers be neutral between deference to God's will as literally revealed in the Bible or authoritatively interpreted by a fundamentalist church and rational inquiry or mutual respect among persons. Liberals think of themselves as committed only to the latter set of virtues—rational inquiry and mutual respect—but the logic of liberal neutrality does not support their commitment in politics. The content of public schooling cannot be neutral among competing conceptions of the good life. And if it could, we would not and should not care to support it.

It is not for democrats to deny fundamentalist parents the right to draw the wrong line for their children in their homes and churches. Parental freedom entails this (limited) right.[21] But it is for democrats to say that parents do not have a right to veto a line drawn by public schools unless that line is repressive or discriminatory. If parents, judges, or philosopher-kings are allowed to veto lines drawn by public schools when those lines are neither repressive nor discriminatory, then democratic institutions are denied their legitimate role in shaping the character of citizens.

But is democracy not repressive if it denies the teaching of Christian fundamentalist convictions within public school, or, what amounts to the same thing, if it requires the teaching of views inimical to fundamentalist convictions? This challenge to democratic education rests on a serious misunderstanding: that a policy is repressive simply because it prevents parents from teaching their sincerely held beliefs or requires the teaching of views inimical to, or undermining of, those beliefs within publicly funded or subsidized schools. Non-repression requires the prevention of repressive practices, that is, practices that stifle rational understanding and inquiry. It is a reductio ad absurdum to claim that preventing such prevention itself constitutes repression.

Some critics sidestep this claim by doubting that any educational practice is more or less repressive than any other. Education necessarily focuses on some subset of reasonable worlds, a subset often chosen (again necessarily) for particularistic rather than universalistic reasons. (How would a school decide on universalistic grounds which among all possible histories and languages to teach and how much time to devote to each?) It does not follow that all education is equally repressive by virtue of excluding consideration of some reasonable worlds and privileging others with greater attention. This conclusion is plausible, if at all, only in abstraction. It is absurd to claim that the Holt, Rinehart texts are as repressive as a set of readers that do not "expose children to other forms of religion and to the feelings, attitudes and values of other students that contradict the [parents'] religious views without a statement that the other views are incorrect and that the [parents'] views are the correct ones."[22] If there is no such thing as a completely nonrepressive education, then there are surely kinds of repression. Unlike the education defended by the Hawkins County Board of Education, the education demanded by the plaintiff parents in the Mozert case—which does not permit children to reason about the merits of religions and values different from those of their parents (or offers only reasons that favor the parents' point of view)—is incompatible with teaching rational inquiry and mutual understanding in a religiously pluralistic society.

Upholding the right of schools to teach what might be called democratic humanism is consistent with criticizing schools that fall short of the democratic ideal in ways rarely considered by courts. It is by now a commonplace that many American schools, especially those in urban areas, are overly centralized and bureaucratized. Such schools are unconducive to the exercise of democratic deliberation by citizens and democratic professionalism by teachers. Democratic professionalism authorizes teachers, at the same time as it obligates them, to cultivate in future citizens the capacity for critical reflection on their culture. The professional responsibility of teachers, too simply summarized, is to uphold the principle of nonrepression by fostering the knowledge, skills, and habits of democratic deliberation. The ideal of democratic education also constrains citizens and public officials to create working conditions that support the democratic role of teachers.

The democratic principles of nondiscrimination and nonrepression serve not only as constraints on authority but also as sources of authorization for more democratic action. This is perhaps most striking in the realm of culture, where public support can serve as a means of preventing the rich (or any other self-appointed group, including artists themselves) from monopolizing influence over and access to high culture. By increasing direct subsidies without increasing control over the arts, a democratic government can decrease the dependence of art institutions on private patrons. The less a museum or an opera house must depend on a few wealthy patrons for its financial well-being, the less pressure it will feel to accept aid tied to demands that violate its own artistic standards.

By itself, increasing direct public aid to the arts is unlikely to avoid all repressive practices. As long as there are relatively few wealthy citizens willing to donate millions to the arts, substantial pressure will still be brought to bear on art institutions to accept improperly tied aid. Other forms of democratic action can further decrease the attractiveness of such private repression. Legislatures can, for example, expose private patronage to closer public scrutiny by placing greater disclosure requirements on tax-deductible donations, thereby increasing the likelihood that improperly tied aid will attract adverse publicity. From a democratic perspective this is a desirable policy for several reasons. First, citizens are entitled to "a clear picture of what is done with money that otherwise would be collected as taxes."[23] Second, a clear public picture would pressure private patrons to live up to the principle of nonrepression. (In most cases, the credible threat of adverse publicity is sufficient to prevent repression.) Third, better disclosure requirements would make it more difficult for patrons to use the indirect subsidy system to defraud the government by over-pricing their donations and entering into illegal deals with art insti-tutions, practices that are now almost impossible to uncover unless the Internal Revenue Service decides to conduct an audit.[24]

Public repression is also possible. But the historical record of public support for the arts even in imperfectly democratic countries, in-cluding the United States, should allay the common concern that governmental subsidy entails governmental control.[25] The evidence does not even suggest that public support has lowered the quality of high culture in this country. The less common concern may be more warranted: that a high culture will deteriorate in democratic societies unless governments take a substantial interest in supporting expensive forms of art and making them part of a common culture. Although the creation of a more democratic culture is certainly not a sufficient condition for maintaining an artistically high culture, it is probably a necessary condition in the United States today.

Democratic societies as a whole may still be less conducive to high culture than undemocratic societies that concentrate power, wealth, and prestige among the few. Both conservative and liberal critics express this reasonable reservation about democracy. Democratic principles are incompatible with the perfectionist view that because high culture is intrinsically good, it should be supported even at the expense of democracy. So conceived, perfectionism cedes political priority to philosophy over democracy. The deliberation necessary and sufficient to support high culture can be conducted exclusively by philosophers; the best philosophical argument should then win out politically.

Democratic perfectionism also accepts the intrinsic value of high culture, but by contrast it denies that this value is sufficient to override duly constituted democratic authority. It is no less objectionable for philosophers than for parents to usurp democratic authority. Dem-ocratic perfectionism sanctions state subsidy of high culture, if, but only if, it is publicly approved (and satisfies the standards of non-repression and nondiscrimination). There is, as T. M. Scanlon points out, "nothing objectionable about an argument among equal citizens about what is to be recognized as good."[26] From a democratic perspective, there is something valuable about such public deliberation and decisionmaking.

The democratic case for subsidizing high culture goes beyond the traditional philosophical understanding of perfectionism in yet another way. High culture helps make a society worthy of the collective pride of citizens. If the citizens of Geneva would support the theater, D'Alembert argued in the article of the *Encyclopedie* that prompted Rousseau's critical letter, "Geneva would join to the prudence of Lacedaemon the urbanity of Athens . . . This city, which many Frenchmen consider dull because they are deprived of the theatre, would then become the seat of decent pleasures, just as it is now the seat of philosophy and liberty."[27] Becoming the seat of decent pleasures, or of high culture, is not essential to the creation of a just society, any more than enjoying the higher pleasures is essential to becoming a just person. But, like individuals, societies that enjoy decent pleasures and appreciate high culture may be more desirable than those that do not. Although democratic perfectionism does not promise that democracies will support high culture, it gives them good reasons to do so, and encourages those citizens who most appreciate the rarest treasures of human culture to rave about them in public rather than rant in private against the philistinism of the public.[28]

The defense of democracy in recent years has taken the form of a priority principle: democracy has priority over philosophy, that is, what citizens decide is right takes precedence over what philosophers demonstrate to be right.[29] The case for democratic education and democracy more generally does not entail giving priority to democracy over philosophy. The priority principle misleads us about both philosophy and democracy. If the wisest philosophers, like Socrates, are distinguished not just by knowing what they do not know but also by publicly admitting the limits of their knowledge, then, far from subordinating itself to democracy, philosophy is the source of democracy's strongest moral defense. Philosophy defends democracy when it discovered that the best life and the best society to which we can aspire must be among those that we recognize and claim as our own. Philosophers cannot simply give citizens a good society, anymore than parents can give their children a good life. One reason for this inherent limit on the power of philosophers, and parents, is that a good life must be one that people live from the inside, by accepting and identifying it as their own. Another reason is that any credible standard for a good life will leave room for discretionary choices on the part of the people who are living those lives. Philosophers and parents who would tell people precisely how to live their lives are morally pretentious. Democratic education embraces this liberal insight, but it rejects the view that individual freedom is the only legitimate end of education.

Two of the most distinctive features of democratic education are its simultaneous refusal to dissolve the tensions between individual freedom and civic virtue in a potent philosophical solution, and its insistence on finding a principled rather than simply pragmatic way of living with the tensions. Living with tensions is not easy, nor is it without sacrifices in freedom and virtue. But the alternatives to democratic education that promise an escape from these tensions and sacrifices are far worse.

· FIVE ·

Civic Education in the Liberal State

WILLIAM GALSTON

In most times and places the necessity and appropriateness of civic education has been accepted without question. It has been taken for granted that young human beings must be shaped into citizens and that public institutions have both the right and the responsibility to take the lead. In the United States today, however, civic education has become intensely controversial. Some skeptics believe that our political and social arrangements can function perfectly well without publicly defined (or directed) civic education. Others doubt that any one specification of civic education can be devised for a liberal polity in which individuals, families, and communities embrace fundamentally differing conceptions of choiceworthy lives. Still others argue that any unitary civic education violates the autonomy and conscience of many individuals and groups in a diverse society.

These objections are mistaken. It is both necessary and possible to carry out civic education in the liberal state. To do so properly, however, the partial truth of the critics' contentions must be recognized in the content and the conduct of that education.

Philosophic Education Versus Civic Education

Let me begin with a distinction between two very different kinds of education. Philosophic education has as its basic objectives, first, the disposition to seek truth, and, second, the capacity to conduct rational inquiry. Training scientists, for example, requires the inculcation both of an ethic of inquiry—do not fabricate or distort results, take care to prevent your hypotheses (or desires) from affecting your observations—and the techniques of inquiry appropriate to the discipline.

There are of course many different forms of philosophic education, corresponding to the numerous ways in which truth may be pursued. Nevertheless, these forms of education share two key features. First, they are not decisively shaped by the specific social or political circumstances in which they are conducted, or, to put it the other way around, they are perverted when such circumstances come to have a substantive effect. There is no valid distinction between "Jewish" and "Aryan" physics, or between "bourgeois" and "socialist" biology; truth is one and universal. Second, and relatedly, philosophic education can have corrosive consequences for political communities in which it is allowed to take place. The pursuit of truth—scientific, historical, moral, or whatever—can undermine structures of unexamined but socially central belief.

Civic education differs from philosophic education in all these respects. Its purpose is not the pursuit and acquisition of truth, but rather the formation of individuals who can effectively conduct their lives within, and support, their political community. It is unlikely, to say the least, that the truth will be fully consistent with this purpose. Nor is civic education homogeneous and universal. It is by definition education within, and on behalf of, a particular political order. The conduct and content of civic education within a liberal democracy will therefore differ significantly from civic education within other kinds of polities. Nor, finally, does civic education stand in opposition to its political community. On the contrary, it fails—fundamentally—if it does not support and strengthen that community.

It might be argued that this alleged opposition between civic and philosophic education is far too sweeping. While some societies are dependent on myths and lies, others are far more open to truth. Liberal democracies, in particular, are founded on principles that can survive rational inspection, and their functioning is facilitated (or at least not crucially impaired) by unimpeded inquiry in every domain.

This argument does contain an important element of truth. The understanding of liberal society as an "open" society has important historical roots in early modern struggles against repressive tradition and superstition. It found classic formulation in John Stuart Mill's invocation of Socrates as liberal hero. In principle and in practice, liberal democracy does exhibit a degree of openness to philosophic education, and to its social consequences, that is probably without precedent in human history. This fact constitutes one of the most important arguments in favor of liberal democracy.

But it would be rash to conclude that the clash between rational inquiry and civic education in liberal societies has ceased to exist. On the level of theory, liberalism takes sides in a series of disputes about the meaning of equality, freedom, and the human good—disputes that cannot be regarded as definitively settled from a philosophic point of view. On the practical level, very few individuals will come to embrace the core commitments of liberal society through a process of rational inquiry. If children are to be brought to accept these commitments as valid and binding, it can only be through a pedagogy that is far more rhetorical than rational. For example, rigorous historical research will almost certainly vindicate complex "revisionist" accounts of key figures in American history. Civic education, however, requires a more noble, moralizing history: a pantheon of heroes who confer legitimacy on central institutions and constitute worthy objects of emulation.[1] It is unrealistic to believe that more than a few adult citizens of liberal societies will ever move beyond the kind of civic commitment engendered by such a pedagogy.

The Need for Liberal Democratic Civic Education

There is a tradition of Mandevillean argument that liberal polities do not need—indeed, are distinctive in not needing—civic education directed to the formation of liberal citizens because social processes and political institutions can be arranged so as to render desired collective outcomes independent of individual character and belief. Albert Hirschman has traced the emergence in seventeenth- and eighteenth-century social thought of the thesis that republican government could best be secured not through civic virtue but through the liberation of the commercial-acquisitive "interests" of the middle class in opposition to the politically destructive "passions" of the aristocracy.[2] The most famous of the *Federalist Papers* (10 and 51) contain memorable formulations of the need to counteract interest with interest and passion with passion. Immanuel Kant, who was at once the most profound moral philosopher and the most devoted liberal theorist of his age, argued vigorously for the disjunction between individual virtue and republican government. A liberal government that fully protects individual rights "is only a question of a good organization of the state, whereby the powers of each selfish inclination are so arranged in opposition that one moderates or destroys the ruinous effect of the other. The consequence . . . is the same as if none of them existed, and man is forced to be a good citizen even if not a morally good person."[3]

The proposition that liberal societies are uniquely able to do without the fruits of civic education has been sharply challenged, however. Recent interpretations of the liberal theoretical tradition have emphasized the copresence of institutional and character-based arguments, as have rereadings of the *Federalist*.[4] Recent explorations of public policy problems—crime, drugs, dependency—have focused on the formation of character and belief as well as on the manipulation of incentives.[5] Historical inquiries into American public education have documented the driving role played by the perceived need for a civic pedagogy that could turn immigrants into citizens.[6] Groups across the political spectrum have reemphasized their belief that a refurbished civic education is an urgent necessity: "Democracy's survival depends upon our transmitting to each new generation the political vision of liberty and equality that unites us as Americans . . . Such values are neither revealed truths nor natural habits. There is no evidence that we are born with them. Devotion to human dignity and freedom, to equal rights, to social and economic justice, to the rule of law, to civility and truth, to tolerance of diversity, to mutual assistance, to personal and civic responsibility, to self-restraint and self-respect—all these must be taught and learned."[7]

Common experience buttresses what history and argument suggest: that the operation of liberal institutions and the functioning of liberal society are affected in important ways by the character and belief of individuals (and leaders) within the liberal polity. At some point the attenuation of civic spirit and competence will create pathologies with which liberal institutions, however perfect their technical design, simply cannot cope. To an extent difficult to measure but impossible to ignore, the viability of liberal society depends on its ability effectively to conduct civic education.

The Possibility of Liberal Democratic Civic Education

Liberal democratic civic education may be necessary, but is it possible? In the same way that the religious diversity of liberal society makes it impossible to reach a religious consensus suitable for public endorsement, so too the moral and political diversity of the liberal polity might seem to undermine the possibility of a unitary civic pedagogy acceptable to, and binding on, all groups. Indeed, the movement from the religious neutrality of the liberal state to a wider moral and political neutrality is one of the defining characteristics of liberal theory in our time, a development with roots in the opinions of urban-based social elites.

This generalization of liberal neutrality is neither necessary nor wise. To the extent that we accept a shared citizenship, we have something important in common—a set of political institutions and of principles that underlie them. What we share, beyond all our differences, provides the basis for a civic education valid across the boundaries of our differences.

Some of the virtues needed to sustain the liberal state are requisites of every political community: the willingness to fight on behalf of one's country; the settled disposition to obey the law; and loyalty—the developed capacity to understand, to accept, and to act on the core principles of one's society. Some of the individual traits are specific to liberal society—independence, tolerance, and respect for individual excellences and accomplishments, for example. Still others are entailed by the key features of liberal democratic politics. For citizens, the disposition to respect the rights of others, the capacity to evaluate the talents, character, and performance of public officials, and the ability to moderate public desires in the face of public limits are essential. For leaders, the patience to work within social diversity and the ability to narrow the gap between wise policy and popular consent are fundamental. And the developed capacity to engage in public discourse and to test public policies against our deeper convictions is highly desirable for all members of the liberal community, whatever political station they may occupy.[8]

A leading contemporary theorist of civic education, Amy Gutmann, has reached conclusions parallel to but divergent from the theses just sketched. Her point of departure is democracy, and her argument is that our civic pedagogy should be oriented toward democratic virtue: "the ability to deliberate, and hence to participate in conscious social reproduction."[9] In my view, this is a piece—but only a piece—of the civic education appropriate to our situation, and it becomes a distortion when it is mistaken for the whole.

Let me begin with a methodological point. The adequacy of a conception of civic education cannot be determined in the abstract, but only through its congruence with the basic features of the society it is intended to sustain. To depart significantly from those features is to recommend a conception of civic education suitable for some society other than the one at hand. Differently put, it is to endorse a politics of transformation based on a general conception of the political good external to the concrete polity in question. I do not wish to deny the possibility or appropriateness of such theoretical practices. But I do not want to distinguish between them and the task of fitting pedagogical practices to existing communities.

It is at best a partial truth to characterize the United States as a democracy in Gutmann's sense. To begin with the obvious: in a liberal democracy the concern for individual rights and for what is sometimes called the private sphere entails limits on the legitimate power of majorities, and it suggests that cultivating the disposition to respect rights and privacies is one of the essential goals of liberal democratic civic education. In Gutmann's account, the power of the majority is limited by the requirement of "nonrepression" and "nondiscrimination," but these limits are themselves derived from the conception of a democratic society all of whose members are equipped and authorized to share in ruling.[10] These considerations are not robust enough to generate anything like a liberal account of protections for individuals and groups against the possibility of majority usurpation.

A second liberal reservation against Gutmann's democracy is the distinction between momentary public whim and the settled will—that is, the considered judgment—of the community. This distinction is what underlies the liberal effort to construct a framework of relatively stable institutions partially insulated from shifting majorities. It is, in short, one of the motives for constitutions as distinct from acts of legislation as well as for processes that complicate the task of forging legislative majorities, at least for certain purposes. A form of pedagogy more fully appropriate than Gutmann's to a liberal democratic constitutional order would incorporate an understanding of these limitations on "conscious social reproduction."

Third, in liberal democracies representative institutions replace direct self-government for many purposes. A civic education congruent with such institutions will emphasize, as I have suggested, the virtues and competences needed to select representatives wisely, to relate to them appropriately, and to evaluate their performance in office soberly. These characteristics are related to, but in some respects quite distinct from, the traits needed for direct participation in political affairs. Perhaps it would be fairer to say that the balance between participation and representation is not a settled question, in either theory or practice. A civic pedagogy for us may rightly incorporate participatory virtues. It may even accommodate a politics more hospitable to participation than are our current practices. But it is not free to give participatory virtues pride of place or to remain silent about the virtues that correspond to representative institutions.

Finally, in liberal democracies certain kinds of excellences are acknowledged, at least for certain purposes, to constitute legitimate claims to public authority. That is, in filling offices and settling policy, equalities of will and interest are counterbalanced by inequalities of training and accomplishment. Examples include the technical expertise of the public health official, the interpretive skill of the judge, and even the governance capabilities of political leaders. As paradoxical as it may appear, a tradition of political theory extending back to Aristotle has understood the selection of public officials through popular elections as significantly aristocratic in its effect. In American thought, some of our greatest democrats have embraced this view. Thomas Jefferson once wrote John Adams: "there is a natural aristocracy among men. The grounds of this are virtue and talents . . . May we not even say, that that form of government is best, which provides the most effectively for a pure selection of these natural *aristoi* into the offices of government? . . . I think the best [way of doing this] is exactly that provided by all our constitutions, to leave to the citizens the free election and separation of the *aristoi* from the *pseudo-aristoi*."[11]

To put this point more broadly: the problem that liberal democracy sets itself is to achieve the greatest possible conjunction between good judgment and virtue, on the one hand, and participation and consent on the other. Democratic processes, suitably refined, may hold out the best prospects for accomplishing this goal. But they are not ends in themselves; they are to be judged by their fruits. Liberal democratic civic education must therefore aim to engender, not only the full range of public excellences, but also the widest possible acceptance of the need for such excellences in the conduct of our public life. Populist rancor against the claims of liberal democratic excellence is understandable, and even at times a useful counterweight to arrogance and usurpation. But it cannot be allowed to obliterate the legitimacy of such claims.

Civic Education Versus Liberal Privacy

Civic education poses a special difficulty for liberal democracy. Most forms of government, classical and contemporary, have tacitly embraced the Aristotelian understanding of politics as the architectonic human association to which all others—family, tribe, economic groupings, even religion—are rightly subordinated. For all such political communities the government's authority to conduct civic education is unquestioned, because conflicts between political and subpolitical commitments are resolved by the belief that the political enjoys a principled primacy. In liberal societies, by contrast, the resolution of such conflicts is far less clear-cut. Reservations against public authority in the name of individual autonomy, parental rights, and religious conscience are both frequent and respectable. The liberal tradition is animated by the effort to carve out spheres that are substantially impervious to government—an effort set in motion by the historical lesson that the attempt to impose religious uniformity through public fiat undermines civil order as well as individual conscience. Thus, even if liberal theories, or public authorities moved by such theories, succeed in specifying a core of habits and beliefs supportive of the liberal polity, individuals and groups may nonetheless object to civic education that tries to foster these habits and beliefs universally.

Yet while the liberal tradition is sensitive to the claims of individual conscience, early liberal theorists were equally mindful of the dangers and limits of those claims. John Locke, for example, refused to expand his doctrine of religious toleration into an inviolable private sphere of conscience. On the contrary, he insisted that in cases of conflict, civil authority takes precedence over conscience or faith, however deeply held. The key criterion is the maintenance of civil order. Opinions that threaten the peace of society may be legitimately opposed or even suppressed: "No opinion contrary to human society, or to those moral Rules which are necessary to the preservation of Civil Society, are to be tolerated by the Magistrate." Nor did toleration preclude affirmative public discourse on behalf of those necessary rules. Locke distinguished between coercion and persuasion. The fact that the sovereign cannot legitimately command adherence to a specific belief does not mean that civil authority cannot offer systematic arguments for, or instruction in, that belief.[12] Thus, although Locke thought that in practice civic education would occur in families rather than through state mechanisms, his theory leads directly to the legitimation of the conduct of such education through public means, individual conscience to the contrary notwithstanding.

Two other lines of argument bolster this conclusion. In practice, the private sphere within which conscience is exercised can only be defended within civil society. In the classic American formulation, government is instituted "to secure these rights." It follows that individuals must be willing to surrender whatever portion of these rights must be sacrificed to the requirements of public order and institutional perpetuation. Individuals who seek to exercise, without compromise, the totality of their presocial rights will quickly find that conflict with other rights-bearers impedes the attainment of their ends and the security of their liberty. Even if we begin with a robust conception of individual rights defined theoretically rather than historically or politically, we are forced to conclude that public authority may legitimately restrict those rights in the name of maximizing their effective exercise. In particular, government may properly teach those beliefs and habits needed to bolster the institutions that secure liberal rights, and citizens of liberal polities who resist this civic education would be irrationally contradicting their own self-interest, rightly understood.

The second argument follows hard on the heels of the first. If citizenship means anything, it means a package of benefits and burdens shared, and accepted, by all. To be a citizen of a liberal polity is to be required to surrender so much of your own private conscience as is necessary for the secure enjoyment of what remains. To refuse this surrender is in effect to breach the agreement under which you are entitled to full membership in your community.

Now, it is perfectly possible to petition your community for special relief from the burdens accepted by your fellow citizens: "My conscience makes it impossible for me to fight in battle / pledge allegiance to the flag / or whatever." Public authority may then make a prudential determination as to whether granting your request will or won't impose unacceptable costs on public aims and institutions. If you are part of a small minority, and if the grounds on which you seek exemption from shared burdens are so narrow and idiosyncratic as to suggest that others are unlikely to follow suit, then it may be possible to grant the exemption. But if the facts suggest that acceding to you will open the floodgate for many others, then it would be rational for public authorities to reject your plea. The issue, to repeat, is one of concrete practice rather than general principle.

A variant of this problem arises when individuals or groups are willing to take the next step, abjuring the benefits of citizenship in order to gain release from its burdens. This is in effect to request a kind of resident alien status within one's community: you remain subject to basic laws of civil order, but you are no longer expected to attain the character, beliefs, and competences needed for effective political membership. Your real desire is simply to withdraw, to be left alone. Here again, as before, the issue is practical. If there is reason to believe that granting this request will generate significant ripple effects, there is a rational basis for public authority to resist it. Alternatively, it might be argued that withdrawal is an untenable halfway house between citizenship and actual physical exit. As long as your group remains located within the domain of wider community, it necessarily interacts with, and affects, that community in many ways. While some free-rider problems could be addressed through taxation, other difficulties would prove far less tractable. It is not clear that the political community could afford to remain indifferent to the example you might set for other potential withdrawers. (This is not intended as an argument against the right of physical exit, which rests on quite different foundations and raises different issues. The Soviets have improperly used arguments parallel to those in this paragraph to thwart the emigration of disaffected groups.)

Perhaps the most poignant problem raised by liberal civic education is the clash between the content of that education and the desire of parents to pass their way of life on to their children. Few parents, I suspect, are unaware of or immune to the force of this desire. What could be more natural? If you believe that you are fit to be a parent, you must also believe that at least some of the choices you have made are worthy of emulation by your children, and the freedom to pass on the fruits of those choices must be highly valued. Conversely, who can contemplate without horror totalitarian societies in which families are compelled to yield all moral authority to the state?

Still, your child is at once a future adult and a future citizen. Your authority as a parent is limited by both these facts. For example, you are not free to treat your child in a manner that impedes normal development. You may not legitimately starve or beat your child or thwart the acquisition of basic linguistic and social skills. The systematic violation of these and related norms suffices to warrant state intervention. Similarly, you are not free to impede the child's acquisition of a basic civic education—the beliefs and habits that support the polity and enable individuals to function competently in public affairs. In particular, you are not free to act in ways that will lead your child to impose significant and avoidable burdens on the community. For example, the liberal state has a right to teach all children respect for the law, and you have no opposing right as a parent to undermine that respect. Similarly, the liberal state has a right to inculcate the expectation that all normal children will become adults capable of caring for themselves and their families.

Thus far the argument is reasonably strong and uncontroversial. But how much further may the liberal state go? Amy Gutmann argues that children must be taught both "mutual respect among persons" and "rational deliberation among ways of life," and that parents are unlikely to do this on their own. It is precisely because communities such as the Old Order Amish are morally committed to shielding their children from influences that might weaken their faith that the state is compelled to step in: "The same principle that requires a state to grant adults personal and political freedom also commits it to assuring children an education that makes those freedoms both possible and meaningful in the future. A state makes choice possible by teaching its future citizens respect for opposing points of view and ways of life. It makes choice meaningful by equipping children with the intellectual skills necessary to evaluate ways of life different from that of their parents."[13]

I do not believe that this argument can be sustained. In a liberal democratic polity, to be sure, the fact of social diversity means that the willingness to coexist peacefully with ways of life very different from one's own is essential. Further, the need for public evaluation of leaders and policies means that the state has an interest in developing citizens with at least the minimal conditions of reasonable public judgment. But neither of these civic requirements entails a need for public authority to take an interest in how children think about different ways of life. Civic tolerance of deep differences is perfectly compatible with unswerving belief in the correctness of one's own way of life. It rests on the conviction that the pursuit of the better course should be (and in many cases can only be) the result of persuasion rather than coercion—a classic Lockean premise that the liberal state *does* have an interest in articulating. Civic deliberation is also compatible with unshakable personal commitments. It requires only that each citizen accept the minimal civic commitments, already outlined, without which the liberal polity cannot long endure. In short, the civic standpoint does not warrant the conclusion that the state must (or may) structure public education to foster in children skeptical reflection on ways of life inherited from parents or local communities.

It is hardly accidental that Gutmann takes the argument in this direction. At the heart of much modern liberal democratic thought is a (sometimes tacit) commitment to the Socratic proposition that the unexamined life is an unworthy life, that individual freedom is incompatible with ways of life guided by unquestioned authority or unswerving faith. As philosophic conclusions these commitments have much to recommend them. The question, though, is whether the liberal state is justified in building them into its system of public education. The answer is that it cannot do so without throwing its weight behind a conception of the human good unrelated to the functional needs of its sociopolitical institutions and at odds with the deep beliefs of many of its loyal citizens. As a political matter liberal freedom entails the right to live unexamined as well as examined lives—a right whose effective exercise may require parental bulwarks against the corrosive influence of modernist skepticism. I might add that, in practice, there is today a widespread perception that our system of public education already embodies a bias against authority and faith. This perception, in large measure, is what underlies the controversy over "secular humanism" that is so incomprehensible to liberal elites.

It is not difficult to anticipate the objections that will be raised against the argument I have just advanced. There are, after all, three parties to the educational transaction: children, their parents, and the state. Perhaps the state has no direct right to shape public education in accordance with the norms of Socratic self-examination. But doesn't liberal freedom mean that children have the right to be exposed to a range of possible ways of life? If parents thwart this right by attempting, as we would say, to "brainwash" their children, doesn't the state have a right—indeed, a duty—to step in?

The answer is no on both counts. Children do have a wide range of rights that parents are bound to respect and that government is bound to enforce against parental violation. As I argued earlier, parents may not rightly impede the normal physical, intellectual, and emotional development of their children. Nor may they impede the acquisition of civic competence and loyalty. The state may act *in loco parentis* to overcome family-based obstacles to normal development. And it may use public instrumentalities, including the system of education, to promote the attainment by all children of the basic requisites of citizenship. These are legitimate intrusive state powers. But they are limited by their own inner logic. In a liberal state interventions that cannot be justified on this basis cannot be justified at all. That is how liberal democracies must draw the line between parental and public authority over the education of children, or, to put it less confrontationally, that is the principle on the basis of which such authority must be shared.[14]

But doesn't this position evade the emotional force of the objection? Does it legitimate parental brainwashing of children, which is a terrible thing? Again, the answer is no, for two reasons. First, the simple fact that authority is divided means that, from an early age, every child will see that he or she is answerable to institutions other than the family—institutions whose substantive requirements may well cut across the grain of parental wishes and beliefs. Some measure of reflection—or at least critical distance—is the likely result. Second, the basic features of liberal society make it virtually impossible for parents to seal their children off from knowledge of other ways of life. And, as every parent knows, possibilities that are known but forbidden take on an allure out of all proportion to their intrinsic merits.

To these points I would add a basic fact of liberal sociology: the greatest threat to children in modern liberal societies is not that they will believe in something too deeply, but that they will believe in nothing very deeply at all. Even to achieve the kind of free self-reflection that many liberals prize, it is better to begin by believing something. Rational deliberation among ways of life is far more meaningful (I am tempted to say that it can *only* be meaningful) if the stakes are meaningful—that is, if the deliberator has strong convictions against which competing claims can be weighed. The role of parents in fostering such convictions should be welcomed, not feared.

Despite the pluralism of liberal societies, it is perfectly possible to identify a core of civic commitments and competences whose broad acceptance undergirds a well-ordered liberal polity. The state has a right to ensure that this core is generally and effectively disseminated, either directly, through public civic education, or indirectly, through the regulation of private education. In cases of conflict this civic core takes priority over individual or group commitments (even the demands of conscience), and the state may legitimately use coercive mechanisms to enforce it.

But the liberal state must not venture beyond this point. It must not throw its weight behind ideals of personal excellence outside the shared understanding of civic excellence, and it must not give pride of place to understandings of personal freedom outside the shared understanding of civic freedom. For if it does so, the liberal state prescribes, as valid for and binding on all, a single debatable conception of how human beings should lead their lives. In the name of liberalism, it becomes totalitarian. It betrays its own deepest—and most defensible—principles.

· III ·

Moral Conflict

Class Conflict and Constitutionalism in J. S. Mill's Thought

RICHARD ASHCRAFT

Within the tradition of liberalism as a political theory, class conflict as a social problem, if recognized at all, has occupied a place of marginal importance. This is hardly surprising, since liberalism not only seeks to institutionalize a moral life without class conflict, it also presupposes an analysis of social relations in terms of the pluralistic associations of individuals, a theoretical framework within which the notion of class conflict can claim no conceptual legitimacy.

I propose to consider an exceptional case to my descriptive characterization of liberalism. Class conflict in capitalist society is a problem of central importance to the political theory of John Stuart Mill. An examination of Mill's effort to think through the various implications of this problem will not only assist us in understanding his political theory, but will also enable us to appreciate some of the difficulties that a recognition of class conflict poses for any liberal democratic perspective.

The Social Foundations of Political Theory

It would be claiming too much to say that Mill could not have recognized the importance of class conflict had he not experienced the "crisis" in his mental history described in his *Autobiography*. But what is true is that Mill's redefinition of "political theory" in the wake of that crisis supplied the necessary intellectual framework for perceiving the problem of class conflict if it should arise in his society—as indeed it did. For reasons which I hope will become clearer as the argument proceeds, it is not a digression, in the case of Mill, to begin with a consideration of certain methodological and conceptual issues which, in Mill's view, were inextricably linked with one's definition of political theory. By 1829 Macaulay's critique of James Mill's *Essay on Government* and his reading of the writings of the St. Simonians had convinced Mill that "the theory of government laid down in Bentham's and my father's writing" omitted "many things" which their political theory "ought to have made room for, and did not."[1] That Bentham's political theory was too narrowly constructed is a criticism that for more than forty years Mill repeatedly directed against that thinker.[2] The essential break with traditional liberal theory, according to him, was exemplified in the writings of nineteenth-century French thinkers. The St. Simonians had developed "a new mode of political thinking," and Tocqueville's *Democracy in America,* Mill declared, "changed the face of political philosophy."[3]

Mill not only recognized the need for a more comprehensive conception of political theory than the one he had inherited from his father or Bentham, he especially emphasized three specific features—actually, a set of interrelated beliefs—that characterized French political philosophy which he believed had been ignored by traditional liberal thinkers.[4] It is worthwhile paying close attention to these omissions, for although the three propositions can be simply stated, each of them embodies several implications. Mill was quite right to believe that, taken together, they represent a significant theoretical critique of the then dominant form of liberalism.

The view that all the elements of social life form an interrelated whole, such that any discussion of political institutions presupposes a theoretical analysis of how social power is distributed in a particular society, made a deep impression upon Mill. Similarly, he immediately saw the force of the argument that the development of society is a process marked by historical stages and, therefore, some theory of history is an essential ingredient of a political theory. Finally, Mill perceived that, methodologically speaking, a political theory is simply an analysis of empirically observable tendencies which, in ensemble, constitute the social system.

Recalling this period of his intellectual development, Mill wrote in his *Autobiography* that he learned from the St. Simonians that "government is always either in the hands, or passing into the hands of whatever is the strongest power in society," and that "whatever is the growing power in society will force its way into the government," because "the distribution of constitutional power cannot long continue very different from that of real power, without a convulsion."[5] "Underneath all political philosophy," he argued, "there must be a *social* philosophy—a study of agencies lying deeper than forms of government, which, working through forms of government," produce their effects.[6] Such a viewpoint undermined any belief in the autonomy of politics. "There can be no separate science of government," Mill insisted, once one sees that political phenomena are shaped and constituted by sociological phenomena. Hence, politics is simply "part of the general science of society, not [a] separate branch of it."[7] In other words, politics was redefined as the science of man in society, or sociology.[8]

Just as he broadened his conception of political economy, which became social economy, so Mill enlarged his view of politics and of political theory.[9] The latter became identical with a theory of how society was constituted: that is, of what social classes it is composed, and what their relations to each other are. How is wealth produced and distributed? What are the dominant beliefs held by individuals in society? What is the level of their intellectual and cultural development?[10] These were just a few of the questions, according to Mill, to which any prospective political theorist would have to supply answers in order to formulate meaningful statements regarding the political institutions in a particular society.

Political theory—now defined as "social science"—was for Mill the most complicated expression of human knowledge.[11] In part, this was because it included so many specialized areas of information— economics, ethics, history, anthropology, science, and philosophy. As Mill's second essay on Bentham (1838) made clear, he could not accept the view that human nature could be reduced to a few philosophical precepts analytically stated in the language of universality. Rather, he insisted, human beings are what they are because their characters have been shaped by the habits, beliefs, and social institutions transmitted to them by previous generations.[12]

The shift from philosophy to sociology not only increased the complexity of any theory of human nature, it also awakened in Mill a deep appreciation for the value of history that went far beyond any understanding of history he had derived from his "course in Benthamism." Here too it was the French who demonstrated the importance of history to an understanding of politics.[13] "Any general theory or philosophy of politics," Mill declared, "supposes a previous theory of human progress, and . . . this is the same thing with a philosophy of history."[14] Nor did he hesitate to insist upon "the necessity of historical studies as the foundation" for political theory.[15] The latter, therefore, could not be formulated in abstract or absolutist terminology; rather, political theory had to be seen "as a question of time, place, and circumstance."[16] Political philosophy was a "convention" created by "the wants of the time" rooted in "the conditions of [the] society" in which it was developed. This perspective expressed "the whole spirit of the new historical school" of French thinkers.[17] That political "truths" are "strictly relative . . . [and] correlative [to] a given state or situation of society" states "one of the principal differences between the political philosophy of the present time and that of the past."[18] "The science of politics," in other words, must be seen as "fluctuating with the exigencies of society."[19]

This contextualization of political theory placed a decisive emphasis upon the empirical investigation of social phenomena, but what exactly did such an investigation uncover? The mere accumulation of facts would, Mill argued, amount to nothing more than the crudest empiricism. Besides, the notion that an "affect" was the result of a singular "cause" was a far too simplistic conception of causality to be applicable to human affairs. To Mill there was little point in abandoning a simplified view of human nature while retaining such a simplistic methodological characterization of human action as causal events. If human nature as the ensemble of influences acting upon individuals in society was complicated, it was because the interaction of all the elements that constitute society was itself a complicated process. The latter could best be understood in terms of a plurality or composition of causes.[20] Even this expression does not adequately comprehend the extent to which there are counteracting causes, or the degree to which, from a contextualist standpoint, it is "capricious" to draw a hard and fast "distinction between the cause of a phenomenon and its conditions."[21] Thus, Mill argued, "all laws of causation, in consequence of their liability to be counteracted, require to be stated in words affirmative of tendencies only, and not of actual results."[22]

Political theory, therefore, must be formulated in terms of the observable tendencies at work in society; it is composed of "approximate generalizations" and conditional projections. There are, according to Mill, no universal tendencies or certainties with respect to human behavior. Social science is, fundamentally, a science of probabilities.[23] Political theory rests upon empirical laws—observed uniformities—and these laws, Mill maintained, "can only be received as true within the limits of time and place in which they have been found true by observations."[24] The fact is, he declared, "human interests are so complicated, and the effects of any incident whatever so multitudinous, that if it touches mankind at all, its influence on them is, in the great majority of cases, both good and bad."[25] The task of the political theorist is to analyze the tendencies in society relative to each other, to determine the good and bad effects of each, and to state, in conditional language, the probable future outcome if these tendencies continue to operate as they appear to be operating in the present. Tocqueville's *Democracy in America* drew so much praise from Mill because the work was written from this standpoint; from the perspective, that is, of the "new political philosophy."[26]

Mill's aim was to provide an empirically grounded basis for a theory of social structures. Hence, some tendencies were certainly long-term ones, and, with respect to human endeavor, they were, for all practical purposes, irreversible. Yet, because "the science of politics, or of human society . . . is principally concerned with the actions not of solitary individuals, but of masses," to know that most people act in a certain way most of the time generally is a sufficient epistemological foundation for the realization of the practical objectives of that science.[27] The objective of a political theory as an instrument of practical politics is "to surround any given society with the greatest possible number of circumstances of which the tendencies are beneficial, and to remove or counteract, as far as practicable, those of which the tendencies are injurious."[28] This application of political theory naturally relied upon the investigatory techniques and the methodological assumption that Mill built into his definition. Stated in its broadest formulation, "the fundamental problem, therefore, of the social science, is to find the laws according to which any state of society produces the state which succeeds it and takes its place."[29]

It is true, Mill conceded, that the complicated and comprehensive knowledge demands social science places upon its practitioners produces an inescapable condition of uncertainty attached to the pronouncements of political theorists; that is, it makes it less likely that "two inquirers equally competent and equally disinterested will take the same view of the evidence, or arrive at the same conclusion." When "to this intrinsic difficulty is added the infinitely greater extent to which personal or class interests and predilections interfere with impartial judgment," it is evident that "political theory," so defined, is deeply rooted in the structural conditions of political controversy.[30]

How these methodological presuppositions are expressed in Mill's analysis of nineteenth-century British society will be discussed later. Here my purpose is to indicate the importance that Mill's redefinition of political theory had as a prolegomena to that analysis. If class conflict were a structural feature of capitalist society, and if it played a role within a theory of social change, then a contextual, historical, sociological approach to the study of politics certainly supplied the intellectual framework in terms of which these issues could be investigated.

I do not wish to draw a sharp distinction between the "philosophical" elements of Mill's thought—concepts he borrowed from other thinkers—and the "sociological" observations he made with respect to the prevailing conditions in his own society, but, in tracing the emergence of a concept of "class interest" in his political theory, let us begin with Mill's interesting interpretation of Bentham's political thought. In his essay on Bentham, Mill draws a critical distinction between cultural or "spiritual interests" and the "material interests" of society. Bentham's philosophy has little to say about the former, but, Mill observes, "it can teach the means of organizing and regulating the merely business part of the social arrangements" between individuals. That is, it can "indicate means by which . . . the material interests of society can be protected."[31] Less emphasized in the secondary literature on Mill is his commentary on what Bentham's philosophy really means if these "social arrangements" are analyzed in greater detail. In the political world of mass and collective action, what the Benthamite pursuit of self-interest means "is selfish interest in the form of class interest, and the class morality founded thereon." That "the social feelings of members of the class are made to play into the hands of their selfish ones," resulting in "the most odious class-selfishness," Mill insists, "was one of Bentham's leading ideas."[32] As he himself put it in his Benthamite period, "in every class, the purely selfish [individuals] always form a large majority."[33] In one sense this proposition he borrowed from Bentham remained a keystone of Mill's thought throughout his life. At the same time, he concluded from the mere existence of classes in society that social institutions had not been properly constituted to realize the general good of society.[34]

If classes were organized collective pursuits of selfish interests, it followed for Mill that they would employ any political power placed in their hands to advance those interests, and they would do so at the expense or through the oppression of classes that were politically weaker than themselves.[35] The very principle of constitutional government, Mill wrote in the *Considerations,* "requires it to be assumed that political power will be abused," and, as he specifically noted, this means that it will be abused in the form of "class legislation."[36] Nor will the use of this power be confined within the boundaries of the law. "Wherever there is an ascendant class, a large portion of the morality of the country emanates from its class interest and its feeling of class superiority."[37] That observation on the exercise of class power occurs in *On Liberty,* where Mill is especially concerned not so much with governmental authority as with the social forces that shape public opinion and the everyday activities of social life. In other words, as Mill developed the insights he gained from French political thought, he increasingly translated the general relationship between "social power" and "constitutional power" into a form of political analysis that specifically singled out "the class which wields the strongest power in society."[38]

Mill's essay on the "Reorganization of the Reform Party" is a brilliant illustration of an analysis of political power in terms of the social class support for three political parties (Whigs, Tories, Radicals) with representatives in Parliament. The "permanent causes" of the divisions expressed as contending political viewpoints, Mill argues, "are for the most part" to be identified with the class interests of individuals and their "class feelings" that those interests can be advanced through the organization and policies of a particular political party.[39] Moreover, if, for example, one's analysis revealed that the middle class was the most powerful class in society, "any counterbalancing power can henceforth exist only by the sufferance of the commercial class."[40] That the tendencies of one class to dominate society could only be offset or counterbalanced by developing tendencies that favor another class with opposing interests is an important point, to which I shall return.

I am not suggesting that Mill would have subscribed to Marx's statement the "all history is the history of class struggle" as a general proposition of his theory of history—though he does characterize all historical forms of representative government as "a standing league of class interests."[41] He certainly did believe, however, that "the ruling principle in the government of this country is not the public good, but the particular interests of certain classes, who command a majority . . . [in] Parliament."[42] What I am suggesting is that when Mill employed his revised definition of political theory and the methodological tools of social science in an analysis of nineteenth-century British society, he was quite prepared to discuss political power in terms of the class interests that structured and exercised it.

Thus, although it is an oversimplification to say that all Mill had to do in order to fit the conflict between the working class and the capitalist class into this framework was to observe its empirical manifestations, nevertheless, it is true that this particular expression of class conflict posed no novel or unique problems from the standpoint of Mill's theoretical analysis of his society, though this conflict did present him with considerable difficulties in his endeavor to find a theoretical solution to it. "Chartism," he wrote in an essay on "The Claims of Labor" published in 1845, "was the first open separation of interest, feeling, and opinion, between the laboring portion of the commonwealth and all above them. It was a revolt of nearly all the active talent, and a great part of the physical force, of the working classes, against their whole relation to society."[43] Notwithstanding the fact that Chartism was avowedly a movement to win political power for the working class, Mill recognized that the working class was preoccupied "with one subject—the relation between laborers and employers."[44] Moreover, there is "no sense of co-operation and common interest" between workers and their employers; their relation to each other is that of "hostile rivals."[45]

Even if such a thing were possible, it is not my concern here to state the precise moment when the pervasiveness of class conflict became apparent to Mill. Suffice it to say that he was a sufficiently keen social observer to recognize that "the most deep-rooted distrusts and aversions which exist in society" were grounded in "the opposition between capitalist and laborers."[46] Thus, there is an "animosity which is universal in this country towards the whole class of employers in the whole class of the employed."[47] Chartism demonstrated not only that "the working classes have taken their interests into their own hands," but also that "they think the interests of their employers not identical with their own, but opposite to them."[48] Yet this opposition was not rooted in—only intensified by—the unequal distribution of political power between classes in Victorian England, nor would extension of the franchise to the working class remove the source of this class conflict. In this respect, Mill's understanding of the situation paralleled that of the radical Chartists, such as Ernest Jones, or Owenite Socialists, both of whom maintained against their suffrage-minded colleagues in the working class that only a restructuring of the system of economic production would put an end to the opposition of class interests.

In the 1860s, long after the Chartists has spent themselves as a political force, Mill believed the capitalist-labor conflict was worsening. "The most important questions in practical politics," he declared, "are coming to be those in which the working classes as a body are arranged on one side, and the employers as a body on the other."[49] Six months later he wrote another correspondent that "the division between labor and employers of labor seems to me to be increasing in importance, and gradually swallowing up all others, and I believe it will be always widening and deepening unless, or until, the growth of Cooperation practically merges both classes into one."[50] There are numerous reaffirmations of this point in Mill's writing and correspondence of the 1860s.[51] Two years before his death he singled out "the land question and the relation between labor and capital" as "the points on which the whole of politics will shortly turn." They were "questions involving the whole structure of society."[52]

At the time of his death Mill was writing a book on socialism which, according to his design, would have been a substantially longer work than any he had hitherto written. In the opening pages of that unfinished manuscript, he explains that, with the passage of the 1867 Reform Bill and the likelihood of further extensions of its provisions in the near future, the working class would soon exercise predominant political power in society. Since "they believe, rightly or wrongly, that the interests and opinions of the other powerful classes are opposed to theirs," workers will use "their collective electoral power," for "the promotion of their collective objects"—that is, for the advancement of their class interests. Not only does the working class have special interests, but they also have "definite political doctrines . . . organized into systems and creeds," which can claim the status of "political philosophy." For, Mill observes, politics is "now scientifically studied from the point of view of the working classes." Hence, by the 1870s to Mill class conflict meant not merely a conflict of interests, the existence of which he had long recognized, but also, and perhaps more important from his standpoint, a conflict between competing class-oriented political theories. In response to this situation, Mill argued, "the discussion that is now required is one that must go down to the very first principles of existing society." By that he meant the principles defining the "rights" attached to property, because, he explained, the conflict between the working class and the property-owning classes centered on the question of who controlled the system of production and how it was to be organized.[53]

Before considering Mill's response to this challenge, it is important to recognize the clarity of his perception of the conflict between the working class and the capitalist class, the seriousness with which he treated the problem as being crucial to an understanding of the structure of society and of the scientific claims of political theory, and the degree to which he believed that this problem claimed priority over other problems in requiring a practical political solution.

Social Conflict, Liberty, and Socialism

Given the precepts of Mill's methodology and the aims of social science, it is surprising that he never systematically explored or elaborated upon the *causes* of the social conflict between workers and capitalists to which he attributed such practical importance. Mill accepted the Ricardian proposition that an inverse relationship obtained between wages and profits, and, at least until his rejection of the wage fund theory in 1869, he apparently believed that this relationship, supported by the scientific laws of the marketplace, supplied a sufficient explanation for the "opposite interests" of workers and their employers.[54] Mill certainly did not accept what he called the "irritating cant" repeated by many of his contemporaries to the effect that "the interest of laborers and employers . . . is one and the same." He thought this a ridiculous proposition, for, "to say that they have the same interest . . . is to say that it is the same thing to a person's interest whether a sum of money belongs to him or to someone else."[55] It was pointless to *imagine* that a harmonious alliance of interests existed when it was obvious (to Mill) that a real conflict, in the form of strikes, lockouts, and trade-union demonstrations characterized the relations between workers and capitalists. The only question worth considering, therefore, was on what grounds one could render a decision respecting the conflicting claims of workers and their employers to possession of the same sum of money, which was the product of the joint production of capital and labor?

In order to answer this question and, in general, to offer an assessment of the conflict of interests between workers and capitalists, Mill argued, one would have to have "a clear view of the causes which govern the bargains between them." In other words, there must be a theory of how wages are determined.[56] The conventional view among nineteenth-century political economists—Mill included—was that the price of labor, like the price of all other commodities, was determined by the laws of supply and demand. When Mill, in his review of W. T. Thorton's *On Labor* (1869), repudiated or, rather, modified his previous position on this issue, he realized that since there was no longer a "scientific foundation" in the "necessities of political economy" for the heretofore accepted causal explanation of wages, any new theory of wages would have to emerge from a consideration of those causes which operate within the realm of politics, broadly defined. Because "the price of labor is decided by a conflict of wills between employers and laborers," Mill wrote, "it is necessary, as in every other case of human voluntary action, to ascertain the moral principles by which this conflict ought to be regulated."[57]

If wages were "decided by a conflict of wills between employers and laborers," it was also true that "every opinion as to the relative rights of laborers and employers involves expressly or tacitly some theory of justice."[58] In 1861, reflecting upon this class conflict, Mill wrote to a correspondent that the difficulty was to find some *principle* of equity between the claims of workers not to starve and the claims of employers that they should receive some remuneration (profit) for their efforts. Yet, he confessed, "between these limits I do not see what standard of equity can possibly be laid down." Looking to the future, Mill said, "I can conceive Socialism" supplying a general rule of equity that would resolve the conflict; but, for the present, "under a system of private property in past accumulations in which no general rule can be laid down," it was not at all clear how "the quarrel between capital and labor" was to be resolved. Since neither party in the dispute was likely to submit to another's arbitrarily imposed "views of equity" as to their competing claims, Mill concluded that "the only thing which people will in these circumstances submit to as final, is the law of necessity, that is, the demand and supply of the market."[59]

But of course these remarks were made prior to Mill's recantation of the wage fund doctrine and his recognition that strikes, trade-union organization, and the exercise of political power *could* affect bargaining outcomes between workers and capitalists.[60] He now saw that "the law of necessity" and market determination neither reigned in fact, nor, from the phenomenological viewpoint, would "the market" be consciously accepted (and especially not by the working class) as a functional principle of equity for resolving this class conflict. What this signified to him, therefore, was a renewed sense of urgency associated with the endeavor to find some "standard of equity," some set of "moral principles by which this conflict ought to be regulated." A situation in which, in addition to the actual physical hardships imposed by strikes, lockouts, and unemployment, there were two conflicting class-based theories of justice was hardly conducive to the maintenance of social peace, not to mention the realization of the greatest good for the community.

Of course Mill believed that relations between workers and capitalists, like all social relations, ought to be governed by the general principle of utility—the happiness of mankind. But he was not such a fool to believe that, stated abstractly in this manner, the utilitarian principle contributed in any *specific* way to the resolution of this class conflict.[61] In general, I believe that Mill's sociological realism has been greatly underestimated by interpreters of his thought making their way across the arid desert of philosophy with their divining rod of logical consistency. Mill could see that, in fact, both workers and employers had more regard for their respective class interests than for the "permanent interest" of the community as a whole. Nevertheless, he argued, "it cannot be right that a contest between two portions of society as to the terms on which they will cooperate, should be settled by impairing the efficacy of their joint action," for example, through strikes.[62] Mill was not opposed to strikes—indeed, he was part of a small minority of those outside the working class who resolutely defended workers' rights to engage in strikes.[63] He simply wanted to make the point that "there must be some better mode of sharing the fruits of human productive power" than according to the practices that presently govern the conflict of wills between workers and capitalists.[64]

This "state of war" could and would be brought to an end, Mill believed, if a system of cooperative socialism replaced the capitalist mode of production. Cooperative socialism expressed that "principle of justice" and equity, he argued, according to which "the great economic problem of modern life," the conflict between labor and capital, could be resolved.[65] "Nothing that I can imagine except cooperation," Mill declared, "would entirely take away the antagonism" or the "opposition of interests between employers and employed."[66] Cooperative socialism, he insisted, is "the real and only thorough means of healing the feud between capitalists and laborers."[67]

There were several versions of socialism current in the nineteenth century, and, commenting upon them, Mill states what he believes they all have in common. "What is characteristic of socialism," he observes, "is the joint ownership by all the members of the community of the instruments and means of production."[68] This is the situation, according to Mill, that must obtain if there is to be a solution to the problem of class conflict. In addition to recognizing cooperative socialism as a practical response to the conflict between workers and capitalists, Mill subscribed to it as a principle of justice, whose implementation would produce a moral revolution in social relations.[69]

It is a perfectly acceptable procedure, Mill wrote, to begin with a "standard of absolute justice" and then consider what "practical obstacles" stand in the way of its realization.[70] This is the procedure he adopts in the *Considerations,* where he is attempting to "work towards . . . the true ideal of representative government . . . by the best practical contrivances which can be found" within the context of a particular set of social conditions.[71] In 1851 Mill declared: "It appears to us that nothing valid can be said against socialism in principle; and that the attempts to assail it, or to defend private property, on the ground of justice, must inevitably fail." The inequalities created by that system of private property are so "obviously unjust" that no sensible person would include them in "the rudest imaginings of a perfectly just state of society." They "could only be defended," Mill argued, "as an affect of causes in other respects beneficial."[72] In other words, the inequalities of the private ownership of the means of production must be counterbalanced by some beneficial effect *sufficiently proximate to the system of private property that it would disappear if the latter were abolished.* Only then, Mill argues—and it should be noted that he is speaking hypothetically—could a defense be provided for existing social institutions. At the same time, he maintained that "The reasonable objections to socialism are altogether practical, consisting in some difficulties to be surmounted."[73] Hence, both the benefits of private property and the deficiencies of socialism could be assessed in terms of practical expediency, but, as competing principles of justice, socialism was clearly the superior of the two.[74] "The rough method of settling the laborer's share of the produce, the competition of the market," Mill wrote, "may represent a practical necessity, but certainly not a moral ideal." Echoing the language he had used nearly twenty years earlier, he added that it was nothing more than a "rude approach to an equitable distribution," compared to the ethical principle of cooperative socialism.[75]

Mill's practical objections to socialism, expressed in his earliest and in his last writings, display a remarkable consistency. For the most part he concentrates upon the difficulty of inducing individuals to act for motives higher than that of self-interest. Yet, since *he* never ceased to insist that the foundations of morality must be laid deeper than "the calculations of self-interest," this "difficulty" could never, in itself, constitute a sufficient ground for rejecting socialism.[76] Mill was convinced that individuals could be educated, through various social practices, to act for the common good. "Everybody," he insisted, "has selfish and unselfish interests, and a selfish man has cultivated the habit of caring for the former, and not caring for the latter."⁷⁷ Thus, "education, habit, and the cultivation of the sentiments will make a common man dig or weave for his country, as readily as fight for his country." A change in the habits, and therefore in the character, of individuals may take some time, "but the hindrance is not the essential constitution of human nature. Interest in the common good is at present so weak a motive" in individuals, "not because it can never be otherwise, but because the mind is not accustomed to dwell on it as it dwells from morning till night on things which tend only to personal advantage." If, as Mill insists, "the deep-rooted selfishness which forms the general character of the existing state of society is so deeply rooted only because the whole course of the existing institutions tend to foster it," then it is easy to appreciate his identification of social reform with the practical realization of the imperatives of a higher morality.⁷⁸ And, given the importance Mill assigned to socialism within the general project of social reform, it is understandable why his objections to socialism—with one important exception to be discussed later—had to assume the form of practical expediencies, as temporary obstacles to be overcome.

Suppose, however, one accepted the constraints imposed by "the vulgar incentives of individual interest," which manifest themselves socially in the form of class interests and in the conflict between opposing class interests.⁷⁹ What are the prospects that justice can be realized in such a society? We have seen that, on the most fundamental level of social relations, Mill denied that class conflict was compatible with his principle of justice, nor was it conducive to the happiness of mankind. Still, reform of existing political institutions might be effected even within a society marred by defective social relations. Hence, the question to be considered—discussed at length by Mill in the *Considerations on Representative Government*—is: How can democratic political institutions be established in a society characterized by class conflict?

In an early comment on the general problem, Mill wrote that "when different sections of the community have clashing interests, and are ranged under hostile banners, the proper place of government is not in the ranks of either body, but between them"; that is, it should assume the role of "a mediator and peace-maker."⁸⁰ Later, and with specific reference to the conflict between laborers and capitalists, he repeated the point that "it is the grand business of government to attempt to reconcile" these conflicting social forces.⁸¹ By the 1860s, as we have seen, it was "above all" this conflict between classes that "requires an arbiter," deciding the issues in dispute between workers and capitalists according to "general rules and comprehensive views." And, Mill added, "when properly constituted . . . the government . . . is that arbiter."[82] But how "properly constituted"?

Since the fatal defect of all forms of government, according to Mill, is that of "class legislation," it follows that "in determining the best constitution of a representative government," the question is, "how to provide efficacious securities against this evil?"[83] We may put aside, as Mill does, any consideration of this problem outside the framework of democracy, for it is obvious to him that the absence of universal suffrage insures class domination in that society.[84] Given a class-divided democratic society, therefore, "the desirable object would be that no class, and no combination of classes" could exercise a preponderant influence in the government."[85] Since Mill strongly disliked the idea of "class representation," it is clear that this "ideal," even if realized, operates under seriously defective social conditions. For, in a true democracy, there should be no social classes to be "combined."[86]

Be that as it may, in a society divided between classes of workers and capitalists, "if the representative system could be made ideally perfect . . . its organization must be such, that those two classes . . . should be, in the arrangement of the representative system, equally balanced, each influencing about an equal number of votes in Parliament." This arrangement remained as close as possible to the prevailing tendencies in Mill's society by "assuming that the majority of each class, in any difference between them, would be mainly governed by their class interests." The "ideal" aspect of this constitutional system only required that a minority of individuals within each represented class subordinate their class interests "to reason, justice, and the good of the whole." Their votes on a particular issue would thus tip the balance in favor of justice, thereby avoiding the evil of class subjection as a systemic feature of representative government.[87] Balancing evils against each other, Mill conceded, is much less desirable than the process of synthesizing goods, but his limited objective in the *Considerations* was to describe the "relative perfection" of "a political constitution" for a society with the sociological tendencies present in Victorian England.[88]

If we view justice emanating from this model as the outcome of practical expediencies rather than "permanent causes"—who could be sure that each class would elect as representatives a minority of relatively classless intellectuals?—there is, nevertheless, one positive principle that is actually constitutive in this form of government. It is that the free expression of different and conflicting opinions in Parliament is *guaranteed under* the arrangement described by Mill. More than a decade before writing the *Considerations,* he had asked: "Ought not parliament to be the place of discussion for adverse interests and principles, the arena where opposing forces should meet and fight out their battles?"[89] Mill realized that unless representatives from the working class acting for the working class were elected to Parliament, this goal was unobtainable.[90] He accepted the relative evil of class representation for the sake of obtaining the greater good of gaining a hearing for workers' views.[91] To this end he personally contributed funds to support the parliamentary candidacies of working-class individuals, and, notwithstanding his own relatively classless status as a spokesman for working-class interests, offered to stand down himself as a parliamentary candidate if a member of the working class could be induced to run in his place.[92] But the point, to emphasize it once more, was to ensure that adversaries had to listen to each others' views and to defend their own proposals with reasons and well-constructed arguments.[93]

Anyone passably familiar with *On Liberty* recalls those passages in which Mill affirms that "truth" almost never appears to mankind as a unity because, generally speaking, "conflicting doctrines . . . share the truth between them." These partial perspectives arise from the "standing antagonisms of practical life." Thus, "Truth, in the great practical concerns of life, is so much a question of the reconciling and combining of opposites, that very few have minds sufficiently capacious and impartial to make the adjustment with an approach to correctness, and it has to be made by the rough process of a struggle between combatants fighting under hostile banners." If these statements are read in the context of the argument Mill advances in the *Considerations*—not an unreasonable suggestion in view of other sentences contained in this passage from *On Liberty*—it appears that the diversity of opinion can not only be preserved, but might even be strengthened, through the constitutional recognition through representation of class conflict.[94]

In order to appreciate this somewhat paradoxical defense of liberty, it is necessary to consider one of Mill's oft-repeated sociological pronouncements regarding the historical development of society (though I will not reproduce the several perturbations through which it passed during his intellectual development). Stated succinctly (in the *Considerations*), it is this: "No community has ever long continued progressive, but while a conflict was going on between the strongest power in the community and some rival power." Without some form of social conflict, "a social support" for "opinions and interests" opposed to the dominant tendencies in society, that society will stagnate and decay.[95] Some mechanism is needed in order to generate that "systematic antagonism" of ideas upon which, in Mill's view, the progressive development of the community as a whole depends.[96] Naturally he allowed that the specific form assumed by this principle of antagonism varied through history relative to the contextual circumstances of particular societies. Even in the earliest examples he cited, however, this form included, but was not limited to, a conflict between classes.[97]

Within the framework of democracy, Mill wanted to place his hopes upon a "learned class," an "instructed minority," acting to check the impulses of a popular majority.[98] Yet he realized that, sociologically and politically speaking, it was futile to imagine that a "separate organization of the instructed classes" could be constitutionally incorporated into the structure of a democratic government.[99] Various contrivances—plural voting, personal representation—might be tried experimentally as a means of ensuring that some intellectuals were elected to Parliament; but even if they were, Mill's sociological analysis no longer supposed that "the standing antagonisms of practical life" *arose* from a conflict between the opinions held by an intellectual minority and the opinions subscribed to by the majority of citizens.[100] Intellectuals in Parliament might articulate their class-oriented positions as well as those positions could be stated, but Mill expected very few conversions to occur across class lines as a consequence of even the most reasoned discussion.[101] The "permanent causes" of social conflict were rooted in the social relations underlying the form of government.

Of course there is no analytical necessity for the diversity of opinion, individual spontaneity, and the conflict of ideas to be tied to the social conflict between classes. Religious beliefs and gender-based interests also foster differences of opinion. Yet, neither of these phenomena were likely to generate that systematic form of antagonism needed to propel a society forward if, in fact, that society had resolved the problem of class conflict.[102] What, then, would serve as a functional replacement for the latter with respect to the preservation and development of liberty?

The one principled, and not merely practical, objection Mill consistently directed against socialism concerned its inability to provide for "individuality of character" or a "variety of intellectual points of view" as a structural feature of society.[103] This last proviso is important, because it is a mistake to assume that the dimensions of this problem were, in Mill's view, confined to the *intentions* of his socialist contemporaries. True, their beliefs, insofar as they did undervalue liberty and individual agency, represented a practical obstacle to be overcome.[104] But, setting aside the specific influence exercised by Owen, St. Simon, Comte, or other individuals, what was even more worrisome to Mill was the "oppressive yoke of uniformity in opinion and practice," viewed as the unintended consequence—that is, as a social tendency—of "the inevitable growth of social equality."[105] Given Mill's definition of social science, it is not difficult to see why this should be so. In a famous passage in *On Liberty,* reflecting upon one possible outcome of this tendency, he declares: "If the roads, the railways, the banks, the insurance offices, the great joint-stock companies, the universities, and the public charities, were all of them branches of the government; if, in addition, the municipal corporations and local boards, with all that now devolves on them, became departments of the central administration; if the employees of all these different enterprises were appointed and paid by the government, and looked to the government for every rise in life; not all the freedom of the press and popular constitution of the legislature would make this or any other country free otherwise than in name."[106] The question I wish to raise is, why not? Why, in a democratic society, with a free press and free elections—assuming the cognate freedoms of assembly, speech, and religious belief, as I believe Mill does in this passage—are the citizens not "free"?

Mill's most general answer is that in such a situation the "energy" of the community at large has disappeared, and it is "chiefly the qualities of mental activity, enterprise, and courage" that are needed to avoid a condition of social stagnation.[107] The latter might be the consequence either of a "tame uniformity of thought, feelings, and actions," arising from the oppressive yoke of public opinion, or of a centralization of power in the hands of a government bureaucracy managing the "collective interests" of society.[108] Much, if not all, of Mill's criticism of socialism can be accounted for in terms of the projected development of these two tendencies in a socialist society. With the record of twentieth-century socialism before us, the prescience of Mill's warning is obvious. Indeed, it is generally from the perspective of hindsight that most interpreters of Mill's thought have read his strictures against bureaucracy and conformity as being equitable with an attack upon socialism. This is not an accurate representation of Mill's critical assessment of these phenomena. He had Tocqueville to remind him—as we have Weber to remind us—that these tendencies are "glaring evils of the existing state of society."[109] The difficulty for Mill, as for us, is to locate those countertendencies in a democratic society which —as Mill's remark seems to imply— operate at a more fundamental level than free elections or a free press to preserve "individual agency."

When the issue is phrased in this way, it is easy to see why so many interpreters of Mill are disposed to rest their case for individual liberty upon the social institution of private property. It appears that a structural defense of individual liberty depends upon such an interconnection. Mill, however, not only does not make, but explicitly rejects, such an argument in *On Liberty*. Rather surprisingly, he claims that the doctrine of free trade in commerce "rests on grounds different from . . . the principles of individual liberty asserted in this essay."[110] Even questions of how "great enterprises of industry" are to be conducted "are not questions of liberty," but of development.[111] This is not to say that there are not statements in Mill's writings, especially in the *Principles of Political Economy,* that support the view that some relationship exists between individual agency and private property. But virtually all of these remarks are imbued with a Lockean quality; that is, that individuals are entitled to own what they produce through their personal labor.[112] What does this maxim have to do with the private ownership of the means of capitalist production? For, as Mill recognized, and as Marx noted in the *Communist Manifesto,* if "individuality" and "freedom" depend upon the ownership and control of private property in capitalist society, then the overwhelming majority of the members of that society are neither free nor do they possess the means to develop their individuality. "The generality of laborers in this and most other countries," Mill observed, "have as little choice of occupation or freedom" of movement, and are as dependent "on the will of others, as they could be in any system short of actual slavery." They "have not enough of—personal and mental freedom—to deserve the name."[113]

In both *On Liberty* and *Considerations,* Mill attacks a "numerous bureaucracy," in whatever form of society it exists, and to which he juxtaposes the democratic participation of individuals.[114] It is the "administrative skill" of "trained officials," or professional managers, versus the self-management of institutions through democratic participation, that is the focus of his argument.[115] Participatory democracy is, for Mill, a practical school educating individuals in public affairs.[116] There is very little in the ordinary work activities of individuals "to give any largeness either to their conceptions or to their sentiments. Their work is a routine," performed for motives of self-interest. "Every thought or feeling— is absorbed in the individual and in the family." The person "never thinks of any collective interest, of any objects to be pursued jointly with others, but only in competition with them, and in some measure at their expense. A neighbor, not being an ally or an associate, is therefore only a rival." The means by which "the manual laborer, whose employment is routine," and "whose daily occupations concentrate his interests in a small circle round himself," escapes these deadening limitations is through obtaining "a share of sovereign power" and through participating in collective action. Only then will he or she cease to feel like an outsider, for whom the management of affairs is of no concern because it is someone else's responsibility.[117] Mill's argument, reduced to its simplest terms, is that participatory democracy engenders a sense of collective concern for the general good, while bureaucratic administration fosters alienation and a narrow range within which individuals pursue their self-interests.

To return to the question raised earlier, What is the difference between large-scale capitalist enterprises bureaucratically managed and bureaucracy-ridden governments, of which Mill is so critical? Business enterprises in which workers have no personal interest no more inspire enlarged conceptions of the collective interest than does a despotic bureaucracy. "A factory operative," Mill argues, "has less personal interest in his work than a member of a Communist association, since he is not, like him, working for a partnership of which he is himself a member." Indeed, "how small a part of all the labor performed in England, from the lowest-paid to the highest, is done by persons working for their own benefit."[118] With respect to the cultivation of the individual's mental and moral capacities—and even in terms of the efficiency of management—Mill maintains that there is really no difference between a corporate and a governmental bureaucracy.[119] In short, there is nothing in his criticism of the effects of bureaucracy in destroying "individuality" in the *Considerations on Representative Government* that does not apply with equal force to the relationship between the individual worker and Exxon or IBM.

The cure for this malady is exactly the same: democratization through participatory control over his "common undertaking." What is truly "distinctive" about a free society, Mill argues, is the "discussion and management of collective interests" by the people.[120] When he describes cooperative socialism, it is a system in which workers "collectively owning the capital" choose "managers elected and removable by themselves."[121] Neither in politics nor in socioeconomic relations, did Mill believe that there were any practical benefits attached to monopolistic or oligarchical control that outweighed the value of democratic control. If he, unlike Marx, underestimated the extent to which the development of monopolies or oligopolistic industrial enterprises is a prevalent tendency in capitalist society, Mill did not hesitate to assert the right of the government to regulate—or even take over—such concerns on behalf of the common interest of society.[122]

Although the institutions of liberal society could tolerate the existence of class conflict in the short term, ultimately, for Mill, the latter was incompatible with the values he associated with participatory democracy and cooperative social relations. To put it simply, class conflict destroys the moral life of liberalism. By extending the meaning of the radical elements of liberal political theory—its moral egalitarianism, the belief that individuals can and do act for the public good, the conviction that political power rightfully lies in the hands of the people—Mill laid the foundations for a democratic socialist perspective. Of course, other aspects of his thought, viewed as a whole, must be regarded as qualifications which he placed upon the development of these tendencies. In the end, however, both Mill's moral conviction and his sociological analysis reinforced his belief that the future of industrial society could be described in terms of the extension of the democratic—radical—features of liberalism into the socioeconomic areas of life.

A society in which there is class conflict between workers and capitalists, in which great inequalities of wealth and opportunity exist, in which there is little or no public debate regarding the basic standing antagonisms of practical life that arise from these social divisions, in which the legislature is not balanced in terms of the representation of class interests, in which gigantic corporations are conducted with little regard for the common good or for the mental and moral development of their employees, and in which a governmental bureaucracy has extended the scope of its powers at the expense of democratic control is not a society for which Mill's political theory is likely to provide a comforting defense. It is an injustice to Mill—and not to him alone, but to those historical dimensions of liberalism which have not always been so dormant as they presently are—simply to conscript him as a defender of twentieth-century Anglo-American political and social institutions. If modern liberals have, to a significant degree, misunderstood the radical dimensions of Mill's political thought, it is because, unlike him, they have demonstrated little interest in exposing and criticizing the fundamental defects and injustices of the institutions that shape their daily lives.

Making Sense of Moral Conflict

STEVEN LUKES

The title of this chapter might suggest that there is a phenomenon, or set of phenomena, that can be recognized as moral conflict and a separate question, namely: How is one to make sense of it? That would be misleading. For the recognition of moral conflict cannot be separated from making sense of it. What sense, if any, one makes of it, will determine the range of recognizable instances. Indeed, there are several well-known ways of making no sense of it at all.

In such cases what we have are at most instances of merely apparent moral conflict—of ignorance or error, or of individual or social pathology. In either case, it is an affliction to be overcome. Thus, Aristotle saw conflicting moral beliefs as a mark of ignorance, never as a recognition of conflicting moral requirements, while Aquinas further thought that the moral virtues formed a harmonious unity and could not exclude one another.[1] Plato followed early Greek thought in contrasting the valid norm of *nomos* with its deformation, *anomia,* which he identified variously with injustice, godlessness, impiety and iniquity, the less beneficial, terrible and fierce desires, cruelty, anarchy, and disorder.[2] In modern times utilitarianism and Kantianism have advanced comprehensive moral theories, each of which proposes an overarching principle that purports to accommodate or else force us to revise our existing moral intuitions, providing us with a practical decision procedure for all moral situations. As Charles Larmore writes: "when moral theories of this monistic sort have run up against recalcitrant moral intuitions that conflict with their favored higher-order principle, they have too often resorted to the tactic of denying those intuitions their very status as 'moral' ones. (Recall the charges of squeamishness and rule-worship that many utilitarians have leveled against those who morally reject an action knowingly injuring another, even though it happens to maximize the general happiness; recall also the censure of principlelessness that Kantians have often directed toward those that have held that sometimes a great good should be obtained at the price of doing evil)."[3]

Ethical relativism is another way of depriving moral conflict of any sense, for the point of relativism is to explain it *away* by proposing a structure in which apparently conflicting claims are each acceptable in their own place. The trouble is that this raises the puzzle, which relativism finds hard to solve, of explaining why the claims appeared to conflict in the first place. Worse, it fails to take such claims seriously by denying their applicability beyond cultural boundaries (assuming these are not in dispute). Nor is it clear how ethical relativism can handle conflicts *within* such boundaries. Finally, subjectivist ethical theories of various sorts constitute a further way of depriving moral conflict of sense, by removing the notion of conflicting *claims* based on reasons. For instance, emotivism, in its various forms, sees morality as just a way of expressing or inducing states of mind and feeling. But, as Bernard Williams compellingly argues, if anything attests to the objectivity of ethics, it is the experience of moral conflict: "That there is nothing that one decently, honourably or adequately *can* do seems a kind of truth as firmly independent of the will and inclination as anything in morality."[4]

In short, none of these attempts to make nonsense of moral conflict seems to succeed. None is adequate to our moral experience, to what has been called "the fragmentation of value" or the "heterogeneity of morality" as we know it in our personal and public lives. Accordingly, I shall ask three questions: What kinds of moral conflict could there be? What kinds of important or significant moral conflicts are there and why should we believe they are important? What bearing does making sense of such conflicts have upon the defense of liberty and of a liberal political order?

Is moral conflict possible and what forms could it take? In addressing these questions, I am concerned with the possibility of conflicting moral claims or requirements that face agents, individual or collective, not with how to reconcile or regulate interpersonal or social conflicts between individuals, between individuals and groups and communities, or between groups and communities. Moral conflicts are conflicts between moral claims that may face persons or groups or communities or governments representing them, when individually or collectively they deliberate about what to do. Sometimes these are experienced as one-person conflicts, when individuals experience the pull of conflicting demands, as in the case of tragic dilemmas of choice or where people—the children of immigrants, for instance—have internalized the requirements of mutually incompatible cultural traditions. Accordingly, I shall now ask: What are such conflicts between? In what exactly does the conflict consist?

The Sources Of Conflict

The form of conflict to which moral philosophers have paid most attention is that of conflicting obligations. Here the conflict consists, not in an incompatibility between duties abstractly defined, but between the actions they require in a given situation. Sartre's pupil could not both go to England to fight with the Free French Forces *and* stay with his mother, deeply affected by the semi-treason of his father and by the death of her eldest son, and thereby help her to survive. The state of the world generated the conflict, and no ethical standpoint, certainly neither the Kantian nor the Christian (this was Sartre's point), can remove it without *mauvaise foi*—partly (as Sartre says) because values are too "vague," too "general for such a precise and concrete case,"[5] but also because each action involves the violation of an obligation. Here, as in other such cases, there is no way of avoiding moral loss, of not committing an uncanceled wrong.

Secondly, there are conflicts between purposes, ends, goals, or (more vaguely still) "values." These too are best thought of, not as instances of inconsistency, but as yielding incompatible directives for action or policy, given the way the world is. This is what Sir Isaiah Berlin had in mind when he wrote that "ends may clash irreconcilably": "Should democracy in a given situation be promoted at the expense of individual freedom; or equality at the expense of artistic achievement; or mercy at the expense of justice; or spontaneity at the expense of efficiency; or happiness, loyalty, innocence, at the expense of knowledge and truth? The simple point which I am concerned to make is that where ultimate values are irreconcilable, clear-cut solutions cannot, in principle, be found."[6]

And it is what Leszek Kolakowski doubtless meant when he wrote: "If socialism is to be anything more than a totalitarian prison, it can only be a system of compromises between different values that limit one another. All-embracing economic planning, even if it were possible to achieve—and there is almost universal agreement that it is

not—is incompatible with the autonomy of small producers and re-
gional units, and this autonomy is a traditional value of socialism,
though not of Marxist socialism. Technical progress cannot co-exist
with absolute security of living conditions for everyone. Conflicts
inevitably arise between freedom and equality, planning and the autonomy of small groups, economic democracy and efficient management, and these conflicts can always be mitigated by compromise
and partial solutions." There are also, Kolakowski argues, "internally
inconsistent" values such as "the ideal of perfect equality," but this
is not, as he says, "contradictory in itself." Rather, it involves conflict
because, given the way the world is, it yields incompatible policies.
It implies "more equality and less government," but "in real life,
more equality means more government, and absolute equality means
absolute government."[7]

Thirdly, there are even more holistic and less well-defined entities
between which moral conflicts may be thought to hold: moral codes
or systems or world views or, in Rawls's phrase, "conceptions of the
good." These are what Pascal may have had in mind when he observed that what is truth on one side of the Pyrenees is error on the
other.[8] (What he meant was perhaps that what is seen as truth on one
side is seen as error on the other.) Conflicts of this sort are marked
by incompatibilities of perception and belief, in particular over "how
good and evil are to be recognised and distinguished from each other."
Such cultural differences of moral perception can certainly seem real
enough. As Kolakowski remarks, they cannot be removed by re-
treating to some common ground which the adversaries share or by
appealing, as in science, to some "higher tribunal" capable of an
intersubjective adjudication of controversies.[9] But, as Pascal and Voltaire in his *Essai sur les moeurs* assumed, and as Allan Bloom and
Kolakowski both rightly insist, real confrontations between culturally
defined moral perceptions in no way imply relativism of moral judgment.[10] As Kolakowski rather dramatically puts it, "I may perceive,
say, the evil of killing malformed babies, but I have to admit that
this kind of perception is not universal and that people in other civ-
ilisations—which I am perfectly entitled to describe in pejorative
terms and call barbarous—see things differently."[11] The example is
extreme and does not capture a real confrontation that many face.
Inhabitants of multiethnic or religiously divided societies or societies
caught between secularism and religiosity can think of many more
familiar and mundane instances—as when communities disagree over
what constitutes respect for women or parents, or the centrality of

religious instruction to education, or the right to free choice in marriage.

Finally, and most interestingly, there are conflicts between different kinds of moral claim. A number of writers have pointed to the irreconcilability of the conflict between consequentialism and deontology, and I have already referred to the way in which utilitarians (who embody the dominant form of consequentialism in Anglo-Saxon cultures) and Kantians seek to deny its very existence. Consequentialism requires that the agent maximize the overall good (on some interpretation of that good), by so acting as to produce the best outcome, all things considered, for all those affected by this action. Deontology, by contrast, proposes a set of (sometimes absolute) side-constraints on action done to others, set by the requirements of the Moral Law or by divine prohibitions or by their moral rights, whatever the consequences to them or to others may be.

The irresolvability of this conflict was perhaps foreshadowed in Machiavelli's dictum that "While the act accuses, the result excuses," if we interpret it to mean that, while the act is (consequentially) justified in retrospect, the accusation *stands*.[12] And indeed, the problem of dirty hands in politics is the *locus classicus* of this kind of clash of moral claims—a clash inadequately captured by the so-called problem of "means and ends." It is perhaps rather the problem of bringing together Lenin's question "What is to be done?" with another that Lenin certainly never asked, namely, "What is not to be done?"— or, as Machiavelli put it, of the Prince learning, "among so many who are not good," how to enter evil when necessity commands for the good of the Republic.[13] Politics, as Max Weber saw, is the arena in which such dilemmas can take their most dramatic form, though they reappear in all areas of life, wherever doing what is best overall requires the committing of a wrong, or the violation of a right.

For utilitarians and some other consequentialists (among whom I include Marxists, for reasons mentioned later) such dilemmas cannot exist, if the appropriate calculations for measuring the best overall outcome, all things considered, have been correctly made. (Of course consequentialists could deny value monism, if they were to recognize types of outcome as ineliminably pluralistic. Generally, however, they do not.) If the consequentially right answer to the question "What is it right to do?" requires one to override the constraints of ordinary morality, then in that case to do so could not be wrong, and neither guilt nor regret would be appropriate. Apparently dirty hands are clean. For Kantian and other deontologists—exponents of what

Trotsky called "Kantian-priestly and vegetarian-Quaker prattle"[14]—
following the appropriate maxim is all that is required in cases of
moral choice, thereby relieving the moral agent of the need to take
responsibility for consequences that, in any case, flow in part from
the choices and actions of others. The moral agent takes responsibility
only for what he alone does. On this view, one's hands must always
be clean, whatever the consequences.

All this is familiar, if contested, ground, but in *Patterns of Moral
Complexity* Charles Larmore advances the discussion by suggesting
that we are caught up in conflicts between three equally objective
practical demands or principles of practical reasoning which urge
independent claims upon us (we cannot plausibly see one as a means
for promoting another) and so can draw us in irreconcilable ways.
These are the principles of deontology, consequentialism, and partiality. The principle of partiality underlies "particularistic duties."
For example, "Partiality requires that we show an overriding concern
for the interests of those who stand to us in some particular relation
of affection. There are, for example, the duties of friendship and the
demands that stem from our participation in some concrete way of
life or institution, to protect and foster it. There are also the obligations that arise from more abstract commitments, as when we speak
of an artist's duty to his art." The duties encompassed by this principle
"arise from the commitment to some substantial ideal of the good
life. The other two principles are universalistic and support categorical
obligations."[15]

I cannot here pursue Larmore's interesting exploration of the ways
in which the claims of partiality—our commitments to particularistic
projects—can conflict, on the one hand, with consequentialism ("If
we were only consequentialists, we constantly would have to set aside
our own projects and friendships, since each of us has countless opportunities for increasing preference-satisfaction within a wider
sphere") and, on the other, with deontology (against Kant, not every
categorical duty, say keeping a promise, overrides every particularistic
commitment).[16] Nor can I discuss his interesting, but I suspect mistaken, suggestion that in a liberal political order neutrally justifiable
principles of justice, whether consequentialist or deontological, must
always rank higher than the principle of partiality (how else could
the foreign-aid budget be limited?). Larmore succeeds admirably in
developing the arguments of others for the view that the basic sources
of morality are plural and against the belief that human beings could
inhabit a world without moral loss and unsettleable conflict.

The Nature of Conflict

In what do such conflicts consist? I suggest that various senses of "conflict" can be ranged along a scale of increasing intractability. Conflict may signify diversity, incompatibility, or incommensurability.

Diversity. First, there is what used to be called "the diversity of morals," a topic of profound interest to early anthropologists and sociologists, much discussed in the late nineteenth and early twentieth centuries by Wilhelm Wundt, Lucien Levy-Bruhl, W.G. Sumner, L.T. Hobhouse, Edward Westermarck, and Morris Ginsberg and still intermittently addressed by social anthropologists and some sociologists,[17] but somehow lost as a central topic for systematic social inquiry. I shall allude later to the interpretation of the data and the inherent difficulties of discerning the actual range of such diversity. Here I simply observe that mere diversity becomes a form of conflict when notional confrontations become real, that is, where in a confrontation between two outlooks, "there is a group of people for whom each of the outlooks is a real option." An outlook is a real option for a group "either if it is already in their outlook or if they could go over to it; and they could go over to it if they could live inside it in their actual historical circumstances and retain their hold on reality, not engage in extensive self-deception, etc."[18]

In such cases—as opposed, say, to our contemplation of Athenian democracy or life among the Incas—conflict involves a more or less deep but relevant difference of life-world and life-style, that may be responded to in various ways. Among these ways are rejection, conversion, and various kinds of syncretistic adaptation. Not all moral diversity, in short, is conflictual. Nor does all conflictual diversity issue in incompatible ways of living.

Incompatibility. Some moral conflicts are instances of incompatibility. I have already alluded to some of them. Antigone cannot both obey the dictates of family loyalty by burying Polynices and those of the law decreed by Creon. Agamemnon at Aulis cannot save both his fleet and his daughter. Sartre's pupil cannot both join the Free French and console his mother. Likewise, there are what are significantly called trade-offs between policies designed to promote democracy, equality, liberty, and so on, and other trade-offs internal to the pursuit of any one of them. Alternative conceptions of the good can turn out to dictate incompatible ways of treating persons in particular situations. Should the immigrant's daughter attend college? Should the sick Amish child go to hospital? Should abortion be permitted?

These undoubted incompatibilities are not yet incommensurable. All moralists and most moral philosophers will assume that they are not, that there is always a point of view from which they are amenable to the discovery of the "right answer." (The law of course is one such point of view, by the very reason of its social role.[19]) Indeed, it is generally assumed that to assert the contrary is a form of irrationalism. Buried very deep in our philosophical consciousness and implicit in our social scientific practice is the nearly universal presumption that consistency of preference and of ethical beliefs is a mark of our rationality. But is it?

Incommensurability. Incompatible moral claims become incommensurable when the trade-offs become unavailable because there is no comon currency. In recent times several writers have appealed to this difficult notion. Berlin writes: "If the claims of two (or more than two) types of liberty prove incompatible in a particular case, and if this is an instance of the clash of values at once absolute and incommensurable, it is better to face this intellectually uncomfortable fact than to ignore it, or automatically attribute it to some deficiency on our part which could be eliminated by an increase in skill or knowledge; or, what is worse still, suppress one of the competing values altogether by pretending that it is identical with its rival—and so end by distorting both."[20]

Williams, citing Berlin, writes that "values, or at least the most basic values, are not only plural but in a real sense incommensurable," adding that this claim says "something true and important."[21] For Rawls, a "workable conception of political justice" must allow for "a diversity of doctrines and the plurality of conflicting, and indeed incommensurable, conceptions of the good affirmed by the members of existing democratic societies.[22] For Thomas Nagel, "values come from a number of viewpoints, some more personal than others, which cannot be reduced to a common denominator," and when "faced with conflicting and incommensurable claims, we still have to do something—even if it is only to do nothing." For Nagel, the "fragmentation of value" encompasses conflicts *between* "moral and other motivational claims of very different kinds" coming from "many perspectives—individual, relational, impersonal, ideal, etc."[23] This is to deepen and broaden the issue we are seeking to confront. And Larmore advocates that we "suspend the monistic assumption underlying so much of moral theory" and "acknowledge that not everything is good or right to the extent that it is commensurable with respect to any single standard."[24]

The key idea, then, is that there is no single currency or scale on which conflicting values can be measured, and that where a conflict occurs no rationally compelling appeal can be made to some value that will resolve it. Neither is superior to the other, nor are they equal in value. To believe in incommensurability is not to hold that all or even most value conflicts or even more conflicts are of this sort; only that some are and that they are nontrivial. Conflicts could be trivially incommensurable where preference rankings are indeterminate because incomplete or discontinuous, as where I just don't know how much more I value Mozart than Bach or how much the weather must improve before I prefer a walk in the park to staying at home with a book.[25] But they could also be nontrivially so if and when I cannot appeal to some single value standard to determine whether, say, E. M. Forster was right to place the value of friendship above patriotism, or how far local autonomy should be protected against policies of equalization, or how things stand between your belief in the fetus' right to life and mine in the mother's right to choose. The fact that one must decide in such cases, in favor of one or the other or by appeal to some value independent of both (such as maximizing utility or well-being), does not show which is worth more. That question does not admit of a "right answer," refusal to accept which is a sure sign of irrationality. However one decides, it will be *from* and not just *for,* one of the viewpoints in contention, or from a further viewpoint that is no less contentious.

So far I have sought to suggest the *possibility* of moral conflict, in all the senses I have distinguished. I have done this in two ways: by seeking to discredit various attempts (by Aristotelians, Platonists, Kantians, utilitarians, relativists, and subjectivists) to make nonsense of such conflicts; and by suggesting that our moral experience bears witness to their presence and to their importance. In doing this, I have enlisted, by citing them, various recent allies in this argument against the prevailing view in both philosophy and social science. I now wish further to motivate the thought that the possibility is actualized and that it is central to our personal and public lives.

Consider first the diversity of morals. Those who have sought to deny, or minimize, this have, appealing to Hume's thought that "mankind is much the same in all times and places,"[26] interpreted differences of belief and practice as best explained by differences in the circumstances human beings face. There is a deep interpretive problem here. Any study of the moral thought and action of others is inexorably caught up in a hermeneutic circle: Is there any way into, say, Navaho or Hopi ethics that does not already presuppose our moral categories and distinctions? Is there, in other words, any way that such a study could avoid John Ladd's criticism of Richard Brandt's study of Hopi ethics, that it "consists in a cross-cultural investigation of the extent to which the Hopi accept principles like our own"?[27] Or, more deeply and worryingly, that they should emerge as reflecting some recognizable fragment of our own moral world? The problem is only deepened by the plausible suggestion that it is a condition of successful translation that "the imputed pattern of relations between beliefs, desires and the world be as similar to our own as possible."[28] If all this is so, perhaps it is no accident that Brandt's Hopi end up as impartial and disinterested and Ladd's Navaho as egoistic prudentialists.

These are deep waters into which I propose to go no further except to suggest that the diversity of morals reveals itself clearly in what, following Bernard Williams, I have called "real confrontations," as in intercultural conflicts within and between contemporary societies. It is possible but not easy to deny the diversity of morals when contemplating cultural conflicts in South Africa or Northern Ireland or the Middle East and the clash between secularism and the various forms of religious fundamentalism.

As for moral conflict as incompatibility, that too is surely a pervasive feature of the modern world. There are two ways of taking the sting out of this, neither of which looks very plausible in the late twentieth century. One is to deny its reality via theodicy: by believing, as Bishop Butler did, that God has so arranged the world and our natures that, though in acting morally we may appear to follow divergent moral principles that exclude general benevolence, nevertheless, *sub specie aeternitatis,* the general happiness is secured.[29] Leszek Kolakowski has well said, "in an apologist's eyes God's inscrutable ways can always be plausibly defended."[30]

The other implausible way of removing the sting from moral conflict as incompatibility is to deny, not its reality, but its necessity via the secular inheritance of theodicy: moral utopianism. A moral utopian believes that there is in prospect a perfect world in which all actual moral incompatibilities will be overcome because the subjective and objective conditions of life will render them impossible, even inconceivable. Like Kolakowski, I think that Marxism is committed to such a belief: for the present to a kind of long-term consequentialism in which pursuing the perfectionist goal of human emancipation is the overriding practical guide to action; and for the future, the undefended and indefensible hope that under "truly human" conditions there will be (1) a maximization of overall good (welfare and perfectionist achievement); (2) a transcendence of the conditions that have made the lawlike ethics of obligations, justice, and rights necessary; and (3) an overcoming of the conditions that render partial obligations and commitments to particular communities and groups incompatible with universal ones.[31] Neither the conceivability nor the feasibility nor indeed the desirability of such a reconciliatory future can any longer be plausibly defended.

I turn finally to the difficult issue of incommensurability. Why should we believe that significant incommensurabilities exist between the apparently conflicting moral claims we face? I suggest that there are two main reasons for believing this. First, as Max Weber and Kolakowski have powerfully argued, in a disenchanted world, there is no longer any reason to believe in the commensurability of basic values.[32] As Weber, "speaking directly," memorably put it "the ultimately possible attitudes towards life are irreconcilable, and hence their struggle can never be brought to a final conclusion. Thus it is necessary to make a decisive choice." What man, he asks, "will take upon himself the attempt to 'refute scientifically' the ethic of the Sermon on the Mount? For instance, the sentence 'resist no evil,' or the image of turning the other cheek? And yet it is clear, in mundane perspective, that this is an ethic of undignified conduct: one has to choose between the religious dignity which this ethic confers and the dignity of manly conduct which preaches something quite different: 'resist evil—lest you be co-responsible for an overpowering evil.' According to our ultimate standpoint, the one is the devil and the other the God, and the individual has to decide which is God for him and which is the devil. And so it goes throughout all the orders of life."[33]

Some believe that this position amounts to a denial that moral judgment can be rationally based and others believe further that it leads somehow inexorably to moral anarchy or fascism or at least to the inability to resist them. (By contrast, I believe it to be essential to a properly defended liberalism.) Bloom, rightly seeing Nietzsche behind Weber, objects that, on that kind of view, "it is our *decision* to esteem that makes something estimable," that "the objects of men's reverence" become "projections of what is most powerful in man and serve to satisfy his strongest needs or desires," that "values are not discovered by reason, and it is fruitless to seek them, to find the truth or the good life," that "producing values and believing in them are acts of the will" and that we have thereby abandoned "the distinction between true and false in political and moral matters," that the choice lies between Plato and Nietzsche and that by choosing against the former, we have thereby sacrified "reason."[34] Alasdair MacIntyre argues, in a not dissimilar way, that, by choosing Nietzsche and Weber, in his case against Aristotle, we have abandoned the possibility of a rational foundation for ethics. He seeks to vindicate Aristotle's "pre-modern view of morals and politics" against the central thesis that he takes to underpin Nietzsche's position—"that all rational vindications of morality manifestly fail and that *therefore* belief in the tenets of morality need to be explained in terms of a set of rationalisations which conceal the fundamentally non-rational phenomena of the will."[35]

Jürgen Habermas, from a very different standpoint, nevertheless holds to a "cognitivist position . . . that there is a universal core of moral intuition in all times and in all societies" and thus rejects "the Weberian pluralism of value systems, gods and demons" and the "empiricist and/or decisionist barriers, which immunize the so-called pluralism of values against the efforts of practical reason."[36] (Here, I believe, he wrongly identifies Weber's position with that of Carl Schmitt.) He proposes, through the utopianism of a counterfactually posited "ideal speech situation," to "vindicate the power of discursively attained rational consensus" and show that "practical questions admit of truth."[37]

But Weber, for what it is worth, did not derive values from decisions and the will. Quite the contrary, decisions, based on moral judgment, are needed just because conflicting values, some objective, some not, are incommensurable. Neither going back (in Bloom's words) to "great wise men in other places and times who can reveal the truth about life"[38] nor looking forward to the imagined consensus of ideal speech serves to gainsay this uncomfortably objective truth.

A second reason for holding that incommensurability is both real and important to our contemporary lives is suggested by Joseph Raz in *The Morality of Freedom*. It applies more particularly to that which holds between partiality, on the one hand, and deontology or consequentialism, on the other. Many of the commitments, loyalties, and obligations that we have to relationships and activities that matter to us consist in part in a refusal to engage in the very kind of trade-off that full commensurability would require. If I were prepared even to consider how much the obligations of friendship are worth in relation to some greater future good to persons unknown, or whether my parental duties can be traded for some greater overall benefit, or against, say, some promise I have made, that might only show that I am not a true friend or parent. Such refusals to compare suggest that constitutive attachments are what they are in part by virtue of their very incommensurability with more universalistic moral claims. To engage in such forms of thinking is itself an expression of the weakening or absence of those very relationships or else a degraded simulacrum of them. The very assumption of commensurability would subvert certain values, which are what they are in part just because they deny it. If all this is right, then we can only conclude that modernity—in which the separation between the partial and the universal, like that between fact and value, has become a prevalent cultural fact—renders incommensurability inescapable. There is no route back from modernity.

What, finally, does the recognition of moral conflict have to do with the defense of liberalism? Liberalism was born out of religious conflict and the attempt to tame it by accommodating it within the framework of the nation-state. The case for religious toleration was central to its development; and out of that there developed the crucial but complex thought that civil society is an arena of conflicts, which should be coordinated and regulated by the constitutional state. In part that conflict is, as Hume saw, a result of scarcity and conflicting claims that arise out of selfishness and competing interests. But, more deeply, it also arises out of conflicting moral claims, which raises the problem of how to treat these justly within a framework of social unity and mutually acceptable laws and principles of distribution. Given all this, the prospects for a morally based defense of liberalism—a defense that derives from a comprehensive or all-embracing moral view— look dim, even self-contradictory.

This has led critics of liberalism to condemn it for being anemic, pale, morally half-hearted, skeptical, even indifferent. Others, notably Kant and the utilitarians, and in some moods John Stuart Mill, defend it by appealing to just such a comprehensive moral theory. But it leads others to argue that its proper defense requires that such a defense be unavailable. Thus, Isaiah Berlin attacks those he calls "single-minded monists," arguing that "The notion that there must exist final objective answers to normative questions, truths that can be demonstrated or directly intuited, that it is in principle possible to discover a harmonious pattern in which all values are reconciled, and that it is toward this unique goal that we must make; that we can uncover some single central principle that shapes this vision, a principle which, once found, will govern our lives—this ancient and almost universal belief, on which so much traditional thought and action and philosophical doctrine rests, seems to me invalid, and at times to have led (and still to lead) to absurdities in theory and barbarous consequences in practice."[39]

Rawls too distinguishes between "those that allow for a plurality of opposing and even incommensurable conceptions of the good and those that hold that there is but one conception of the good and which is to be recognized by all persons, so far as they are fully rational." He sees the latter as the "dominant tradition," which includes Plato, Aristotle, the Christian tradition as represented by Augustine and Aquinas, and classical utilitarianism. He contrasts that tradition with liberalism as a political doctrine, which holds that "there are many conflicting and incommensurable conceptions of the good, each compatible with the full rationality of human persons" and that "the question the dominant tradition has tried to answer has no practicable answer. . . for a political conception of justice for a democratic society."[40]

Allan Bloom, by contrast, while defending "liberal education," is plainly a monist and a full subscriber to the "dominant tradition." I doubt that there could be a more devout form of adherence to that tradition than the Straussianism he has so successfully popularized. For him, the Rawlsian defense of liberalism is nothing short of a plea for moral indifference and skepticism, even "value-relativism." Rawls's *A Theory of Justice,* he writes, argues that "the physicist or the poet should not look down on the man who spends his life counting blades of grass or performing any other frivolous or corrupt activity. Indeed, he should be esteemed, since esteem from others, as opposed to self-esteem, is a basic need of all men. So indiscriminateness is a moral imperative because its opposite is discrimination. This folly means that men are not permitted to seek for the natural human good and admire it when found, for such discovery is coeval with the discovery of the bad and contempt for it."[41]

This is certainly an imaginative Straussian reading of the inner meaning of Rawls's text, which explicitly and repeatedly states the contrary. More important, it misses the point and the force of Rawls's defense of liberalism altogether. Fortunately, in anticipation of such a charge, Rawls has fully answered it and I will quote him doing so. He has forthrightly denied advocating "either skepticism or indifference about religious, philosophical, or moral doctrines. We do not say that they are all doubtful or false, or address questions to which truth and falsehood do not apply. Instead, long historical experience suggests, and many philosophical reflections confirm, that on such doctrines reasoned and uncoerced agreement is not to be expected. Religious and philosophical views express outlooks toward the world and our life with one another, severally and collectively, as a whole. Our individual and associative points of view, intellectual affinities and affective attachments are too diverse, especially in a free democratic society, to allow of lasting and reasoned agreement. Many conceptions of the world can plausibly be constructed from different standpoints. Diversity naturally arises from our limited powers and distinct perspectives; it is unrealistic to suppose that all our differences are rooted solely in ignorance and perversity, or else in the rivalries that result from scarcity. Justice as fairness tries to construct a conception of justice that takes deep and unresolvable differences on matters of fundamental significance as a permanent condition of human life. Indeed, this condition may have its good side, if only we can delineate the character of social arrangements that enable us to appreciate its possible benefits."[42]

This raises the deep and difficult issue of specifying just what sense liberalism is to make of moral, and more generally value, conflicts. Some, most obviously some religious conflicts, cannot be resolved, because their justification seems to be internal all the way down: what is to count as good or overriding reasons remains to the end internal to the opposed parties and not susceptible to common or public argument.[43] Others—and these are what Rawls has in mind in the passage quoted—are so susceptible but are nevertheless irresolvable because there is no prospect of publicly available evidence and argument yielding uniquely determinate solutions rationally compelling upon all.[44] For the state to impose any single solution on some of its citizens is thus (not only from their standpoint) unreasonable. Hence the liberal's commitment to impartiality, at the level of social and political institutions, among such conflicting conceptions of the good—and the right— as are compatible with the survival of a liberal order. The question of how far that commitment is a merely strategic one (as a means to securing a modus vivendi) and how far, and in what ways, itself a substantive moral one (appealing, for instance, to an interpretation of the Kantian categorical imperative) is one I cannot explore further here.

This, then, is how moral conflict bears on the proper defense of liberalism. That defense cannot, for the reasons I have sought to develop, rely on the gleaning of ineffable truths from ancient texts or on the elaboration of comprehensive moral theories. It cannot be based on either a return to or a contemporary restatement of Plato or Aristotle or Natural Law or Kantianism or utilitarianism; or on a resort of relativism or subjectivism or an appeal to theodicy or moral utopianism. It can rest only on taking moral conflict seriously and making sense of it.

Liberal Dialogue Versus a Critical Theory of Discursive Legitimation

SEYLA BENHABIB

Power is a social resource and a social relation in need of legitimation. Legitimacy means that there are good and justifiable reasons why one set of power relations and institutional arrangements are better than and to be preferred to others. Conceptions of legitimacy consist of normative arguments, defending the justice and fairness of a particular set of institutions, relations, and arrangements. I maintain that the legitimation of power should be thought of as a public dialogue. In this chapter I shall defend a "dialogic" or "discourse model of legitimacy" by contrasting it with alternative views of legitimacy prevalant in contemporary liberal political theory.

Proceduralist Ethics and the Idea of Dialogue

We can identify three dominant models of legitimacy in contemporary political thought. I suggest that we view these models as "neo-Kantian" approaches to the relation between morality and politics. First, one could argue that there is a continuity between Kant's universalist and procedural moral philosophy based on the value of the autonomous personality and his theory of justice of such a nature that political institutions must be viewed—in Kantian language—as embodying those "external conditions of freedom" most compatible with the dignity of the autonomous person.[1] This connection between the moral worth of the autonomous personality and the institutions of a just society remains the guiding and constant theme of the Rawlsian view of justice.[2] According to this view, the principles of justice most compatible with the value of the autonomous personality can be specified via a model of collective choice constrained by certain procedural rules. These are deemed to be reasonable limitations on choice, defining the circumstances of justice. Although procedural, this Rawlsian model of legitimacy is not dialogic. The choice of the principles of justice is not thought to result from any kind of dialogue among the parties to the original position.[3]

Let me contrast this view with the model of procedural dialogue developed by Karl-Otto Apel and Jürgen Habermas who view normative justification as a public dialogue. The sum of those procedural constraints to be respected in such situations of dialogue are referred to by Apel as "the ideal communication community," and by Habermas as the model of the "ideal speech situation."[4] Both can be viewed as going back to what Kant calls the "transcendental condition of publicity," namely, that "All actions affecting the rights of other human beings are wrong if their maxim is not compatible with their being made public."[5] The emphasis in this model is not so much on those institutions most compatible with the "coexistence of the will of one with the will of all under conditions of external freedom," but rather on the question: Which norms and which institutional arrangements would individuals who engage in a practical discourse, governed by the procedural constraints of an ideal speech situation, accept as legitimate? This model is both procedural and dialogic.

There is a third way to conceive of the relation between morality and politics within Kantian thought. This is the idea of a "republic of devils." Kant defines it as follows: "As hard as it may sound, the problem of setting up a state can be solved even by a nation of devils (so long as they possess understanding). It may be stated as follows: 'In order to organize a group of rational beings who together require universal laws for their survival, but of whom each separate individual is secretly inclined to exempt himself from them, the constitution must be so designed that, although the citizens are opposed to one another in their private attitudes, these opposing views may inhibit one another in such a way that the public conduct of the citizens will be the same as if they did not have such evil attitudes.' "[6] According to this view, a just constitution need not make strong moral assumptions about the person and motivations of individuals. In fact, assuming the worst about them, one must be able to come up with a set of public rules that would ensure public order, continuity, and stability. I suggest that Bruce Ackerman's conception of modus vivendi liberalism, as defended in *Social Justice in the Liberal State*[7] and in his article "Why Dialogue?"[8] represents this position.

For Ackerman liberalism is a form of political culture in which the question of legitimacy is paramount. In *Social Justice in the Liberal State* he writes: "Whenever anybody questions the legitimacy of another's power, the power holder must respond not by suppressing the questioner but by giving a reason that explains why he is more entitled to the resource than the questioner is."[9] Ackerman understands liberalism as a way of talking about power, as a political culture of public dialogue based on certain kinds of conversational constraints. The most significant conversational constraint in liberalism is neutrality which rules that no reason advanced within a discourse of legitimation can be a good reason if it requires the power holder to assert two claims: that his conception of the good is better than that asserted by his fellow citizens; or that, regardless of his conception of the good, he is intrinsically superior to one or more of his fellow citizens.[10] In "Why Dialogue?" Ackerman presents a pragmatic-political as opposed to moral justification of the idea of a public dialogue based on the conversational constraint of neutrality.

Since Ackerman's ideal of liberal dialogue articulates a procedural, public discourse of legitimation, it is instructive to contrast it with the "discourse model of legitimacy." Such a contrast is a useful starting point for highlighting some of the differences between liberal models of legitimacy and a discourse theory of legitimacy.

Although we are both committed to a dialogic model of legitimacy, I disagree with Ackerman on two points: first, his model of "conversational restraints" imposes arbitrary as opposed to reasonable and defensible limits on the content and scope of public dialogue; and second, the superiority of the Habermasian model of an "ideal speech situation" is precisely that it allows us to publicly thematize what Ackerman's model privatizes. As opposed to the model of public dialogue based on conversational restraints, the ideal speech situation or the "discourse model of legitimacy," is reflexive, that is, it allows radical self-questioning; it is critical, which is to say that it allows us to challenge precisely existing forms of power relations that hinder the conversation from being fair, just, and genuinely open.

Modus Vivendi Liberalism Versus a Discourse Model of Legitimacy

Bruce Ackerman bases his case for public dialogue, "not on some general feature of the moral life, but upon the distinctive way liberalism conceives of the problem of public order."[11] His question is how different primary groups, about which we know only that they share the same conception of the good, can "resolve the problem of coexistence in a *reasonable* way."[12] Ackerman believes that citizens in a liberal state must be guided by a Supreme Pragmatic Imperative (SPI) which states that they must be willing to participate in an ongoing dialogue about their conception of the good with others who are not members of their primary group.

Ackerman is concerned to find a justification of this imperative that will not fall into the three traps that traditionally affect moral philosophies of liberalism. One must find a justification of the SPI that is not based on trumping, that is, already asserting as supreme one moral view over others. Furthermore, one cannot assume, as utilitarians do, that there is a translation manual neutral enough in its language and in terms of which all our various moral commitments can be stated. According to Ackerman, such a translation manual would violate one of the parties' sense of the good. Finally, one cannot ask the parties to assume a "transcendental perspective" as the precondition for entering into dialogue. Such a transcendental perspective, let us say the point of view of the "original position" or that of the "ideal speech situation," abstracts so radically from the condition of existing differences that it forces the parties to the public dialogue to assent to moral truths which they do not hold.

The way out is the path of "conversational restraint." "When you and I learn that we disagree about one or another dimension of the moral truth, we should not search for some common value that will trump this disagreement; nor should we try to translate our moral disagreement into some putatively neutral framework; nor should we seek to transcend our disagreement by talking about how some hypothetical creature would resolve it. We should simply say *nothing at all* about this disagreement and try to solve our problem by invoking premises that we *do* agree upon. In restraining ourselves in this way, we need *not* lose the chance to talk to one another about our deepest, moral disagreements in countless other, more private, contexts . . . Having constrained the conversation in this way, we may instead use dialogue for pragmatically productive purposes: to identify normative premises all political participants find reasonable (or at least, not unreasonable)."[13] I want to challenge this argument.

First, the pragmatic justification of "conversational restraint" is not morally neutral; this justification both trumps and transcends. The idea of a supreme categorical imperative governed by conversational restraint can appear as a reasonable, pragmatic approach only when the primary groups regard public peace and order as the supreme good. If peace is not the supreme moral good, then there is no reason to engage in such a public conversation; our vision of the good may in effect dictate that the disruption of the seeming tranquility and civility of this order is the supreme good. In the view of such groups as the Dadaists of the early twentieth century to various separatist movements in our own days, submitting to such a conversational restraint would simply perpetuate the false peace we want to destroy.

Second, the pragmatic justification not only trumps but also "transcends," for it asks the parties to the conversation to agree to "say nothing at all about" fundamental disagreements. It is unclear to me why this agreement not to talk about fundamental disagreements in public is any less loaded or controversial an assumption than the idea of a "veil of ignorance" which asks us to feign ignorance about our conception of the good. If I am deeply committed to the belief that prevalent conceptions of sexual division of labor in our societies are morally wrong because they oppress women and hinder their full expression of themselves as human beings, why should I agree not to do the best I can to make this a public issue and to convince others of my point of view? Or suppose I am a member of the Israeli opposition to the occupation of the territories. I consider this occupation wrong not on pragmatic grounds but on moral ones, because I believe that the occupation is corrupting the ethical values of the Jewish people. I may well be aware that under current conditions public opinion is so divided that I stand no chance of winning assent; nevertheless, is it unreasonable of me to seek the widest possible forum of public discussion and participation to air my views, rather than to agree with you, as Ackerman advocates, not to talk about what is of most concern to me. Either Ackerman's justification of the SPI is based on stronger moral grounds than he admits to or it cannot claim the supreme status it is supposed to enjoy.[14]

I see no way of justifying a dialogic or discursive model of legitimacy—including Ackerman's—without making some strong assumptions both about morality and about rationality. No procedural theory can be developed without making some substantive assumptions. If a procedural ethical theory is going to say anything worthwhile, it will have to make a number of controversial substantive commitments. This, though unavoidable, is not as damaging to the case for proceduralism as it is usually thought to be. For we can then do two things. First, we can allow the conditions of the procedure to be thematized within the dialogue situation itself. The dialogue must be so open that we can even discuss how the rules of dialogue are set up, while seeing, however, that we are in Neurath's boat, that we can throw overboard only some of the planks at certain points in time, but that we cannot remove all the planks of the boat and continue to remain afloat. In other words, even while challenging the rules of dialogue we have to respect some rules to keep the conversation going. Second, we must seek to justify the presuppositions of dialogue in the context of our most explicit assumptions about human nature, history, and society. Proceduralism does not imply formalism and ahistoricism, as it is usually thought to do. There is no reason why a procedural theory cannot be part of a more general theory of the self, historical change, and social structure.

But is the path of conversational restraint so arbitrary? Why can it not be regarded as one of those procedural constraints on dialogue that we all have to agree to on reasonable, moral grounds, even if not wholly pragmatic ones? My answer is that the idea of conversational restraint presupposes a questionable moral epistemology and that it implicitly justifies a separation between the public and the private that is oppressive to the concerns of certain groups.

By the "moral epistemology" of the conversational restraint model I mean the following. The liberal theorist of conversational restraint presupposes that the primary groups to the conversation already know what their deepest disagreements are even before they have engaged in the conversation. These groups already seem convinced that a particular problem is a moral, religious, or aesthetic issue as opposed to an issue of distributive justice or public policy. We can legitimately discuss the second, says the liberal theorist, but let us abstract the first. Take, however, issues like abortion, pornography, and domestic violence. What kind of issues are they? Are they questions of "justice" or of the "good life"? I have no more definitive answers to these questions than anybody else at this stage in the debate, but what I am suggesting is that the very process of unconstrained public dialogue will help us define the nature of the issues we are debating. The distinction between issues of justice and those of the good life cannot be decided by some moral geometry. I suggest that all issues that participants in a practical discourse agree cannot be universalized and be subject to legal norms constitute issues of the good life; the rest are issues of justice. This means that citizens must indeed feel free to introduce, as Bruce Ackerman says, "all kinds of moral arguments into the discussion. For it is only after the dialogue has been opened in this radical fashion that we can be sure that we do agree upon a mutually acceptable definition of the problem rather than reaching some compromise consenses.

The issue of pornography illustrates my point well. This question has been so divisive and has created such strange and unholy alliances—Andrea Dworkin and Jerry Falwell, for example—that it is the paradigm example of the kind of moral disagreement that the modus vivendi liberal may urge us to agree not to publicly disagree about. This, however, is precisely what we should not do at this stage of the debate. Whether pornography is to be defined as a question of the reasonable limitations to be imposed upon the First Amendment right of free speech; whether pornography is to be thought of as a private, moral issue concerning matters of sexual taste and style; whether pornography is to be thought of as a matter of aesthetic-cultural sensibility and as a question of artistic fantasy—these we simply cannot know before the process of unconstrained public dialogue has run its course. Now I no more want to live in a society which cannot distinguish between *Hustler* magazine and Salinger's *Catcher in the Rye* than Ackerman does, or in a society that would place Henry Miller and D. H. Lawrence in the company of "Deep Throat." As sensitive as one may be, however, to the traditional liberal fear that unlimited public conversation might erode those few constitutional guarantees we can rely upon, I think that the reprivatization of issues that have become public only generates conceptual confusion, political resentment, and moral outrage. I consider limitations upon the content and scope of public dialogue, other than constitutional guarantees of free speech, to be unnecessary. A normative theory of such conversational constraints fails to become a critical model of legitimation.

The Discourse Model of Legitimacy

The discourse model of legitimacy, based on the procedural constraints of the ideal speech situation, places no such limits upon the content and scope of the public conversation. Ackerman considers this model hopelessly utopian, and maybe even politically pernicious. The "ideal speech situation" is so counterfactual, in his view, that it trumps, translates, and transcends. Or it is so devoid of content that it is irrelevant for the resolution of public issues.[15] I suggest that one can offer a moral justification of this model that neither trumps, translates, nor transcends. Furthermore, this model appears empty only because its critics have not appreciated that the purpose of the discourse theory of legitimacy is not to develop a blueprint for social order but to suggest a critical vantage point from which to judge power relations in our societies.[16]

The procedural constraints of the "ideal speech situation" are that each participant must have an equal chance to initiate and to continue communication. Each must have an equal chance to make assertions, recommendations, and explanations. All must have equal chances to express their wishes, desires, and feelings. And finally, within the situation of dialogue speakers must feel free to thematize those power relations which in ordinary contexts would constrain the wholly free articulation of opinions and positions. Together these conditions specify a norm of communication that can be named one of *egalitarian reciprocity*. Although I cannot expand on the differences here, let me state that as opposed to Apel in particular, who claims to justify this model via a "transcendental" argument, I prefer a "weak" justification strategy which functions more like a "coherence test."[17]

The discourse model of legitimacy is an aspect of a communicative theory of ethics. The discourse model develops the basic idea of this theory in its application to institutional life. Communicative ethics is first and foremost a theory of moral justification. The question from which it proceeds is how to defend the cognitive or rational kernel of moral judgments without assimilating these either into statements about the world (naturalism) or into statements about my preferences (emotivism). Briefly, the answer is that we should view moral judgments and other statements defending the validity of norms as assertions whose justifiability we can establish via moral argumentations named "discourses." Moral justification amounts to a form of moral argumentation. This is the fundamental principle governing a discourse ethic. Habermas names it D, and I see no reason to depart from this: "only those norms can be called valid, which all concerned agree to (or would agree to) as participants in a practical discourse."[18]

The justification for D involves an epistemic account of what it means to raise validity claims and how one redeems them. This justification is part of the transcendental and universal pragmatic reformulation of the concepts of truth and rationality which Apel and Habermas have undertaken. A major consequence of this "pragmatic turn" in critical theory is that theoretical truth as well as normative claims should be viewed as "discursively redeemable assertions." In fact, from an epistemic standpoint there is no difference between the kinds of argumentative processes through which truth claims are debated and those through which normative assertions are examined.

In addition, the justification for D must be supported by reference to aspects of our moral experience. It must be shown that D reflects or expresses some feature of our moral experience that we can all recognize. Habermas and Apel at this juncture have appealed to Lawrence Kohlberg's moral theory and have maintained that D corresponds to the moral experience of "post-conventional" moral reasoning. This is the stage when a disjunction occurs between "social acceptance" *(soziale Geltung)* and "moral validity" *(morale Gültigkeit)*. Having come to doubt the moral validity of societally given norms, roles, and expectations, the individual moves to a "principled" standpoint of justifying moral validity via appeal to principles that have certain formal features, such as impartiality and the ability to be generalized and reversed. Norms are valid because they would apply to all; judgments are impartial because we could all agree to them; and norms and judgments are reversible because they would be seen to be fair from the perspective of all involved. But Lawrence Kohlberg's theory of moral development per se does not justify the specific formulation of the postconventional moral standpoint suggested by communicative ethics. It is maintained only that communicative ethics is a plausible, even if not the singular, account of postconventional moral reasoning and argument.

There are thus two presuppositions of a weak justification program: the epistemic-pragmatic reformulation of truth and rationality in terms of a discourse theory, and the plausibility of communicative ethics to serve as an account of postconventional moral reasoning. The steps guiding this reformulation can be formalized as follows:

1. A philosophical theory of morality must show wherein the justifiability of moral judgments and/or normative assertions reside.

2. To justify means to show that if you and I argue about a particular moral judgment—it was wrong not to help the refugees and to let them die on the wide sea—and a set of normative assertions—education should be free for all for the first eighteen years of their lives—we could in principle come to reasonable agreement *(rationales Einverständnis)*.

3. A "reasonable agreement," however, must satisfy some conditions which, in principle, correspond to our idea of a fair debate.

4. These rules of fair debate can be formulated as the "universal-pragmatic" presuppositions of argumentative speech, which can be stated as a set of procedural rules.

5. These rules reflect the moral idea that we ought to respect each other as beings whose viewpoint is worthy of equal consideration (the principle of reciprocal recognition as moral beings and the norm of egalitarian reciprocity) and that furthermore,

6. We should treat each other as concrete human beings whose capacity to express this viewpoint we should enhance by creating, whenever possible, social practices embodying the discursive ideal (the utopian dimension of communicative ethics).

As I have reformulated the weak justification program, steps 5 and 6 are substantive moral norms. Step 5 is the norm of equal, reciprocal respect. What is the force of the "ought" which attaches to it? This "ought" is not arrived at by a philosophical deduction from steps 1 to 4. A weak justification strategy consists in showing that there is not a single deductive chain of reasoning establishing this principle, but that there are a family of arguments and considerations, each supporting the centrality of this principle as a basic moral norm. One of the arguments leading to the plausibility of the norm of egalitarian respect is indeed a "universal pragmatic" one. It goes as follows: All argumentation entails respect for one's conversation partners; such respect belongs to the idea of fair argumentation; to be a competent partner in such a conversation entails recognizing the principle of equal mutual respect. Step 5 in this sense is an explication of the material normative content of the idea of argument, fair debate, and so on.

A second argument leading to the idea of egalitarian reciprocity derives from social action theory. I agree with Habermas that "reciprocity" is embedded in the very structures of communicative action into which we are all socialized, for reciprocity entails that insofar as we are a member of a particular human group, we be treated by others equally.[19] All communicative action entails symmetry and reciprocity of normative expectations from group members. In fact, to become a member of a human group involves our being treated in accordance with such reciprocity. "Respect" is an attitude and a moral feeling first acquired through such processes of communicative socialization. This implies that the basis for respect can be disturbed if the conditions for developing a sense of self-worth and appreciation from others are lacking. Respect may cease to be an aspect of our life experience under conditions of extreme war and hostility leading to the breakdown of mutuality, or it may shrivel in a culture given to extreme indifference and extreme forms of atomized individualism.

An additional argument supporting the principle of "egalitarian reciprocity" is provided by analyzing how rationality and freedom entail each other. The claim that a particular moral principle, norm of action, or set of institutional arrangements are "rational" entails the belief that those to whom they are addressed can be convinced that this is the case. Rationality claims entail the possibility of free assent. Assent given under conditions which violate the free exercise of such assent cannot be deemed rational.

Now defenders of inegalitarianism—men and women are "by nature" different and hence must be assigned different rights and privileges; the white race is "by nature" superior to others and hence must be granted "higher" rights than other races; practitioners of the "one true" religion are closer to the truths of God and hence must have more authority than practitioners of other false religions in determining collective moral matters—combine with such claims also the belief that they can be demonstrated to be "valid" even to members of those groups singled out for unequal treatment. Only the very extreme cases of sexism, racism, and religious bigotry consider any kind of argument futile or unnecessary. Women should not only be treated differently but they should "want" to be treated differently by assenting to the fact that this is "natural"; nonwhite peoples should willingly accept the superiority of the white man and be grateful for it; infidels should be converted to see the true path to God. Inegalitarian arguments also usually require that others "see" the validity of these principles. And herein lies the paradox of such inegalitarianism. If such inegalitarianism is to be "rational," it must seek the assent of those who will be treated unequally, but to seek such assent means admitting the "others" to the conversation. But if these "others" can see the rationality of the inegalitarian position, they can also dispute its justice. To assent entails just as much the capacity to dissent, to say no. Therefore, either inegalitarianism is irrational, that is, it cannot win the assent of those it addresses, or it is unjust because it precludes the possibility that its addressees will reject it.

Of course one should notice the historical conceit of stating such an argument in purely "conversational" terms. In the true Hegelian sense of the term, such conversations of equality and inequality are less conversations but more historical struggles for recognition, battles, and debates. The reciprocal recognition of equal mutual respect is a principle which the social struggles of history have established. However, "world history" should not be "the court of the world," and for this reason moral philosophy cannot proceed from the factual existence of reciprocal recognition but is always in the position of arguing for its ever wider universal extension and continuous practice. Thus, in this "weak justification" of the principle of egalitarian reciprocity, universal-pragmatic arguments, arguments from social-action theory, and philosophical analyses of rationality claims come together.

Many consider this model hopelessly utopian and unreachable, but this is partly because the purpose of the discourse of legitimacy is not to draw a blueprint for a well-ordered society. Rather, the purpose is to develop a model of public dialogue such as to demystify existing power relations and the current public dialogue which sanctifies them. This involves: identifying those issues which are prevented from becoming public because of existing power constellations; identifying those groups that have not had access to means of public expression and advocating their inclusion in the discourse of legitimacy; distinguishing between genuine agreement and pseudo-compromises based on the intractability of power relations; and saying what is in the public interest as opposed to the universalization of what is only the interest of a particular group.

The Meta-Politics of the Liberal Model of Dialogue

Proponents of liberal dialogue are not sensitive enough to the fact that a theory of conversational restraint may be damaging precisely to the interests of those groups that have not been traditional actors in the public space of liberalism—like women, nonwhite peoples, and sometimes nonpropertied males. It is characteristic of most social and political movements since the French Revolution that they demand the entry of excluded groups into the public realm and that they also require a restructuring of the boundary between the private and the public, such that what had hitherto been considered private becomes a matter of public justice. Socialist movements in the past have demanded that work conditions and the terms of the contract regulating the labor-capital relation be made public issues, that is to say, issues of general concern to all and subject of public regulation and legislation. Anticolonialist movements and the civil rights movement have not only demanded the universal extension of civil and political rights to nonwhite peoples but have also required the sensitization of the public to the representation of members of these groups in racist, demeaning, and pejorative terms and categories. Similarly, the second wave of the women's movement since the end of World War II is not only asking for the creation of conditions that would allow and protect the position of women in the public sphere as citizens and wage earners. Women also want to have the lines between public and private debate redrawn in such a way that issues like domestic violence, child abuse, the sexual division of labor in the family become matters of public concern. Social struggles both extend the participants of the public realm and extend the scope of the conversation in the public realm.

It is therefore important that we cease thinking of the public realm solely in terms of the domain of legislative or state activity. The original sense of res publica is the "public thing" that can be shared by all. Sharing by all means first and foremost that certain issues become matters of public conversation, and that, in Hannah Arendt's terms, they leave the sphere of private shame, embarassment, silence, and humiliation to which they have been confined. In making public those issues and relations that had condemned us to shame, silence, and humilation, we are restoring the public dignity of those who have suffered from neglect. I do not want to be misunderstood: all human societies live with a boundary between the public and the private; there will always be a realm that we simply will not want to share with others and that we will wish to be protected from the intrusion of others. Where I differ from the liberal political theorist is that, whereas he or she seems to be sure where these boundaries ought to lie, I am deeply suspicious of the implicit politics of a certainty attained without truly open public debate.

Power is not only a social resource to be distributed, say, like bread or automobiles. It is also a sociocultural grid of interpretation and communication. Public dialogue is not external to but constitutive of power relations. As Nancy Fraser has observed, there are offically recognized vocabularies in which one can press claims; idioms for interpreting and communicating one's needs; established narrative conventions for constructing individual and collective identities; paradigms of argumentations accepted as authoritative in adjudicating conflicting claims; a repertory of available rhetorical devices.[20] These constitute the "meta-politics of dialogue," and as a critical theorist I am interested in identifying the present social relations, power structures, and sociocultural grids of communication and interpretation that limit the identity of the parties to the public dialogue, that set the agenda for what is considered appropriate or inappropriate matters of public debate, and that sanctify the speech of some over the speech of others as being the language of the public. I believe that the res publica can be truly identified only after the unreasonable constraints on public conversation have been removed. I consider the discourse model of legitimacy to be more conducive to the achievement of such an ideal than the model of liberal dialogue based on conversational constraints.

· IV ·

Repairing Individualist and Communitarian Failings

· N I N E ·

Cross-Purposes:
The Liberal-Communitarian Debate

CHARLES TAYLOR

We often hear talk of the difference between "communitarians" and "liberals" in social theory, and in particular in the theory of justice.[1] Certainly a debate seems to have been engaged between two "teams," with people like Rawls, Dworkin, Nagel, and Scanlon on one side (team L), and Sandel, MacIntyre, and Walzer on the other (team C). There are genuine differences, but I think there are also a lot of cross-purposes, and just plain confusion in this debate. That is because two quite different issues tend to get run together in it. We can call these, respectively, ontological issues and advocacy issues.

The ontological questions concern what you recognize as the factors you will invoke to account for social life. Or, put in the "formal mode," they concern the terms you accept as ultimate in the order of explanation. The big debate in this area, which has been raging now for more than three centuries, divides atomists from holists, as I propose to call them.[2] The former are often referred to as methodological individualists. They believe that in (a), the order of explanation, you can and ought to account for social actions, structures, and conditions, in terms of properties of the constituent individuals; and in (b), the order of deliberation, you can and ought to account for social goods in terms of concatenations of individual goods. In recent decades, Popper has declared himself a militant advocate of (a), while (b) is a key component of what Amartya Sen has defined as "welfarism," a central if often inarticulate belief of most writers in the field of welfare economics.[3]

Advocacy issues concern the moral stand or policy one adopts. Here there is a gamut of positions, which at one end give primacy to individual rights and freedom, and at the other give higher priority community life or the good of collectivities. We could describe the positions on this scale as more or less individualist and collectivist. At one extreme we would find people like Nozick and Friedman and other libertarians; at the other, Enver Hodja's Albania, or the Red Guards of the cultural revolution define the ultimate benchmarks. Of course most sane people, when not in the grip of some relentless ideology, find themselves much closer to the middle; but there are still significant differences between, say, liberals à la Dworkin who believe that the state should be neutral between the different conceptions of the good life espoused by individuals, on one hand,[4] and those who believe that a democratic society needs some commonly recognized definition of the good life, on the other—a view which later I will defend.

The relation between these two congeries of issues is complex. On the one hand, they are distinct, in the sense that taking a position on one does not force your hand on the other. On the other hand, they are not completely independent, in that the stand one takes on the ontological level can be part of the essential background of the view one advocates. Both these relations, the distinctness and the connection, are inadequately appreciated, and this confuses the debate.

Now when people refer to "liberals" and "communitarians," they often talk as though each of these terms describes a package of views, linking the two issues. The underlying assumption seems to be that they aren't distinct, that a given position on one commits you to a corresponding view on the other. Thus, while the principal point of Michael Sandel's important book *Liberalism and the Limits of Justice*[5] is ontological in my terms, the liberal response to it has generally been as a work of advocacy.[6] Sandel tries to show how the different models of the way we live together in society—atomist and holist— are linked with different understandings of self and identity: "unencumbered" versus situated selves. This is a contribution to social ontology, which can be developed in a number of directions. It could be used to argue that because a totally unencumbered self is a human impossibility, the extreme atomist model of society is a chimaera. Or one could argue that both (relatively) unencumbered and situated selves are possibilities, as would be then also (relatively) atomist- and holist-based societies, but that the viable combinations between these two levels are restricted: a highly collectivist society would be hard to combine with an unencumbered identity, or a very individualist life-form would be impossible where selves are thickly situated.

Taken in either of these directions, the tenor of these theses about identity would still be purely ontological. They still don't amount to an advocacy of anything. What they do purport to do, like any good ontological thesis, is to structure the field of possibilities in a more perspicuous way. But this precisely leaves us with choices, which we need some normative, deliberative, arguments to resolve. Even taken in the first direction, which purports to show the impossibility of atomist society, it leaves us with important choices between more or less liberal societies; while the second direction is concerned precisely to define options of this kind.

Both the relations I have mentioned are illustrated here. Taking an ontological position does not amount to advocating something; but at the same time, the ontological does help to define the options which it is meaningful to support by advocacy. This latter connection explains how ontological theses can be far from innocent. Your ontological proposition, if true, can show that your neighbor's favorite social order is an impossiblity or carries a price that he or she did not count with. But this should not induce us to think that the proposition *amounts to* the advocacy of some alternative.

Both this impact of the ontological and the misperception of it can be seen in the debate around Sandel's book. Sandel made a point about Rawls's invocation of the Humean "conditions of justice." According to these, justice is a relevant virtue where there are scarcities, and people are not spontaneously moved by ties of affection to mutual benevolence. Where the former does not hold, there is no point dividing up shares; and where the latter does not hold, there is no call to hold people to some rule of distribution. What is more, in this second case, trying to enforce a rule will quite possibly disrupt the existing ties: to insist punctiliously on sharing expenses with a friend is to imply that the links of mutual benevolence are somehow lacking or inadequate. There is no faster way of losing friends.[7] Similarly, insistence on clearly defined rights can create distance in a close family.

Sandel has sometimes been read as though his point was to *advocate* a society that would have close relations analogous to a family, and thus would not need to concern itself with justice. This proposal has been, rightly, ridiculed. But this seems to me to miss the relevance of his argument. First we have to see that the choice is not simply between a close, familylike community and a modern, impersonal society. Even within the latter, there are important choices about how zealously we entrench in legislation, or enforce through judicial action, various facets of equality which justice might dictate. What do we entrust to the spirit of social solidarity and the social mores which emerge from it? In certain societies the answer may be: very little. But that will be where this spirit is weak or lacking. Where it is strong, there may be problems with overenforcement of our intuitions about fair dealing. Trying to define and enforce in detail some of our common feelings about equality may weaken the common sense of moral commitment and mutual solidarity from which these feelings grow. Sometimes of course legislation can help to crystallize a growing consensus: the civil-rights laws in the United States in the 1960s are a good example. But sometimes overenforcement can work the other way. Sandel's point about the conditions of justice should serve to open up this whole issue, which gets left in the shade if we just ask what the principles of justice ought to be between mutually indifferent contracting individuals.

I will come back to this point from another angle later, when I consider the relative advantages of two kinds of model of citizen dignity, one based on political participation, and the other on judicial retrieval.

The same point about the impact of the ontological emerges even more clearly from one of Sandel's central criticisms of Rawls.[8] He argues that Rawls's very egalitarian difference principle, which involves treating the endowment of each as part of the jointly held resources for the benefit of society as a whole,[9] presupposes a high degree of solidarity among the participants. This sense of mutual commitment could be sustained only by encumbered selves who shared a strong sense of community. And yet the contractors are defined very much as mutually indifferent. Here again, it is clear that the point of the argument, whether right or wrong, is to define the alternatives in an important choice. Sandel's point pushes us toward the issue of whether the kind of egalitarian redistribution Rawls recommends can be sustained in a society which is not bound together in solidarity through a strong sense of community; and whether, in turn, a strong community of this kind can be forged around a common understanding which makes justice the principal virtue of social life, or whether some other good does not have to figure as well in the definition of community life. My point is just that this kind of choice-definition is the central function of what I have been calling ontological propositions. This is how Sandel's critique of Rawls has to be read on this score, not as a counteradvocacy.

This is not to say that Sandel does not also want to make an important normative statement about the future course of American society. This has become more and more evident with what he has written since.[10] It is simply that his contribution to the ontological debate should not be lost from view behind them. This would be a loss, not just because this contribution is important in its own right, but also because it is part of the background to what he advocates, and grasping this relation helps us to understand exactly what his normative position is. Whereas when these normative points are misconstrued as recommendations, the most bizarre interpretations emerge, and the debate is beclouded beyond hope of recovery.

My belief is that the misconstruals occur because there has been widespread insensitivity to the difference between the two kinds of issue. The portmanteau terms "liberal" and "communitarian" will probably have to be scrapped before we can get over this, because they carry the implication that there is only one issue here, or that someone's position on one determines what he holds on the other. But a cursory look at the gamut of actual philosophical positions shows exactly the contrary. Either stand on the atomism–holism debate can be combined with either stand on the individualist–collectivist question. There are not only atomist individualists (Nozick) and holist collectivists (Marx), but also holist individualists, like Humboldt— and even atomist collectivists, as in the nightmare, programmed utopia of B. F. Skinner, "beyond freedom and dignity."[11] This last category may be of interest only for the student of the bizarre or the monstrous, but I would argue that Humboldt and his ilk occupy an extremely important place in the development of modern liberalism. They represent a trend of thought that is fully aware of the (ontological) social embedding of human agents, but at the same time prizes liberty and individual differences very highly. Humboldt was one of the important sources for Mill's doctrine of liberty. In the face of this, it is astonishing that anyone should read a defense of holism as entailing an advocacy of collectivism. But the rich tradition that Humboldt represents seems to have been forgotten by Mill's heirs in the English-speaking world.

Recovering the distinction I am making here is therefore worth the trouble, if it can allow this tradition to return to its rightful place in the debate. This is a big part of my (not so hidden) agenda, because it is the line of thought that I identify with. But I also believe that the confusion of issues has contributed to a kind of eclipse of ontological thinking in social theory. Since this is the level at which we face important questions about the real choices open to us, the eclipse is a real misfortune. Sandel's first book was very important because he put on the agenda some issues that a properly aware liberalism ought to face. The reaction of the "liberal" consensus (to use one of the portmanteau terms I have just impugned) was that to obtrude issues about identity and community into the debate on justice was an irrelevancy. My thesis is that, quite the contrary, these matters are highly relevant, and the only alternative to discussing them is relying on an implicit and unexamined view of them. Moreover, in that the unexamined views on these matters in Anglo-Saxon philosophical culture tend to be heavily infected with atomist prejudices, the implicit understanding tends to be—according to my, holistic outlook—wrong. The result is that an ontologically disinterested liberalism tends to be blind to certain important questions. I would like in the remainder of this chapter to try to sketch why I think this is so.

There is a family of theories of liberalism that is now very popular, not to say dominant, in the English-speaking world, which I want to call "procedural." It sees society as an association of individuals, each of whom has his or her conception of a good or worthwhile life, and correspondingly, his or her life plan. The function of society ought to be to facilitate these life plans, as much as possible, and following some principle of equality. That is, the facilitation ought not to be discriminatory, although there is obviously some room for serious question as to exactly what this means: whether the facilitation ought to aim at equality of results, or of resources, or of opportunities, or of capacities, or whatever.[12] But many writers seem to agree on the proposition that the principle of equality or nondiscrimination would be breached if society itself espoused one or other conception of the good life. This would amount to discrimination, because we assume that in a modern pluralist society, there is a wide gamut of views about what makes a good life. Any view endorsed by society as a whole would be that of some citizens and not others. These latter, in seeing their views denied official favor, would not in effect be treated with equal respect in relation to their compatriots espousing the established view.

Thus, it is argued, a liberal society should not be founded on any particular notion of the good life. The ethic central to a liberal society is an ethic of the right, rather than the good. That is, its basic principles concern how society should respond to and arbitrate the competing demands of individuals. These principles would obviously include the respect of individual rights and freedoms, but central to any set that could be called liberal would be the principle of maximal and equal facilitation. This does not in the first instance define what goods the society will further, but rather how it will determine the goods to be advanced, given the aspirations and demands of its component individuals. What is crucial here are the procedures of decision, which is why I want to call this brand of liberal theory "procedural."[13]

There are grave problems with this model of liberalism, which only can be properly articulated when one opens up the ontological issues of identity and community I have been referring to. There are questions about the viability of a society which would really meet these specifications, and an issue about the applicability of this formula in societies other than the United States (and perhaps also Britain), where it has been mainly developed, which also have a prima facie right to be called liberal. In other words, the theory can be taxed with being unrealistic and ethnocentric. Both of these objections are directed against procedural liberalism's exclusion of a socially endorsed conception of the good.

1. The viability issue has been raised by thinkers in the civic humanist tradition. One of the central themes of this line of thought concerns the conditions for a free society. "Free" is understood here not in the modern sense of negative liberty, but more as the antonym to "despotic." Ancient writers, followed by such moderns as Machiavelli, Montesquieu, and Tocqueville, have all tried to define the conditions in terms of political culture in which a participatory regime can flourish. The underlying reasoning, in its different forms, has been of the following sort: every political society requires some sacrifices and demands some disciplines from its members: they have to pay taxes, or serve in the armed forces, and in general observe certain restraints. In a despotism, a regime where the mass of citizens are subject to the rule of a single master, or a clique, the requisite disciplines are maintained by coercion. In order to have a free society, one has to replace this coercion with something else. This can only be a willing identification with the polis on the part of the citizens, a sense that the political institutions in which they live are an expression of themselves. The "laws" have to be seen as reflecting and entrenching their dignity as citizens, and hence to be in a sense extensions of themselves. This understanding that the political institutions are a common bulwark of citizen dignity is the basis of what Montesquieu called "vertu," the patriotism which is "une préférence continuelle de l'intérêt public au sien propre,"[14] an impulse which cannot be placed neatly in the (very modern) classification egoistic-altruistic. It transcends egoism in the sense that people are really attached to the *common* good, to *general* liberty. But it is quite unlike

the apolitical attachment to universal principle that the Stoics advocated, or that is central to modern ethics of the right.

The difference is that patriotism is based on an identification with others in a particular common enterprise. I am not dedicated to defending the liberty of just anyone, but I feel the bond of solidarity with my compatriots in our common enterprise, the common expression of our respective dignity. Patriotism is somewhere between friendship, or family feeling, on one side, and altruistic dedication on the other. The latter has no concern for the particular: I am inclined to act for the good of anyone anywhere. The former attach me to particular people. My patriotic allegiance does not bind me to individual people in this familial way; I may not know most of my compatriots, and may not particularly want them as friends when I do meet them. But particularity enters in because my bond to these people passes through our participation in a common political entity. Functioning republics are like families in this crucial respect, that part of what binds people together is their common history. Family ties or old friendships are deep because of what we have lived through together, and republics are bonded by time and climactic transitions.

Here is where we find ourselves pushed back into the ontological issues of community and identity I have been discussing. Of course there was a (premodern) time in the history of our civilization when patriotism was intellectually unproblematic. But the last three centuries have seen the growing power of atomist modes of thought, particularly in the English-speaking world, and more, these have fostered the constitution of an unreflecting common sense which is shot through with atomist prejudices. According to this outlook, there are individuals, who have inclinations and goals and life plans. These inclinations include affection for others, which may be mutual and hence bring about bonding. Families and friendships thus find a place. But beyond these, common institutional structures have to be understood as in the nature of collective instruments. Political societies in the understanding of Hobbes, Locke, Bentham, or the twentieth-century common sense that they have helped shape are established by collections of individuals to obtain benefits through common action that they could not secure individually. The action is collective, but the point of it remains individual. The common good is constituted out of individual goods, without remainder. This construal of society incorporates the atomist component of Sen's "welfarism" that I have already mentioned.

This implicit ontology has no place for functioning republics, societies bonded by patriotism in the above sense. For these are grounded on a common good of a stronger kind than atomism allows. To see this we have to dive deeper into the ontological level. I want to take a plunge now for a few paragraphs and raise an issue wider than the political, before returning to this question of the nature of republics.

There is a distinction largely ignored, or mischaracterized, in post-Cartesian thought: that between matters which are for me and for you, on one hand, and those which are for us, on the other. This distinction plays a tremendously important and pervasive role in human affairs, in ways both banal and fateful. In a banal context, we transfer matters from one category to the other when we open an ordinary conversation over the back fence. "Fine weather we're having," I say to my neighbor. Prior to this, he was aware of the weather, may have been attending to it; obviously I was as well. It was a matter for him, and also for me. What the conversation-opener does is make it now a matter for *us:* we are attending to it now together. It is important to see that this attending-together is not reducible to an aggregation of attendings-separately. Obviously it involves something more than each of us enjoying the weather on our own. But our atomist prejudices may tempt us to try to account for this more in terms of aggregations of monological mind-states: for example, now I know that you are attending, and you know that I am attending, and you know that I know that you know, and so on.[15] But just adding these monological states does not get us the dialogic condition where things are for us. In certain circumstances, I can know just by seeing you that you are enjoying the weather, and you know the same of me, and since we're both in plain view of each other, each will know that the other knows, and so on. Nevertheless, it is very different when we actually start conversing.

A conversation is not the coordination of actions of different individuals, but a common action in this strong, irreducible sense; it is *our* action. It is of a kind with—to take a more obvious example—the dance of a group or a couple, or the action of two men sawing a log. Opening a conversation is inaugurating a common action. This common action is sustained by little rituals which we barely notice, like the interjections of accord ("unhunh") with which the presently nonspeaking partner punctuates the discourse of the speaker, and with rituals which surround and mediate the switch of the "semantic turn" from one to the other.[16]

This threshold, which conversation takes us over, is one which matters in all sorts of ways and on all sorts of levels in human life. In human terms, we stand on a different footing when we start talking about the weather. That is the main point of conversation, where frequently the actual new information imparted may be sparse or nonexistent. Certainly I do not tell you anything new with my opener. On a deeper level, those whom I talk to about the things that matter to me are my intimates. Intimacy is an essentially dialogic phenomenon: it is a matter of what we share, of what's for us. One could never describe what it is to be on an intimate footing with someone in terms of monological states. On a transpersonal, institutional level, the same difference can play an important role. The steamy personal life of a political candidate may be for long an open secret, known to all insiders, journalists, politicians, even cab drivers in the capital. But a significant line is crossed when it breaks into the media and becomes "public knowledge." This has to do with the number and kind of people (unsophisticated country folks, for example), who know about it of course, but not only. It is also a matter of the way in which even those who "always" knew, now know: it is now for us, out there in public space. Analogous thresholds exist in the diplomatic world between states. Some things unsaid, or kept discreet, can be tolerated, which you have to react to once they are public. The move from the for-me-for-you to the for-us, the move into public space, is one of the most important things we bring about in language, and any theory of language has to take account of this.[17]

I have been looking at an example of a common focus of attention. But the monologic-dialogic distinction is just as evident in relation to goods. Some things have value to me and to you, and some things essentially have value to us. That is, their being for us enters into and constitutes their value for us. On a banal level, jokes are much funnier when they're told in company. The really funny joke is an integral part of a conversation, using this latter word in a broad sense. What raises a smile when I read it alone can put me in stitches mediated in the ritual of telling which puts it in common space. Or again, if we are lovers or close friends, Mozart-with-you is a quite different experience than Mozart-alone. I will call goods of this kind "mediately" common goods. But there are other things we value even more, like friendship itself, where what centrally matters to us is just that there are common actions and meanings. The good is that we share. This I will call an "immediately" common good.

These contrast with other goods which we enjoy collectively, but which I want to call "convergent," to mark the difference. To take the classical examples of welfare economics, we enjoy security from various dangers, through our system of national defense, our police forces, our fire departments, and the like. This is collectively pro-vided, and could not be obtained otherwise.No individual could af-ford it alone. These are classical cases of collective instrumental action as understood in the Hobbes-Locke tradition. We might normally speak of these goods as "common" or "public," to mark that they not only in fact are secured collectively, but that we could not get them any other way. But in my language they are convergent, because all this concerns only how we have to go about providing them. It has nothing to do with what makes them goods. Security as a valued end is always security for A, and for B, and for C. It is in no wise a different good, let alone a more valued one, because it is in fact ensured collectively. In the unlikely event that an individual could secure it for him/herself, he/she would be getting the same valued condition as we all get now from social provision.

A little story may illustrate the difference. Jacques lives in Saint Jérôme, and his greatest desire was to hear the Montreal symphony under Charles Dutoît playing in a live concert. He had heard them on records and the radio, but he was convinced that these media could never give total fidelity, and he wanted to hear the real thing. The obvious solution was to travel to Montreal, but his aged mother would fall into a state of acute anxiety whenever he went farther than Saint Janvier. So Jacques got the idea of recruiting other music lovers in the town to raise the required fee to bring the orchestra to Saint Jérôme. Finally the great moment came. As Jacques walked into the concert that night, he looked on the Montreal Symphony Orchestra visit as a convergent good between him and his fellow subscribers. But then, when he actually experienced his first live concert, he was enraptured not only by the quality of the sound, which was as he had expected quite different from what you get on records, but also by the dialogue between orchestra and audience. His own love of the music fused with that of the crowd in the darkened hall, resonated with theirs, and found expression in an enthusiastic common act of applause at the end. Jacques also enjoyed the concert in a way he had not expected, as a mediately common good.

What has all this to do with republics? That it is essential to them, as I have characterized them, that they are animated by a sense of a shared immediate common good. To that degree, the bond resembles that of friendship, as Aristotle saw.[18] The citizen is attached to the laws as the repository of his and others' citizen dignity. That might sound like the way I'm indebted to the Montreal Urban Community for its police service. But the crucial difference is that the latter relationship secures what we all understand as a merely convergent good, whereas the identification of the citizen with the republic as a common enterprise is essentially the recognition of a comon good. My attachment to the MUC for its police service is based on enlightened self-interest. My (frequently inoperative) moral commitment to the welfare of all humans is altruistic. But the bond of solidarity with my compatriots in a functioning republic is based on a sense of shared fate, where the sharing itself is of value. This is what gives this bond its special importance, what makes my ties with these people and to this enterprise peculiarly binding, what animates my "virtu," or patriotism.

In other words, the very definition of a republican regime as classically understood requires an ontology different from atomism, and which falls outside atomism-infected common sense. It requires that we probe the relations of identity and community, and distinguish the different possibilities, in particular, the possible place of we-identities as against merely convergent I-identities, and the consequent role of common as against convergent goods. If we abstract from all this, then we are in danger of losing the distinction between collective instrumentality and common action, of misconstruing the republic as a hyped-up version of the Montreal Urban Community, delivering a product of much greater importance, and about which the beneficiaries feel (on grounds which are hard to fathom, but which have possibly irrational roots) particularly strongly.[19]

Perhaps this does not matter too much practically, if this kind of regime has no relevance to the modern world. And such is the view of many students of modern politics. But if we are going even to consider the basic thesis of the civic humanist tradition, we cannot simply just assume this from the outset. This thesis, to repeat, is that the essential condition of a free (nondespotic) regime is that the citizens have this kind of patriotic identification. This may have seemed self-evident to them because of their concept of freedom. This was not defined mainly in terms of what we would call negative liberty. Freedom was thought of as citizen liberty, that of the active participant in public affairs. This citizen was "free" in the sense as having a say in the decisions in the political domain, which would shape his and others' lives. Since participatory self-government is itself usually carried out in common actions, it is perhaps normal to see it as properly animated by common identifications. Since one exercises freedom in common actions, it may seem natural that one value it as a common good.

The underlying reasoning of the thesis, as I have said, is that the disciplines that would be externally imposed by fear under a despotism have to be self-imposed in its absence, and only patriotic identification can provide the motivation. But the case could also be argued in slightly different terms. We could say that a free, that is, participatory regime calls on the citizens to provide themselves for things which a despotism may provide for them. The foremost example of this was national defense. A despotic regime may raise money and hire mercenaries to fight for it; a republican regime will generally call on its citizens to fight for their own freedom. The causal links run in both directions. Citizen armies guarantee freedom because they are an obstacle to despotic takeover, just as large armies at the disposal of powerful generals invite a coup, as the agony of the Roman Republic illustrates. But at the same time, only people who live in and cherish a free regime will be motivated to fight for themselves. This relation between citizen armies and freedom was one of the main themes of Machiavelli's work.

So we could say that republican solidarity underpins freedom, because it provides the motivation for self-imposed discipline; or else that it is essential for a free regime, because this calls on its members to do things that mere subjects can avoid. In one case, we think of the demands on members as the same, and the difference concerns the motivation to meet them: fear of punishment versus inwardly generated sense of honor and obligation. In the other, the demands of freedom are defined as more onerous, and the issue concerns what can motivate this extra effort.

The second formulation very much depends on seeing freedom in participatory terms. Free regimes are more onerous, because they require service in public life, both military and political, that the unfree do not. The importance of this latter formulation in the civic humanist tradition shows the degree to which freedom was understood in terms of participation. But one can extract a thesis from this tradition about the essential bases of nondespotic society which is broader than this. The thesis would define nondespotism not just in terms of participation, but by a broader gamut of freedoms, including negative ones. It would draw on the first formulation to argue a link between the solidarity of patriotism and free institutions, on the grounds that a free society needs this kind of motivation to provide what despotisms get through fear; to engender the disciplines, the sacrifices, the essential contributions it needs to keep going, as well as to mobilize support in its defense when threatened.

If we call this basic proposition connecting patriotism and freedom the "republican thesis," then we can speak of narrower and broader forms of this, with the former focused purely on participatory freedom, and the latter taking in the broader gamut of liberties. With all these preliminaries behind us, we can finally address the first criticism of procedural liberalism, that it offers a nonviable formula for a free regime.

We can see right off how this kind of liberalism *seems* to run athwart the republican thesis. It conceives of society as made up of individuals with life plans, based on their conceptions of the good, but without a commonly held conception espoused by the society itself. But that seems to be the formula for an instrumental society, designed to seek merely convergent goods; it seems to exclude the republican form altogether.

This is the usual reaction of people steeped in the civic humanist tradition when they first confront the definitions of procedural liberalism. I confess that I find myself reacting this way. But this criticism as it stands is not quite right. There are confusions here, but what is interesting is that they are not all on one side, not only in the mind of the critic.

What is wrong with the criticism? The liberal can respond to the republican that he is not at all commited to a merely instrumental society. His formula does indeed exclude there being a societally endorsed common *good,* but not at all that there be a common understanding of the *right;* actually, it calls for this. The misunderstanding turns on two senses of "good." In the broad sense, it means anything valuable which we seek; in the narrower sense, it refers to life plans or ways of living which are so valued. Procedural liberalism cannot have a common good in the narrow sense, because society must be neutral on the question of the good life. But in the broader sense, where a rule of right can also count as "good," there can be an extremely important shared good.

So procedural liberalism can parry the objection of nonviability. This objection, to recall, came out of the republican thesis, and reading this type of liberal society as necessarily instrumental, saw it as essentially lacking citizen identification with a common good. But since this is a condition of a nondespotic regime, it judged this form of liberalism to be by its very nature self-undermining. A free society, which thus needs to call on a strong spontaneous allegiance from its members, is eschewing the indispensable basis of this: strong citizen identification around a sense of common good—what I have been calling "patriotism."

One reply to this attack would remain entirely within the assumptions of modern atomism. It would simply reject the republican thesis, and suppose that viable liberal societies can rely on quite different bases: either the eighteeth-century view that the citizens' allegiance could be grounded on enlightened self-interest; or the idea that modern civilization has educated people to higher moral standards, so that citizens are sufficiently imbued with the liberal ethos to support and defend their society; or else the idea current in modern "revisionist" democratic theory, that in fact a mature liberal society does not demand very much of its members, as long as it delivers the goods and makes their lives prosperous and secure. As a matter of fact, on this view it is better if the citizens do not try to participate too actively, but rather elect governments every few years and then let them get on with it.[20]

But procedural liberalism need not reply in this way. It can accept the republican thesis, and plead that it *does* have a place for a common good, and hence patriotism, hence that it can be viable as a free society.

Which reply ought liberalism to make? Those of an atomist outlook will opt for the first. They will think that the republican thesis, whatever its validity in ancient times, is irrelevant in modern mass bureaucratic society. People in the modern age have become individualist, and societies can only be held together in one or other of the ways I have just described. To hanker after the unity of earlier republics is to indulge in bootless nostalgia. If this is right, then all the ontological discussion of the previous pages, designed to make sense of republican societies, is of purely antiquarian interest, and the civic humanist critique of liberalism can be shrugged off.

But plausible as this atomist view might seem to us today, it is wide of the mark. We can see this if we look at the recent history of the United States, which is after all the main society of reference for procedural liberals. Think of the reaction to Watergate and, to a lesser degree, to the Iran-Contra misdemeanors. In the first case, citizen outrage actually drove a president from power. Now I want to make two, admittedly contestable, points about these reactions, which together amount to an important confirmation of the continuing relevance of the republican thesis.

The first is that the capacity of the citizenry to respond with outrage to this kind of abuse is an important bulwark of freedom in modern society. It is true that Americans are perhaps especially sensitive to acts of executive abuse, in comparison to other contemporary democracies—think, for instance, of the (absence of) French reaction to the *Rainbow Warrior* incident. But the general point would be that, although the targets might vary from society to society, most democratic electorates are disposed to react to violations of the norms of liberal self-rule, and this is a crucial supporting factor to the stability of these regimes. Where this disposition has been relatively lacking—as, for example, in a number of Latin American countries, where a large number of people are ready to tolerate "disappearances" perpetrated by semiclandestine arms of the military, or to welcome army putshes—then one is in danger of ending up with an Argentine Junta or a murderous Pinochet regime.

The second point is that this capacity for outrage is not fueled from any of the sources already enumerated that are recognized by atomism. People do not respond this way because they calculate that it is in their long-term interest. Or rather, we should admit that some do, but they are comparatively few. Nor do most people respond just because of their general commitment to the principles of liberal democracy. This too plays a role, but by itself it would not lead to, say, an American reacting more vigorously to Nixon's violations than to Pinochet's or Enver Hodja's. Now there are certainly some people who feel very strongly about the fate of democracy everywhere, but they too are, alas, a relatively small minority of most modern electorates. Thirdly, people would barely respond at all if they thought of their society purely instrumentally, as the dispenser of security and prosperity.

What generates the outrage is something in none of the above categories, neither egoism nor altruism, but a species of patriotic identification. In the case of the United States, there is a widespread identification with "the American way of life," a sense of Americans sharing a common identity and history, defined by a commitment to certain ideals, articulated famously in the Declaration of Independence, Lincoln's Gettysburg address, and such documents, which in turn derive their importance from their connection to certain climactic transitions of this shared history. It is this sense of identity, and the pride and attachment which accompanies it, that is outraged by the shady doings of a Watergate, and this is what provokes the irresistible reaction.

In other terms, my second point is that republican patriotism remains a force in modern society, one that was very palpably operative during the days of Watergate. It goes unnoticed, partly because of the hold of atomist prejudices on modern theoretical thinking, and partly because its forms and focus are somewhat different from those of classical times. But it is still very much with us and plays an essential role in maintaining our contemporary liberal democratic regimes. Of course patriotism is also responsible for a lot of evil, today as at any time. It can also take the form of virulent nationalism, and in its darker forms encourages an Oliver North to violate the norms of a free society, even as it is generating a healthy defense against the danger he creates. But whatever menace the malign effects have spawned, the benign ones have been essential to the maintenance of liberal democracy.[21]

This is my second point. It is of course controversial. It involves a certain reading of recent history, and of its causes, which is far from being universally agreed. But I should like to make the point even stronger. Not only has patriotism been an important bulwark of freedom in the past, but it will remain unsubstitutably so for the future. The various atomist sources of allegiance have not only been insufficient to generate the vigorous defensive reaction à la Watergate; they will never be able to do so, in the nature of things. Pure enlightened self-interest will never move enough people strongly enough to constitute a real threat to potential despots and putschists. Nor will there, alas, be enough people who are moved by universal principle, unalloyed with particular identifications, moral citizens of cosmopolis, Stoic or Kantian, to stop these miscreants in their tracks. As for those who support a society because of the prosperity and security it generates, they are only fair-weather friends and are bound to let you down when you really need them. In other words, I want to claim that the republican thesis is as relevant and true today, in its peculiar contemporary application, as it was in ancient or early modern times, when the paradigm statements of civic humanism were articulated.

If I am right about this, then liberalism cannot answer the charge of nonviability just by assuming atomism and dismissing the republican thesis. To do so would be to be blind to the crucial dynamics of modern society. But that leaves the other answer: that a procedural liberal society can be a republican one in a crucial respect. And indeed, that is one way of reading the Watergate reaction. What the outraged citizens saw as violated was precisely a rule of right, a liberal conception of rule by law. That is what they identified with, and that is what they rose to defend as their common good. We no longer need to argue that, in theory, procedural liberalism allows for patriotism; we have a living case, or at least a close approximation, of such a patriotism of the right. The confusion in the mind of the critic would be to have thought that procedural liberalism entails an atomist ontology, on the grounds that it speaks of individual life plans, and that hence it can only draw allegiance from the atomist sources, which are manifestly inadequate to sustain it. But in fact a procedural liberal can be a holist; what is more, holism captures much better the actual practice of societies that approximate to this model. Thus runs a convincing answer to the critic—which incidentally illustrates again how essential it is not to confuse the ontological issue of atomism-holism with questions of advocacy opposing individualism and collectivism.

Now here it is the critics who seem to have fallen prey to this confusion. But they may not be the only victims. For once we understand procedural liberalism holistically, certain questions arise which its protagonists rarely raise.

(i) We can question whether a patriotic liberal regime really meets the full proceduralist demands. The common good is, indeed, a rule of right. But we have to remember that patriotism involves more than converging moral principles; it is a common allegiance to a particular historical community. Cherishing and sustaining this has to be a common goal, and this is more than just consensus on the rule of right. Put differently, patriotism involves beyond convergent values a love of the particular. Sustaining this specific historical set of institutions and forms is and must be a socially endorsed common end.

In other words, while the procedural liberal state can indeed be neutral between (a) believers and unbelievers in God, or (b) people with homo- and heterosexual orientations, it cannot be between (c) patriots and antipatriots. We can imagine its courts hearing and giving satisfaction to those who, under (a), object to school prayers, or those who, under (b), petition to ban a manual of sex education that treats homosexuality as a perversion. But supposing someone, under (c), objected to the pious tone with which American history and its major figures are presented to the young. The parents might declare themselves ready to abide by the rules of the procedural republic and to educate their children to do so, but this they will do for their own hyper-Augustinian reasons, that in this fallen world of depraved wills, such a modus vivendi is the least dangerous arrangement. But they'll be damned (no mere figure of speech, this!) if they'll let their children be brainwashed into taking as their heroes the infidel Jefferson, and the crypto-freethinker Washington, and indoctrinated into their shallow and impious cant about human perfectibility. Or else we might imagine a less ideological objection, where parents who espouse an apolitical life-style object to the implicit endorsement of active citizenship that flows from the patriots' view of American history.

These examples sound fanciful, and they are, indeed, very unlikely to happen. But why? Is it not because, while fighting about religion in schools has become a very American thing to do and the battle continues well beyond the point where another less litigious people might have settled on a workable compromise, just because Americans on both sides feel that what they advocate is dictated by the constitution, so a questioning of the value of patriotism is profoundly un-American, and is close to unthinkable as a public act?[22] But logically such a challenge is possible, and it would be no more illegitimate on the terms of procedural liberalism than those under (a) and (b). But any court which gave satisfaction to such a suit would be undermining the very regime it was established to interpret. A line has to be drawn here before the demands of proceduralism.

This may not be a major problem. No political theory can be implemented in all the purity of its original model. There have to be some compromises with reality, and a viable procedural republic would have to be non-neutral about its own regime patriotism. But another issue, touched on earlier, must be explored.

(ii) This patriotic liberal regime differs from the traditional republican model. We have imagined that the values enshrined in the historically endorsed institutions are purely those of the rule of right, incorporating something like: the rule of law, individual rights, and some principles of fairness and equal treatment. What this leaves out is the central good of the civic humanist tradition: participatory self-rule. In fact, one could say that the center of gravity of the classical theory was at the opposite end of the spectrum: ancient theories were not concerned with individual rights, and they allowed some pretty hairy procedures judged by our modern standards of personal immunity—such as ostracism. Moreover, their notions of equal treatment applied very selectively from our point of view. But they did think citizen rule was of the very essence of the republic.

Now the question arises of what we make of this good in our modern liberal society. Procedural liberals tend to neglect it, treating self-rule as purely instrumental to the rule of law and equality. And indeed, to treat it as the republican tradition does, which sees self-rule as essential to a life of dignity, as the highest political good in itself, would take us beyond the bounds of procedural liberalism. Because a society organized around this proposition would share and endorse qua society at least this proposition about the good life. This is a clear, unconfused point of conflict between procedural liberals and republicans. Thinkers like Hannah Arendt and Robert Bellah clearly have an incompatible political ideal, which this liberalism cannot incorporate.[23] Well, so what? Why is that a problem for procedural liberalism?

Perhaps it is not, but important questions arise before we can be sure. The issue is, can our patriotism survive the marginalization of participatory self-rule? As we have seen, a patriotism is a common identification with an historical community founded on certain values. These can vary widely, and there can of course be patriotisms of unfree societies, for example, founded on race or blood ties, and finding expression in despotic forms, as in Fascism; or the patriotism of Russians, under tsars and Bolsheviks, which was/is linked to authoritarian forms of rule. A free society requires a patriotism, according to the republican thesis. But it must be one whose core values incorporate freedom. Historically republican patriotism has incorporated self-rule in its definition of freedom. Indeed, as we have seen, this has been at the core of this definition.

Does this have to be so? The point is, that the patriotism of a free society has to celebrate its institutions as realizing a meaningful freedom, one which safeguards the dignity of citizens. Can we define a meaningful freedom in this sense, which can capture people's allegiance, which does not include self-rule as a central element?

We could argue this point in general terms: What will moderns recognize as genuine citizen dignity? This has to be defined not only in terms of what is to be *secured* for a citizen; the modern notion of the dignity of the person is essentially that of an agent, who can affect his or her own condition. Citizen dignity involves a notion of citizen capacity. Two major models are implicit in much of my discussion.

A. One focuses mainly on individual rights and equal treatment, as well as a government performance which takes account of the citizen's preferences. This is what has to be secured. Citizen capacity consists mainly in the power to retrieve these rights and ensure equal treatment, as well as to influence the effective decisionmakers. This retrieval may take place largely through the courts, in systems with a body of entrenched rights, such as we find in the United States (and recently also in Canada). But it will also be effected through representative institutions. Only in the spirit of this model, these institutions have an entirely instrumental significance. They tend to be viewed as they were on the "revisionist" model mentioned earlier. That means that no value is put on participation in rule for its own sake. The ideal is not "ruling and being ruled in turn,"[24] but having clout. This is compatible with not engaging in the participatory system at all, provided one can wield a credible threat to those who are so engaged, so that they will take notice; or with engaging in it in an adversarial way, in which the actual governors are defined as "them" to our "us," and pressured through single-issue campaigns, or petitions or lobbies, to take us into account.

B. The other model, by contrast, defines participation in self-rule as of the essence of freedom, as part of what must be secured. This is thus also seen as an essential component of citizen capacity. In consequence, a society in which the citizen's relation to government is normally adversarial, even where he or she manages to bend it to his or her purposes, has not secured citizen dignity and allows only a low degree of citizen capacity. Full participation in self-rule is seen as being able, at least part of the time, to have some part in the forming of a ruling consensus, with which one can identify along with others. To rule and be ruled in turn means that at least some of the time the governors can be "us," not always "them." The sense of citizen capacity is seen as incompatible with our being part of an alien political universe, which one can perhaps manipulate but never identify with.

These two kinds of capacity are incommensurable. We cannot say *simpliciter* which is greater. For people of an atomist bent, there is no doubt that *A* will seem preferable, and for republicans *B* will seem the only genuine one. But ranking them in the abstract is not the issue. The point is to see which can figure in the definition of citizen dignity in a viable patriotism. This requires us to share an allegiance to and cherish in common a historical set of institutions as the common bulwark of our freedom and citizen dignity. Can definition *A* be the focus of some such common sentiment?

The reasons for being skeptical are that this model of citizen capacity is so adversarial that it would seem impossible to combine it with the sense that our institutions are a shared bulwark of dignity. If I win my way by manipulating the common institutions, how can I see them as reflecting a purpose common to me and those who participate in these institutions? But there are also reasons to be skeptical of a too simple logic. Once again the reality of United States experience gives us pause. One could argue that America has moved in the last century more and more toward a definition of its public life based on *A*. It has become a less participatory and more "procedural" republic.[25] Judicial retrieval has become more important; at the same time, participation in elections seems to be declining. Meanwhile, political action committees (PACs) threaten to increase the leverage of single-issue politics.

These are exactly the developments that republicans deplore, seeing in them a decline in civic spirit, and ultimately a danger for free society. But liberals could counterargue that the continuing vigor of American political life shows that a patriotism of model *A* is viable; that underlying the adversarial relation to the representative institutions is a continuing sense that the political structure of which they are a part remains a common bulwark of freedom. The law invites us to litigate as adversaries to get our way; but it entrenches and enshrines for both sides their freedom and capacity as citizens. After all, they may add, the agon of citizens struggling for office and honor was central to the classical polis. That regime too united adversaries in solidarity.

I do not know who will turn out to be right on this. Republicans argue that the continued growth of bureaucratic, centralized society and the consequent exacerbation of participant alienation cannot but undermine patriotism in the long run. Liberals will reply that the resources of rights retrieval will increase to empower people *pari passu* with the spread of bureaucratic power. Such measures as the freedom of information acts already show that countervailing power can be brought to bear.

But the question cannot be settled in purely general terms. It is not just a matter of whether in the abstract people can accommodate to one or other model of citizen dignity. The question must be particularized to each society's tradition and culture. Procedural liberals seem to assume that something like model *A* is consonant with the American tradition, but this is vigorously contested by others, who argue that participation was an important part of early American patriotism and remains integral to the ideal by which American citizens will ultimately judge their republic.[26]

My aim cannot be to settle this issue. I raise it only to show how placing procedural liberalism against the background of a holist ontology, while answering the oversimple charge of nonviability in principle, opens a whole range of concrete questions about its viability in practice. These questions can be properly addressed only after we have settled issues on the ontological level, in fact in favor of holism. Both my main theses about the relation of the two levels are illustrated here: Once you have opted for holism, extremely important questions remain open on the level of advocacy; but at the same time, one's ontology structures the debate between the alternatives, and forces you to face certain questions. Clarifying the ontological question restructures the debate about advocacy.

When I said that procedural liberals might be confused about these levels, and not only those who proffer the simple republican criticism, I was referring to this. Certainly this liberalism has an answer to the in principle nonviability objection, and perhaps it will prove viable in practice. But procedural liberals seem quite unaware that this issue has to be addressed. Could it be that they are still too much in the thrall of commonsense atomist-infected notions, of the instrumental model of society, or of the various atomist sources of allegiance to see that there are questions here? That they are too insensitive to the ontological issues to see the point of the republican critique? I suspect that this is so. And thus they fail to articulate the distinction between ontological and advocacy questions, and take their communitarian critics to be simply advancing a different *policy,* which they vaguely apprehend as more collectivist; instead of seeing how the challenge is based on a redrawn map of political possibilities.

2. Having gone on at some length about the viability objection, I have little space left to address the charge of ethnocentricity. Fortunately I can make the point tersely, having laid some of the groundwork. Whether or not model *A* is the one entrenched in the American tradition and can ensure a free society in the United States in the future, it is clearly not the only possible model. Other societies are more oriented to model *B,* Canada for instance. Indeed, this makes one of the principal differences between the political culture of our two countries, which expresses itself in all sorts of ways, from the relatively higher voting participations to the greater emphasis on collective provision in Canada, reflected, for instance, in the Canadian public health service.[27]

There are other societies where the fusion between patriotism and the free institutions is not so total as in the United States, whose defining political culture from the beginning was centered on free institutions. There are also modern democratic societies where patriotism centers on a national culture, which in many cases has come (sometimes late and painfully) to incorporate free institutions, but which is also defined in terms of some language or history. Quebec is the prominent example in my experience, but there are many others.

The procedural liberal model cannot fit these societies, because they cannot declare neutrality between all possible definitions of the good life. A society like Quebec cannot but be dedicated to the defense and promotion of French culture and language, even if this involves some restriction on individual freedoms. It cannot make cultural–linguistic orientation a matter of indifference. A government that could ignore this requirement would either not be responding to the majority will, or would reflect a society so deeply demoralized as to be close to dissolution as a viable pole of patriotic allegiance. In either case, the prospects for liberal democracy would not be rosy.

But then one is entitled to raise questions about the procedural model as a definition of *liberal* society tout court. Are these other types of society, organized around model *B* or a national culture, not properly liberal? This could of course be made true by definitional fiat, in which case the claim is uninteresting. But if proceduralism is an attempt to define the essence of modern liberalism, it has to find a place for these alternatives. The discussion up to now has suffered from a certain parochialism. It has to come to terms with the real world of liberal democracy, to echo one of my compatriots, most of which lies outside the borders of the United States.

But these vistas can only be properly opened if we can properly clarify the ontological issues, and allow the debate between "liberals" and "communitarians" to be the complex, many-leveled affair that it really is.

TEN

Democratic Individuality and the Meaning of Rights

GEORGE KATEB

In recent years a number of theorists have insistently challenged individualism. Speaking simply, one could say that the challenge has been made in behalf of four ideals: first, the life of continuous and direct citizenship, with the polis or the revolutionary council held up as a model for close or approximate imitation; second, the feeling of community, with its satisfaction of the need for rootedness, belonging, fraternity, or harmony; third, the transcendence of self in a group identity, understood as the identity in which every individual should find the completion or perfection of his or her personal identity. There is a fourth ideal that seems to be individualist, but that I think is at bottom anti-individualist. That is the affirmation of self-realization when understood primarily as a process of mutual growth achieved in social activities that are publicly defined and publicly supported and even enabled. Obviously this is not an exhaustive list of anti-individualist ideals, but only a representative sampling. Among the theorists who have contributed to them are Hannah Arendt, Sheldon Wolin, John Schaar, Carey McWilliams, Benjamin Barber, Alasdair MacIntyre, Charles Taylor, Michael Sandel, and, to a degree, Michael Walzer. Again, this list is hardly exhaustive.

I dare say that the number of those who have consciously tried to resist these tendencies would be smaller than the number of those who have furthered them—a fact of great symptomatic importance. And I can say this while ignoring two other pronounced tendencies: the anti-individualism of some authoritarian and disciplinarian conservatives; and the wordy, and at crucial moments, practically speechless onslaught on the idea of the individual as subject undertaken by some Marxists, by structuralists, and by Althusser, Foucault, Derrida, and their followers. (The critique of the subject may not affirm any ideal but it certainly works to corrode the individualist ideal.) Let us leave these two latter groups aside and concentrate on the anti-individualist ideals I have just mentioned, all of whose theorists are democrats.

I use the word "individualism" as the name of the common adversary of these ideals rather than "liberalism" because I think that "individualism" is more accurate, and also because "liberalism" is by now so frequently and variously used that we cannot be sure what it means in any given case, without an explicit definition, which is only rarely given. It would also be well to notice that though the four types of anti-individualism that I have singled out are communitarian in some sense, communitarianism in the strict sense is a separate ideal. We can continue to call our matter the debate between liberalism and communitarianism, but it could more precisely be called the debate between individualism and anti-individualism. Anti-individualism is the common element in these four types of idealism, whatever else may unite them or distinguish them. Of course each theorist cannot be reduced to a single type. She or he will most likely show signs of more than one, just as the richness of each work may surpass the specific project of criticizing individualism and affirming an anti-individualist ideal.

These four ideals all go back a long way. But I think that in recent years Rawls's work, the great statement of individualism in this century, has helped many anti-individualist theorists to collect their thoughts and find their voice. Like any genuine work in political theory, *A Theory of Justice* energizes not only its own cause but that of its opponents. It does this not by its deficiencies but by its vulnerability, a vulnerability incurred by its courageous reach and attention to particulars; and even more by its indefinite suggestiveness than by its vulnerability. It instructs its opponents even as it provokes them. Doubtless, the works of Ronald Dworkin and Robert Nozick, among others, have also contributed to the anti-individualist theoretical fire. Yet having said all this, we should keep in mind the long lineage of both individualism and its antitheses. We can always find help for either cause in the remote or nearer past. I hope to do so in this essay.

What we find in recent political theory, then, is the idealism of individualism under attack on a broad front. I worry about the persistence and intensity of the attack as much as I worry about the force of the critical arguments; and I worry about the antithetical idealisms affirmed. My purpose in this chapter is to expose my worries—in particular, my concern that individualism is not always seen in its fullness and thus is disparaged unfairly or at least prematurely, and that the losses that would be sustained if anti-individualist idealisms were to be realized go unremarked, even by those who are more or less friendly to individualism.

My perspective is made up of two types of individualism, historically related. The first is the individualism of personal and political rights, profoundly present in Rawls, Dworkin, and Nozick, but, as we know, the creation of the English Protestant seventeenth century: the work of the Levellers, Roger Williams, Milton, Hobbes, and Locke (among others). This work is carried on, and sometimes improved, by Trenchard and Gordon, Montesquieu, Rousseau, Paine, Kant, Jefferson, Madison, Lincoln, and J. S. Mill (despite his declaimers about believing in abstract rights). The second type is what I have been calling "democratic individuality," an idealism imagined and theorized initially by Emerson, Thoreau, and Whitman, and with a force that has not been equaled since then, must less surpassed.[1]

Actually, it is not easy to say who has even made the effort to further the Emersonian tradition, unless it be poets like Wallace Stevens and Robert Frost, who did so indirectly, even if deliberately. What should one say? Perhaps most of American imaginative literature indirectly furthers the work of the Emersonians, though usually not deliberately; but a lot of American political science and moral philosophy does not even do that.

The connection that I see between the two types of individualism is that democratic individuality is perhaps not the only but probably the best actuality and aspiration that grows or can grow out of a culture in which individual personal and political rights are systematically recognized and appreciated. In other words, the Emersonian tradition is the best working out of the existential meanings of rights-based individualism, the best pursuit of its intimations. This means that democratic individuality could not exist, as an actuality or aspiration, apart from rights-based individualism.

The four anti-individualist ideals that I have mentioned have characteristically directed their critique at the individualism of personal rights, while assuming that those who prize personal rights tend not to be much interested in political rights. As the critics sometimes put it: their critique is aimed at liberalism, not at democracy. But I believe that the whole discourse of rights, political rights included, is found narrow and obstructive by some of those who affirm any of the four antithetical ideals. But whatever the situation is in any given anti-individualist text, the plain fact is that there is scarcely any indication that the critics have democratic individuality in mind. It is as if the Emersonian tradition did not exist. For that reason, I would like to continue the effort of trying to say what the Emersonians were up to. From them one may gather considerations that pertain to my two concerns: the unrecognized nature of individualist idealism; and the size of the loss that would be sustained if, by some mischance, one or more of the four anti-individualist idealisms were to take hold in our individualist culture programmatically. Needless to say, in the debate between the defenders and critics of rights-based individualism the defenders have ample resources at their disposal to fend off the critics, without having to enlist the Emersonians. Still, we should notice that any serious attack on the centrality of rights in political life is also, and necessarily, even if unknowingly, an attack on democratic individuality.

I go on the assumption that Emerson, Thoreau, and Whitman are best understood in relation to each other. Though Emerson is first, and is the great teacher of the other two, Thoreau and Whitman are their own geniuses. And what they say expands or qualifies, enriches or transforms, the thinking of Emerson. They also break new ground. At the same time, I maintain that not only is Whitman a theorist of *democratic* individuality, but so are Emerson and Thoreau, appearances notwithstanding.

What, then, is the theory of democratic individuality? It is, to begin with, an insistence that a society with democratic political institutions—and for the Emersonians, that can mean only the United States—is a culture that is distinctive in major respects. The culture is individualist in ways or in degrees that other cultures that lack democratic political institutions are not. For the Emersonians the newness of the New World and the newness of modern democracy are practically the same thing. Something new is going on; a new sense of life is showing itself. A large part of the explanation is found in the all too obvious fact that the American government is guaranteed its continuous existence only through the will and the suffrage of a population of individuals; and that the government is suffered to exist only because it acknowledges and protects rights and does not try to govern too much. That the government functions because of frequently disgraceful partisan *agon* is all to the good. This way authorities and their enactments, in their confused changeability, lose enough of their dignity so that individuals can keep and increase theirs. The government is their government, but it does not originate or emanate from what is best in them. The real good it does, it does by the manner of its working, by its procedures and processes, much more than by its enactments. Its procedures and processes impersonally and continuously instruct citizens in the dependence of political authority on them, and in the unsolid quality of the results of political activity. Actually the instruction is indistinguishable from remembrance. Citizens already know but can scarcely believe the lessons. In such instruction or remembrance, liberation is found: on the one hand, liberation from feelings of inferiority and from habitual docility, and, on the other hand, possible liberation to a new stage of character—what I have been calling democratic individuality.

For the Emersonians the actual culture shows evidences of such liberation. Their common purpose as philosophers is to theorize a fuller conception of democratic individuality to serve as a reproach and an inspiration. The obstacles are, first, timorousness, which accounts for the strange reluctance of citizens to believe what their own political creation is impersonally teaching them, and thus to accept the opportunity for a larger liberation; and second, the temptations of moneymaking, which threaten forfeiture of democratic individuality by confining individualism to acquisitive and consumerist pursuits. The Emersonians feared the latter obstacle much more than the first. They knew that economic individualism was historically and conceptually separate from rights-based individualism and hence from the democratic individuality that could grow out of it. But they also knew that economic individualism was the most likely deviation.

Before examining the main aspects of democratic individuality, I would like to suggest why rights-based individualism leads—both in the actuality of the culture and in further theoretical aspiration—to democratic individuality. We may ask why the system of rights, housed in democratic political institutions, led the Emersonians to their insistence on recognizing what was going on in the life of their society and to their elaboration of an aspiration; and also why this system can or should lead us, more than a century later, to the same insistence on recognition and the same elaboration of aspiration.

What is the overt as well as the potential meaning of rights-based individualism—or, at least, what is one possible theorization of such meaning? I have in mind especially the right to life, the right to a full range of expression, the right to be let alone, the right to ownership, and the right to equal citizenship in a constitutional representative democracy. To begin with, let us look at the overt meaning of the acknowledgment and protection of such rights, for each individual against the rest where need be, and with the rest where possible; and for all against government, where need be.

Anything I say here is either familiar or fragmentary. I think that the heart of the matter is found in the speeches made at Putney by the spokesman for the so-called Levellers, and in writings by other Levellers like Lilburne and Overton. In a famous but not perhaps sufficiently appreciated sentence, Colonel Rainborough says, "For really I think that the poorest he that is in England hath a life to live, as the greatest he."[2] What meanings are lodged here? Everyone equally has a life to live. To live a life, a person's personal and political rights must be acknowledged and protected. Living a life does not necessarily mean that one will say or do great things, but rather than one will say and do one's own things, or be like the rest only after one has taken some thought. What one claims for oneself one must concede to the rest: to talk of rights at all is to talk of the same rights for all, and everywhere. The point of specifically *political* rights is not to use them in order to press class advantage but to attain a moral status—that of self-governance—that every individual deserves just by being. (The Levellers thus purge democracy of passion for levelling, the grossness of demotic resentment.) Depending on circumstances, one will be entitled to press one's own claim to this or that right, or will feel compelled to assert a claim in behalf of others who may be denied this or that right. There will be mutual recognition, but there need not be very much mutuality beyond that. The great duties that correspond to the great rights are largely abstentionist in nature: to forbear from transgression—though help to the desperate is always obligatory. Above all, the principle is to tolerate others who though different are not other, no matter how foreign.

A sense of life certainly inheres in the theory and practice of rights. The individualism of personal and political rights *is* a sense of life. It is best described in negatives, just as its morality is largely negative. There is no good life, only lives that are not bad. The mere absence of oppression and degradation is sweet. A person's equal acceptance by the rest removes the heavy weight of inferiority, contempt, invisibility. That too is sweet. The weakening of traditional enclosure in status, group, class, locality, ethnicity, race—the whole suffocating network of ascribed artificial, or biological but culturally exaggerated, identity opens life up, at least a bit. The culture of individual rights has lightness of being; free being is light. It seems insubstantial and lacking in positivity. Yet all its negativity, all its avoidances and absences and abstentions, are a life, and a life that it takes patient eyes to see, and a new sense of beauty to admire. The life that is not the good life is good in itself. However, can something even richer come out of it?

The Emersonian writers think so. More than England itself, North America inherited the Levellers. The New World can be the place for the sense of life intrinsic to the individualism of rights to develop itself, despite the constant danger of forfeiture to economic individualism.

I admit that in the account that I am about to give I make the Emersonians more explicit in their attention to the democratic culture of rights than the surface of their writing usually indicates they are. I also schematize, and just by doing that, offend against their own beliefs about proper literary procedure. But I am persuaded that we make a good overall sense of the profoundest elements in these writers when we see them attentive to the democratic culture of rights and struggling to raise it to a more intense awareness of itself and its best possibilities. So, to put it crudely perhaps, the work of Emerson, Thoreau, and Whitman seeks to draw more meaning from the democratic culture of rights. The life lived around them gives a fair amount of evidence that people know the meaning of their rights. But the realization is very imperfect, very impure.

The work of Emerson, Thoreau, and Whitman seeks to suggest that, to begin with, living a life should mean more: a life should gain in definition; it should be more *assertive* or *expressive*. The regime of habit or custom or convention should be shaken; sleep should be "thrown off." The move should not be from feeling oneself as ill-defined to an acceptance of ascribed identity, but from feeling that one has unused powers to an acceptance of experiment. Next, the Emersonians, especially Thoreau, are saying that the readiness to assert a claim in behalf of others who are denied some crucial right should convert itself into the readiness to *resist* political power when it oppresses others, even when oneself and many others like oneself are safe and free. The sense of indirect responsibility is as important as the sense of direct responsibility. And the real grievances of others must be felt as real, must be felt as if they were one's own. Last, Emersonians are suggesting that toleration be transformed into an active generosity of perception, into a *receptivity* or *responsiveness* that aims to take in on its own terms what presents itself; or, if need be, on better terms than the person or creature or thing is already claiming for itself. Put schematically, we may say that the aspiration to a more fully achieved democratic individuality has three components: positive, negative, and impersonal. These terms do not matter. What matters is to see that Emerson, Thoreau, and Whitman undertake a complex conceptualization and that its essence is to draw out of the individualism of personal and political rights a deeper meaning that is there, awaiting its utterance. The formulation will help to move in a faithful direction the life that already gives evidence of some deeper meaning. One possible completion or perfection of rights-based individualism is thus democratic individuality, the life of expression, resistance, and responsiveness, in a constitutional representative democracy. Democratic individuality is what democracy is for.

I think that it is fair to say that the initial component is self-assertion or self-expression: what Emerson in his most famous essay calls self-reliance. It is the initial component in the sense that any individualism starts with oneself and with what one means to do, and in the sense that any society, even a rights-based democracy, tends to be too much for individuals, tends to induce and reward conformity. There is thus a tinge of resistance in expression, something negative in the positive. But because one's commitment to expressing oneself is accompanied by a recognition of everyone else's right to do the same, there is not supposed to be any tinge of insolence. There is all the difference in the world between a culture of expressiveness, in which class stratification standardizes expression for each group, ranks the groups, permits eccentricity for a few inside the few, and encourages the few as a group to use the rest as resources for their own group stylization, and a culture of expressiveness in which democratic respect frames, limits, and inspires self-assertion. Equal rights avoid the kinship to privilege that unequal rights have.

Relatedly, democratic self-assertion is not conceptualized in the Emersonian tradition in a subjectivist way. The stark dualism of ego and other that we associate with the teaching of Fichte and Stirner, and with the antagonism posited by Hegel between lord and bondsman, is not part of the mentality of democratic individuality. On the contrary, the developed individuality of one would not be a threat to others; nor would it quite be an individuality compensatory to the different individuality of others, in either the Aristotelian or the Rawlsian sense. Rather, the concurrence of developed individualities would be more like a riot of colors, a field of wild flowers, or the spangled garment of uncertain taste to which Plato likened democratic culture. Neither the psychology of subjective scarcity nor the aesthetics of formal composition would enable the observer to encompass the scene.

Some of the sentiments of democratic self-assertion or self-reliance, as observed and theorized by the Emersonians, and that still matter, can be clustered as follows:

(1) the wish to be different; the wish to be unique; the wish to go off in one's own direction; the wish to experiment, to wander, to float;

(2) the wish to be let alone; the wish to be uninvolved in somebody else's game; the wish to be unobserved; the wish to be mysterious, to have secrets, to be thought undefined;

(3) the wish to be unbeholden; the wish to own oneself;

(4) the wish to think, judge, and interpret for oneself;

(5) the wish to feel real, not dazed; the wish to live, not play just one lifelong role or perform just one lifelong function;

(6) the wish to go to one's limit; the wish to score, to accumulate heterogenous experiences;

(7) the wish to shape one's life, but not into a well-shaped story, or a well-made work of art; the wish to be fluid, not substantial;

(8) the wish to find oneself, to find the "real me"; to be oneself rather than somebody else's idea of that self; the wish to be reborn as oneself.

These are some of the sentiments that pervade the writings of the Emersonians as they strive to understand American social reality and to coax it further in its own direction. The premise is that if there is strain in trying to become an individual, there is at least as much strain in trying not to become one, in trying, instead, to conform. Strain for strain, there is far more dignity in becoming individual. Yet such dignity is not without cost. There is the cost to the individual, which is paid in loneliness of the Calvinist sort, and in a frequent sense that one is unreal to oneself, that one lacks a continous sense of existing because one is inclined to reject ascribed artificial identity and hence must often improvise without sponsorship. Socially sanctified habit is not always or fully available to thicken one's ego. There is also a cost to the theoretical observers. The secret worm that gnaws at the Emersonians is not respect for an aristocratic culture or for classical virture, but misanthropy. They feel an irritation bred of disappointment with their fellows that sometimes turns into contempt. They see democratic individuals lapsing into economic individuals. The underside of the Emersonians' sense of democratic potentiality is a steady censure, a dislike, almost. But of course these writers are and must be discontented with themselves. They too lapse, if not into economic individualism. They lapse into distraction. Their misanthropy is forgivable as a form of self-doubt. Thoreau says, in *Walden*, "I never knew, and shall never know, a worse man than myself."[3]

For all the salience in the Emersonians of the theme of becoming an individual self, leading a self-assertive or self-expressive life, my judgment is that this component is not the main one. It may seem odd to give it a subordinate place—after all, what is any kind of idealization of individualism but an instigation to become different, to become an individual by one's own definition? Nevertheless, it is possible to read the Emersonians as pointing beyond positive individuality to states of being—they may be only moments or episodes in a life—in which concern for one's project gives way to concern for others in the two special modes to which I have already referred: resistance in behalf of others when they are denied some right and are oppressed; and responsiveness to everything outside oneself.

It may be that the most important reason for cultivating a positive individuality is to effect a break with habit, convention, and custom, all of which work to condition us to accept the oppression of others, on the one hand, and to respond in an impoverished manner to difference, on the other hand. Democratic individuality is not egotism; its highest purpose is to establish a new sort of connectedness, but one that bears little relation to communitarianism in a strict sense or in any loose sense. There are ways of working together by working apart. One must be an individual, must presume to be a self that is no mere resultant of all that has happened to one, if one is to be capable of either disinterested protest or a poetical or philosophical openness to reality. Of course there are many ways of taking others seriously besides the way of democratic individuality; but democratic individuality is one way. Its excellence consists in the refusal to confine concern to those it is easy to care about: oneself, and those like one, or close to one, or dear to one. A radical and secularized reading of the Gospels is thus intrinsic to the components of democratic individuality that transcend one's positive project. The story of the good Samaritan[4] and the precept that the God we should imitate is the God who "maketh his sun to rise on the evil and on the good, and sendeth rain on the just and on the unjust"[5] are quintessential in the teachings of the Emersonians.

Thoreau's great essay on civil disobedience is the central text concerning the theme of resistance in behalf of others. I do not wish to repeat what I have said on other occasions about his doctrine of negative individuality.[6] I only note that Thoreau's whole sense of the need to resist in behalf of others supposes that one is not oppressed. The calculation is that when one's personal and political rights are safe, one should give little thought to what society can do to further one's prosperity or well-being, material or spiritual. The latter is one's own business only. One will not look to society for help in living. It follows that when a dissident presses claims, they must be to basic rights that are denied others. The rights anyone has, others must have. That is democracy. Thoreau insists on *obliging* those who are safe to risk something—not very much: as much as the good Samaritan—for those who are denied. Forbearance from transgression is normally the greatest of all sorts of duty; but some samaritanism is also obligatory. Thoreau, however, extends the sense of responsibility. After all, though he wrote an essay called "Slavery in Massachusetts," there was no slavery in Massachusetts. But Massachusetts' membership in the Union helped to sustain slavery; and Thoreau's membership in Massachusetts helped to sustain Massachusetts. He therefore refused to pay the most general tax, the head tax; he went to jail, prepared to stay, but was released the next day when someone interfered and paid his tax. But Thoreau was prepared to stay; he felt responsible.

The act, which had no influence in its time, has had great influence ever since. What matters, in any case, is not its actual influence, but its possible influence, its meanings. Its first meaning is that the notion of personal responsibility is indispensable to resistance in behalf of others. When Althusser and Foucault, for example, suggest that the sense of responsibility is imaginary and works only to preserve a radically unequal distribution of power and wealth, they are thinking mainly of the impact of the idea of responsibility on the mentality of the disadvantaged. Resistance in their own behalf would be facilitated by rejection of this idea: they are victims and must develop the solidarity of victims. Victims must not blame themselves or hold themselves responsible for their condition. One trouble that I see is that this critique of responsibility can also excuse the privileged. Then too, it can be interpreted as the contribution made by two generous spirits who were trying to help others press their claim for the rights—or, at least, the power and wealth—that they were denied. I think, however, that the charity of Althusser and Foucault is exorbitant.

Even if their doctrine may energize struggle, it teaches people to think of themselves as material or as animals. For that reason, the struggle is guaranteed to produce inhuman effects. Thoreau's idea of responsibility is more efficacious for good, even if it may not be directly efficacious, or very efficacious at all.

The further meaning of Thoreau's act implies an immense individual importance. Thoreau's stance is that of a person who only episodically departs from the state of nature, which is a state of living by one's conscientious understanding of the law of nature, basic morality, the morality that culminates in personal and political rights for all. He gives his assent (never a full consent), he complies when he has to, as long as what government does is congruent with basic morality. So often it is not. When it robs Mexico and keeps slaves it is using democratic forms to eviscerate democracy. Resistance should take the form of breaking the law, when the policies are atrocious, because an individual must make a dramatic reversion to the state of nature, to a politically unpledged situation—at least in some respects. This takes the specific form of refusing to pay the most general tax, which is the instrument and symbol of government as such.

In refusing, Thoreau may be said by us, who ponder his act and the words by which he surrounded it, to disaffiliate, to chastise the authorities, and to constitute himself as a parallel legislature, as a "majority of one." But the new law he lays down is the very law that people profess but disregard. The lawbreaker becomes the upholder of the law when the law is twisted to immoral purposes. If good law is only a memorandum, as Emerson says,[7] the conscientious lawbreaker will be, in reference to certain deeds and policies of government, a memorandum to the custodians of the original memorandum. The appeal in the act, Thoreau says, is an appeal "from them to themselves."[8] From them in a forgetful condition, to themselves when they can be brought to remember, if reproached and allowed to witness the punishment entailed by the free act of the lawbreaker. Emerson said of Thoreau: "It cost him nothing to say No; indeed he found it much easier than to say Yes."[9] But that may be true of anyone who appreciates the meaning of rights and insists that one is truly being an individual when one acts in behalf of those denied them. To borrow from Wallace Stevens:

> under every no
> Lay a passion for yes that had never been broken.[10]

But I grant that even Thoreau's Yes is suspicious of the positive component of individuality. In a sentence in *Walden* that Foucault could almost have written, he says: "Do not seek so anxiously to be developed, to subject yourself to many influences to be played on; it is all dissipation."[11]

We can say, in sum, that Emerson, Thoreau, and Whitman show a valuable diversity concerning the proper nature of self-assertion or self-expression; and that Thoreau, much more than the other two, makes resistance an essential component of democratic individuality. But on the third component in our scheme, they converge. They all think that the fruition of democratic individuality is the achievement of a new relation to reality, what Emerson in his first book, *Nature,* embarrassingly calls "an original relation to the universe."[12] We can also call it a poetical or philosophical relation to reality, to both human and nonhuman reality. The works of all three writers are dominated by the effort to bestow attention, especially on what tends to be taken for granted, or overlooked, or thought unfit or unworthy. Further, when we examine the consummatory passages in the three writers, we find a rapturous contemplation of all existence.[13] I grant that this rapture is sometimes marred by a still-too-religious proclivity to comprehend all phenomena as making up a totality and see them as permeated by something like a divine intelligence. But we can sever the words from their theological or metaphysical preconceptions without violating them. We simply continue the process of secularization of theological and metaphysical insight that the Emersonians did so much to advance. Any of us committed to democratic individuality will want to think with their ecstatic words, even though on our own terms, because they are the best words, in and out of context.

At the same time it is well to recognize that not only is there a romantic, post-Enlightenment theology or metaphysics in the Emersonians, there are also significant traces of an earlier Protestantism. The Emersonians work in their own manner with the idea that the highest relationship is an unmediated relationship between each individual and the most important thing, which must be nonsocial and which includes the nonhuman. For the Emersonians it is not the inscrutable God of Luther and Calvin that is the most important thing; rather, things are the most important thing, things in their beauty, the impulsive succession of human and natural phenomena as they present themselves. The necessary supposition is that a man or woman can become enough of an individual to be able in certain recurrent moods or moments, to imagine that he or she is entitled to consider all immediate and local ties as less than final and venture to marry the world. I exist for nothing less than the world. I exist, and everything else exists. I define myself as existing in the face of everything else. When I am my best self, nothing social, not even intimate or domestic love, can be allowed to interpose itself as supreme. A deliberate self-possession, though only fitful, is needed to fight off the inevitable presence of prejudice, conventionality, acquired distaste, and reflexive disgust that close and enclose one, that impede receptivity or responsiveness. In Protestantism one did not dare to equate oneself to the most important thing. Similarly in the thought of the Emersonians, the responsive individual, in her or his most concentrated impersonal moments or moods, knows eagerly that she or he is not equal to the succession of things that present themselves for contemplative attention. It is not that one is dwarfed by the relationship, it is that one wants to lose oneself in admiration or love or wonder or gratitude. These feelings are the completion or perfection of the tolerance intrinsic to rights-based individualism.

Only a self that is possessed can be truly lost; and it is gained in order to be lost. The consummation of democratic individuality is therefore a passage beyond self-concern. In one of his descriptions of ecstatic contemplation, Emerson says (of course embarrassingly): "all mean egotism vanishes. I become a transparent eyeball; I am nothing; I see all."[14] The Emersonians take to heart a hidden lesson of Plato's parable of the cave, namely, that one can see, one can see things as they are in their true phenomenal beauty instead of their falsely perceived shadowy simulacra, one can see the actual sun, only when one has lost sight of one's social self. Scattered throughout the works of Emerson, Thoreau, and Whitman are renderings of the ecstatic state. But short of the ecstatic state, their more sober and continuous attention is lighted by an unparalleled receptivity or responsiveness.

A particularly important text, in this regard, is Emerson's essay, "Art," from *Essays: First Series.* He says: "it has been the office of art to educate the perception of beauty. We are immersed in beauty, but our eyes have no clear vision. It needs, by the exhibition of single traits, to assist and lead the dormant taste."[15] The passion of the Emersonians—already present in the great 1816 essay "On Imitation," by the English romantic democrat, William Hazlitt[16]—is to see beauty in what is not intended or designed to be beautiful. A person, a creature, a thing in nature, is what it is, or does what it does; it does not aim at being beautiful. It may even be plain or ugly, and even think (when it can think) that it is ugly. But if one attends, much awaits a receptive eye that does not register on a conventional eye. It may be a matter of beholding the surface of someone or something that is making its indeliberate plea to be perceived, to be perceived as beautiful, or at least as worthy of perception. Or it may be a matter of empathic interpretation: such interpretation is also a mode of attention; and it is not creative, it is only patient.

The passion of the Emersonians is to teach us to look at what is not art with an artist's eye and interpret what is not art with an artist's energy. The function of artworks is to train the nonartist's eye and sensibility; to make each individual's relation to reality like that of the painter or the poet or novelist. The function of artworks is to be surpassed because of the perceptual influences they radiate. The greater beauty is found in reality, not in artworks. Truth is beauty. The greater beauty resides in what does not try to be beautiful. It resides in the surface or in the depths of each person or creature or thing.

In one of his letters Keats said that the imagination is like Adam's dream: "he awoke and found it truth."[17] One meaning of this famous passage is that when we awaken, that is, when we throw off the sleep of convention, we see as for the first time. What we see is what is around us. The purpose of the artist's imagination is to awaken us, not to a literally new reality but to reality just as it is, and to see it just as it is, and thus to see it as answering to the imagination, and indeed exceeding its expectations. As Keats says in another letter, "I live in the eye; and my imagination, surpassed, is at rest."[18] Art is not the highest expression in life. The highest art is unpremeditated. Life itself is the highest art. Life need not be beautiful to be beautiful. The artwork is indispensable, but it is only instrumental. It is instrumental to democratic aestheticism. And democratic aestheticism takes things as it finds them; it is the constant disposition to give each person or creature or thing, just as it is, its due, its rights, in the fullest sense. Each is to try to do what Whitman says the great poet actually does: "He bestows on every object its fit proportions neither more nor less."[19] Democratic aestheticism is the culmination of democratic justice. The attempted rupture with social enclosure redeems the social, and everything else besides. The democratic individual most truly is, in Whitman's phrase about the greatest poet, the "complete lover."[20] The complete lover aims not at objectivity, but at a mobile and multiple perspectivism. Such acceptance does not include an acceptance of injustice. If democratic aestheticism inclines toward a universal absolution, a sense of "universal innocence," in Thoreau's words, that does not mean that denial of rights can ever be allowed.[21] Democratic aestheticism presupposes that everyone is already included or on the way to being so. The commitment to equal rights, to say it again, frames, limits, and inspires every component of individuality.

In sum, the aspiration to greater expressiveness, resistance, and responsiveness is the theory of democratic individuality. The theorized aim of greater expressiveness is to come to know oneself, to get to know who one is; but especially to know who one isn't, to know that one is not merely a role or function or ascribed identity, while leaving perpetually unmeasured the possibilities of self-expression. The aim is not necessarily to live more fully or more intensely, but rather to live more honestly, as oneself rather than in "endless imitation." The aim of greater resistance is to avoid involvement in or indifference to the cruelties that come from thoughtlessness, routine, or conformity; or from tribalism; or from the herd mentality with its tendency to trample or stampede. The aim of greater receptivity is to lose oneself in appreciation and admiration, or in empathy, and thus to allow things to be as they must be or to appear at their best. Taken together, these desiderated aspects of democratic individuality point to the democratization of cultivated inwardness, to a richer consciousness and a more deliberate self-consciousness for all.

When we ponder what the Emersonians are saying, we gain, in addition to everything else, a perspective on the anti-individualist ideals that have been pressed so urgently in recent years. From this perspective these ideals, whether the life of continuous citizenship or membership in a tight community or membership in a well-defined group vis-à-vis other groups or a life of collectivized and socialized self-realization, seem to share a common lamentable essence. Abstractly considered, they signify an impoverishment of inwardness, of consciousness and self-consciousness. Despite important differences between them, and also between the several statements of each of them, they all theorize in the direction of making people more shallow. It may even be that the theorists feel that ordinary persons can never be anything but shallow, and hope to enlist them in patterns of life and action that would have the effect of making them do things that are more interesting and aesthetically compelling than what they do when on their own more, when they are individuals. There is a strong anti-individualist wish that people be taken care of in every sense.

The upshot of anti-individualism could be an increased coherence in society, and perhaps an even more well-defined individuation on the part of people; but these results would be hollow. Full-bodied characters, enacting a well-made story, whether in novels or in life, are actually those who forget the difference between themselves and what they do: the more full-bodied, the more mechanical. They are the ones who are most rehearsed, who remember their lines best, who are most theatrical. Enriched inwardness is not likely to make society more shapely, intelligible, or manifestly splendid. It may and does induce a greater lightness, tentativeness, irony, distance, playfulness, uncertainty, awkwardness, looseness. The anti-individualist ideals that I have mentioned seem to suggest that what is done, what is accomplished, matters more than the doer; that the political and social labor or the moral or aesthetic level of the deed matters more than the relation between the individual and the labor to be achieved or the deed to be done. The self-loss that the theorists of anti-individualist ideals seek is losing oneself in what is to be done, losing oneself in the effort to be as adequate as possible. The self-loss present in the third and highest component of democratic individuality, the idea of receptivity or responsiveness, is losing oneself in the effort to let everything that presents itself to a person have its being without the distortions that the egotism of individual or group or species would inflict on it. These are two divergent types of self-loss or self-forgetting. That of anti-individualism proceeds from a diminished inwardness; that of democratic individuality from an enhanced inwardness.

In what I say I here am guided by Henry James, whose reflections on the contrast of the New World and the Old are unsurpassed. For our purposes this contrast is roughly equivalent to that between democratic individuality and recent anti-individualism. In a passage from his autobiographical writing, *The Middle Years,* James compares living in what he calls the "thickness" of European class society as one raised in it with observing it as a sympathetic American raised in the seeming shapelessness and unrootedness of the United States.[22] He knows he lost much in not being habituated; but his own upbringing had prepared him to enter sympathetically into the strange and foreign. American lightness of being allowed his mind "the ideal play of reflection, conclusion, comparison" when it encountered a different and much heavier social order. But he suggests that to be raised, as he was not, in such a social order is to be "immersed," and thus to become less receptive to what is different, to what is outside. To be immersed in a social order is to be unable to see, with Emerson, that one is "immersed in beauty." Even in regard to a person's own New World society, living socially "immersed" exacts the penalties of diminished everyday inwardness that living a less defined and ascribed life tends to avoid. James's reflections on the greater possibilities of inwardness refer not only to himself as an artist and thinker but also to ordinary persons in their New World actuality.

It seems to me that the only way the theorists of anti-individualism can neutralize the charge that they encourage diminished inwardness is to show the truth of the view that expanded consciousness is necessarily an expanded bondage; that the work of introspection is merely self-policing; that honestly pursuing one's genuine responses to things is simply discovering the unrecognized effects of colonization, of suggestions planted in oneself by one or another power technique; that, in short, the more one takes in, the more one is taken in. According to Foucault's conceptualization, the inwardness of democratic individuality is merely and perniciously the type of individualism that is fabricated by the "pastoral" power of the state, as well as by the disciplinary power inherent in all lesser sectors.[23] At best, it is the mere set of effects inexorably produced by culturally specific and altogether transpersonal rules, as if all activity were an involuntary adherence to recipes.[24] Can all this really be proven? I think this is mostly a tactical reductiveness useful for certain kinds of (eventually self-defeating) radicalism.

I do not deny that there is a place, even on individualist grounds, for anti-individualist ideals. They are valuable when theorized in full awareness that in a democratically individualist culture these ideals are and will be best realized only in temporary or local forms. When we see them actually practiced in the United States, we see that they already endure such an individualist reworking. First, the ideal of continuous involvement in the political life of a sovereign entity gives way to episodes of direct involvement in movements, or to local and intermittent participation in such important but unsovereign forums as party caucuses, town meetings, and institutions and work places of every sort. Second, the ideal of permanent and bounded community gives way to temporary, voluntary, and quite intense experiences of staying together for a while and then breaking up. Third, the ideal of completing or perfecting a person's identity in an armed group that is encouraged to be proud of its difference from other groups and ready (perhaps eager) to assert and express itself in relation to other groups and preferably at their expense, gives way to a local or partisan pride that is quite compatible with the sense that playing is itself at least as important as prevailing. Fourth, the ideal of publicly defined and sustained mutual self-realization that promises that one will become a completed person living with other completed persons, and that all will carry on the good life as if life were a lovely ceremony and each a flawless performer in it, gives way to private and porous associations in which one gives and takes, and never dreams (that is, *only* dreams) of being finished. Such individualist, hence limited or temporary enactments of anti-individualist ideals, are compensations for and frequently attractive emanations of lives that are—at least, to some noteworthy degree—democratically individualist.

I do not deny that a person sympathetic to the theory of democratic individuality must retain a concept of citizenship that is more than episodic, a concept of society that attends to long-lasting ties, and a concept of a people that is more than an accidental aggregation (even though it is that, too). (I find no need to accommodate the ideal of mutual self-realization as continuous and societywide.) But the theory not only sponsors the individualist conversion of ideals into temporary and local forms, it suggests an individualist reworking of the concepts of citizenship, society, and people. The good citizen is watchful and independent, though not routinely active. Society works, to an unusual degree, by means of consent and explicitness rather than because of involuntary or unarticulated ties. The people (We, the People) are connected by choice, rather than by blood, faith, or the past.

But the anti-individualist versions of these continuous and society-wide ideals must turn bad. If we consider them not only abstractly but as realized, we can imagine terrible results besides the diminished inwardness to which I have referred. Think first of the impact on rights. In their common disdain for rights, many anti-individualist theorists ignore the danger that docility must increase when individuals stop thinking of themselves as entitled to those fences that protect them from oppression, including the soft oppression that comes from high-minded regulations issuing from a confident and carelessly supervised executive power. The danger does not end there. Even when a particular theorist of these ideals wants to retain the notion of personal rights, they are seen as instrumental to a socially defined purpose. That means that one or another right may be abridged or diluted unless it is clear that the tendency of its use is socially beneficial. What is thought socially beneficial is always some seemingly substantial purpose that may turn out, after a while, to be a good deal less than substantial. Individuals are to be held accountable for the use they make of their rights. All four anti-individualist ideals incline in the direction of the doctrine that Mill powerfully attacks as "monstrous" in chapter four of *On Liberty*: namely, the idea of "social rights" according to which, "it is the absolute social right of every individual, that every other individual shall act in every respect exactly as he ought . . . The doctrine ascribes to all mankind a vested interest in each other's moral, intellectual, and even physical perfection, to be defined by each claimant according to his own standard."[25] The very notion of having a right is thereby denatured. An oppressive sociality must ensue. Further, as I have tried to show, the indispensable core of democratic individuality is undone, and the aspiration itself extinguished—a cost that anti-individualist theorists do not tally.

Nevertheless, if they are not obliged to tally the cost to the democratic individualist aspiration when they condemn the idea of rights, such theorists are obliged to worry about the likely results of the realization of their ideals in a continuous and societywide manner. These anti-individualist ideals not only wash away the idea of human dignity that is contained in the theory and practice of personal and political rights even without the enhancement of that idea attempted by the democratic-individualist theorists. The potentialities harbored in anti-individualist ideals, if realized, would spell the end of those ideals themselves, not just of rights-based individualism and democratic individuality.

I detect in anti-individualist ideals a capacity to do the following. They can make people much more barbarous than we already are. This is latent in the ideals of continuous citizenship and group identity. They can make them more infantile. This is latent in the ideal of tight community, in the ideal of the group which is subconsciously conceived as a natural and discrete substance or a peculiar plant that grows only in its native soil, and in the ideal of socialized self-realization which always implies gentle superintendence by the political power. They can make them much more idolatrous. This is latent in all four ideals because they all welcome closure and certainty and set narrow limits on the restlessness of consciousness. But if people become even more barbarous, infantile, and idolatrous than they—we—already are, then think how yet more virulent many of the worst tendencies of modern life become: war, systemic cruelty, religious zeal, bigotry, nationalism, xenophobia, and fascism. The priority of the good over the right is the priority of the wrong over the right.

I see in all these ideals nothing so much as an inadvertent collusion with everything in modern life that leads to the growth of the power of the state. In that growth even anti-individualist ideals would wither or grow cancerous. If we cannot even ask any theorist to consider that the Emersonian writers may have something to teach, and if we cannot even ask anti-rights theorists to reconsider the idea of human dignity lodged in the theory and practice of individual rights, we can at least ask the critics of individualism to think again about the dangers of statism and the way in which their ideals may contribute to it.

Statism must grow with the growth of belief in the prestige of political life, even if that belief is centered in participation in the act of legislative deliberation rather than in holding administrative office. The results of deliberation need to be carried out, and can be carried out, only administratively. Statism must grow with the belief in the tight community, because a tight community cannot be dissociated from a pervasive censorial authority needed to insure adherence and to inhibit deviance. Statism must grow with the growth of belief in the supremacy of group identity because the societywide group is the armed group possessed of fantasy projects of assertion and expression, of domination, of permanent enmity, of war and its waste. Statism must grow with the growth of belief in socialized self-realization because this sort of self-realization is almost indistinguishable from therapeutic and paternalist condescension to ordinary persons who are secretly thought by theorists to be no better than a plebs. Who but the state can ultimately administer, or at least supervise, therapeutic and paternalist disciplines to a whole society, even though these disciplines are decentralized? I think that rights-based individualism provides the best perspective from which to condemn statism, and also to detect in seemingly nonstatist or even overtly antistatist ideals a terrible statist latency. Yet not only does statism imperil human dignity as conceived in rights-based individualism, and altogether block the Emersonian conception of democratic individuality, it imperils everything minimally decent or tolerable.

One attractive aspect of democratic individuality is that it is not a continuous and societywide ideal in the usual sense. Not only may it be in any of its components an episodic achievement, it is also not striven for by state action, by the content of laws and social policies. It happens as it happens because of the impersonally educative force of political and legal procedures and processes, and because of the general spirit that emerges over time from an individual and governmental commitment to rights that mostly need only forbearance, restraint, and caution to exist.

I do not mean to be intransigent. I concede that the terrible features of modern life are not what they are because of recent anti-individualist idealisms. Rather, the anti-individualist theorists have been insufficiently attentive to the possibility that their studied anti-individualism lessens their ability to protest and resist these features, or to do so consistently. I also concede that it is plausible to hold that some terrible features of modern life seem to come from some type of individualism, whether economic individualism or another. We witness and experience such things as moronic selfishness; social neglect; varieties of alienation such as disquiet, rage, loneliness, all of which may come from the need or the opportunity to make things up (including an identity) as one goes along in an individualist culture; and anomie (that is, moral confusion amid unprecedented powers that often become new sources of fragility, and unprecedented choices that often become dilemmas or aporias). Anti-individualist ideals are meant to mitigate or end these troubles. But the potential cost is intolerably high. Nothing is worse than the horrors that do or would come from the unqualified prestige of participation in sovereign politics, the societywide bond of community, the solidarity of the armed group, and the project of socialized self-realization. They are horrors in themselves and are auxiliaries to the further horrors of statism. The remedies for the troubles must be found, at least in any democratic setting, within rights-based individualism and the aspiration to democratic individuality.

Despite all the troubles, and whatever their sources, we should perceive the evidences of democratic individuality, especially in the United States. Some were seen by the Emersonians and can still be seen by us; others we see a century and a half later. In them may be found help for the troubles—unless one thinks, as some do, that these evidences are themselves evidences of troubles. They are also good as such. Democratic individuality would be utopianism rather than an aspiration, unless the lives lived in the democratic culture of rights already showed evidences of individualist assertion or expression, individualist resistance in behalf of others, and individualist receptivity or responsiveness. It is a matter of our noticing. What can be noticed?

Concerning assertion or expression. There are the characteristic American explorations of nature, on the one hand, and the psyche, on the other. Of course European culture in general sponsors these explorations, but, as Tocqueville and D. H. Lawrence have said, there is a peculiar American intensity in dealing with the obduracy and splendor of nature and psyche that derives from a culture that is fundamentally not social in the Old World sense and that therefore drives many to explore the nonhuman other outside oneself and the nonsocial other inside oneself.[26] The human is not other, but nature and psyche are. Democratic individuality, as an actual though incomplete condition, expects the nonhuman or nonsocial to be strange and wrestles with it as an equal. Destructiveness and self-destructiveness may inhere in such extremism; but so does heroism. And if there is struggle, there is always the appetite for reconciliation. Other evidences of the assertive or expressive life include the stylistic innovation and creative social adaptability of ordinary persons; an easy ability to improvise temporary structures of governance when a new and ungoverned situation calls for them; and the growth of movements that try to democratize or make constitutional all human relations, with the engendering of claims for equal recognition of the *rights* of women, ethnic and racial minorities, homosexuals, handicapped people, prisoners, and so on, and not just for privileges or leniency. The group tendency aspires to the dissolution of the group, of ascribed categorical identity, not merely to the effacement of stigma. There is also principled miscegenation; there are many "melting-pot" phenomena.

Concerning resistance. Constant evidences of the suspicion of political, and other, authority permeate American manners and reflexes. There is widespread attentiveness to official lawlessness and impatience with official secrecy, withholding, and distortion of the truth. There are the great movements of protest and civil disobedience, either in behalf of rights denied others or in behalf of the integrity of the Constitution itself.

Concerning receptivity or responsiveness. There are numerous evidences of the ethic of the open road (to use Whitman's phrase), of openness to experience. Intermittently displayed is a readiness to convert tolerance into recognition; to admire and appreciate, especially that which may be overlooked or despised; to acknowledge that one is not the only real thing in the world, and that others are just as real to themselves. If an individual's knowledge can only go a little way into others, the sense of their equal reality can nevertheless be very deep. The effort to live outside oneself, to lend oneself to the acknowledgment of other persons, to creatures, and things, exists and is underwritten by the sense that one is multiple, various, full of contradictions, full of moods that "do not believe in each other."[27] The steadiness of such an effort may then crystallize in moments of wonder at the mere fact of the abundance of phenomena. American life shows evidences of such a poetical or philosophical relation to reality in its indefatigable capacity to detach a particular from the flow and accord it solicitude or celebrity or admiration and appreciation, if only for an instant.

It seems to me that the democratic individualist life of assertion or expression, resistance, and receptivity or responsiveness is more likely to avoid some of the most terrible possibilities of modern life and to exploit some of the good ones. This life is the best preparation for learning to endure both the shocks and pleasures of modernity—and of postmodernity, if there is such a condition. The more the aspiration to democratic individuality is realized, the better the preparation. It is, and can become even more, a life of pleasures and occasional ecstasies. But, let us admit, it is probably not a life of happiness, and the pains eventually outweigh the pleasures. Perhaps, anyway, happiness has always been a foolish and dishonest ideal, a guarantee of a theorist's bad faith and espousal of the wrong sort of aestheticism. Perhaps anti-individualist idealisms are not purged of an attachment to the standard of happiness. Perhaps the honor of the Emersonians consists in reminding us that a happy life can only be an all too human life, a herd life, a life of diminished inwardness, and therefore a life of diminished dignity.

Pluralism and Self-Defense

NANCY L. ROSENBLUM

Liberal political thought has evolved in reaction to the harsh realities of political arbitrariness and constraint; it has also been positively inspired by visions of enlightenment, autonomy, and self-realization. But political theory sometimes finds additional resources in our purely intuitive responses to political life and to the ideas that justify it. Among our most powerful intuitive responses are romantic aversions to everything cold and instrumental, impersonal and unlovely. Today, these aversions are widespread. We have come to expect them, especially in critics of liberalism.

Familiar Aversions

The relation between liberalism and romanticism is a family one, intimate and tense. When liberalism imposes its severe discipline of legalism, it excites a romantic reaction. Romanticism is the return of the repressed. For its part, romantic expressivism is only expansive and provocative where there is resistance of a particular kind. It erupts in opposition to prosaic utilitarianism; its nemesis is generality and regularity, security of expectation. It is doubtful whether romanticism can survive in any truly repressive medium or produce a constructive politics of its own. Liberalism excites romantic aversions and then asks us to disavow them, leaving other political theories to exploit these discontents.

Mutual repulsion is not the whole story, though. I have argued that liberalism can enlist romantic inclinations, if only it would attend to them.[1] In generating a consensus about essential political principles and institutions, liberalism can win the assent not only of irreconcilable interests and moral opinions but also of conflicting tastes and dispositions, including romantic ones. It can offer romantic sensibilities who feel that individuality and spontaneity have no place in conventional liberal thought reasons to temper their most extravagant claims, and to make their peace. There are good reasons to attend to these claims, not least the fact that romanticism's familiar tendencies—individualist, aesthetic, and affective—can provide motivation and fresh justifications for supporting liberal institutions in practice.

Nothing is more common among North American political theorists today than an edgy, impatient attitude toward liberalism that reflects this dynamic of romantic aversion and reconciliation. In this chapter I want to draw attention to the romantic impulses at work in recent communitarian and individualist thought. Contemporary communitarianism, precisely because of its romantic sources, is more tentative and less wholehearted in its antiliberalism than is often believed. It constitutes a criticism from within. Moreover, both communitarian and individualist responses to liberalism suffer the same, peculiar vulnerability: inclined to emphasize and exploit romantic aversion, they overlook the element of liberalism that remains attractive, even compelling, for romantic sensibilities. They miss the affinity between romanticism and liberal pluralism. In diagnosing liberalism's deficiencies and in formulating their prescriptions, political theorists consistently ignore pluralism. They do not admit the messy reality of pluralism—of shifting involvements among diverse spheres—into their thinking about political freedom or into their theories of the self.

The tendency of communitarians and individualists to disregard pluralism is remarkable since two current themes in political thought—methodological and moral contextualism, and propositions about the "situated" or "constituted" self—could reasonably be expected to draw attention to it as an inescapable reality. After all, the context of moral and political practices is, on any description, pluralist; on any account of personal development, the self is formed from an array of relations in diverse spheres. Ignoring pluralism creates a weakness at the center of communitarian thought in particular, since it promises to provide the strong dose of sociological realism that liberal theory, with its fondness for abstract and universal principles, allegedly lacks. But the crucial vulnerability is that by discounting pluralism it is impossible for individualists and communitarians to fulfill an essential part of their purpose—to speak constructively to romantic discontents. For the romantic self finds its chief self-defense in shifting involvements among plural spheres.

Is it a frivolous distraction, attending to romantic aversions to liberalism? It has been said that these aversions are the luxury of the politically privileged and that political theorists in the grip of romantic longing carelessly disregard the elementary lessons of liberalism's troubled history. Communitarians in particular are preoccupied with what they see as liberalism's intolerable coldness and impersonality. Because of this they have been charged with flirting heedlessly with political danger: the politics that attract them, a politics of solidarity, of belonging to a community that appears incomparably lovely to its members, are threats to personal liberty. But in North America, where both communitarian and individualist theories flourish today, it is hard to see the peril, which is why my objections to contemporary communitarianism and my milder differences with its individualist counterpart are not grimly cautionary. Neither a radical reorientation of commitment to public life, with its attendant threats to personal liberty, nor antipolitical privatization appear imminent. Nor does fascism, or religious civil war, or the awful anarchism of legalism in disarray, which *should* cause political theorists to retrench and focus on essentials: institutional securities against official power and the rule of law.

Romantic aversion, in contrast, is not remote, certainly not for the generation of theorists whose formative political experiences occurred in North America in the 1960s and 70s. It is perfectly appropriate to want to recast political theory to meet the changing political reality of some (admittedly few) societies as well as the changing needs (including psychological needs) of successive generations. My argument with communitarian and individualist critics of liberalism is that they do not understand present needs well enough or recognize the resources liberalism can bring to them.

There should be nothing for orthodox liberals to object to in attempts to reconstruct liberal theory in a fashion sympathetic to romantic sensibilities. Liberalism has always aimed at inclusiveness and rested on eclectic foundations. The urgent problem has never been choosing among justifications for limited government: fear, or natural rights, or the promise of self-realization. The challenge has been to motivate people to pay attention to the political institutions and social conditions without which none of these are conceivable. We do not have to adopt romantic justifications for liberalism to acknowledge characteristic romantic aversions and affinities as potential resources in support of one essential, pluralism, in particular, defined by diversity, social openness, and the experience of shifting involvements among separate public and private spheres.

The Conventional Accommodation of Liberalism and Romanticism: Negative Liberty

Liberalism's dread of arbitrariness, its commitment to impersonal government and the impartial rule of law, make self-expression and arrant emotionalism anathema in public life. (That is the most obvious reason for romantic antipathy to the public ethos of liberalism.) But in limiting the force and range of public power, liberalism secures a free sphere of private life where romantic impulses and expressions of personality reemerge. Historically, attempts to accommodate romanticism and liberalism have centered on negative liberty and the separation of public and private spheres.

The most sanguine accounts see legalistic public life and expressive private life as mutual insurance. On this view, romantic inclinations and aversions are protected by the right to privacy, by being left alone. For its part, romanticism is suspicious of public power, especially of the demands of government presuming to inspire us or call up strong feelings—the most intolerable intrusion is the official mobilization of emotions. In this way, romantic resistance is a force for preserving the boundary between spheres. At the same time, retirement from public life to cultivate one's own emotional and aesthetic garden is said to provide a vital refreshment from the rigorous discipline of tolerance and from utilitarian calculations. It restores us so that we can return again to the good but prosaic business of maximizing public happiness. This picture of a mutually advantageous balance between public and private life (J. S. Mill's picture) draws romanticism into the framework of classical liberal thought as both beneficiary and guarantor of negative liberty and the boundary between spheres. Richard Rorty's reaffirmation of this division of labor and spheres is the most recent: the intellectual's need for the ineffable and sublime, a need to go beyond limits, is met on his own time and in private life within the limits set by Mill's *On Liberty*. Its complement, for Rorty, is pragmatic action to harmonize social purposes, carried on in the public arenas of liberal democracy.[2]

Negative liberty has provided the framework for reconciling liberalism and romanticism, even apart from hopeful visions of harmonious spheres and idealistic views of what goes on within their respective boundaries. For Isaiah Berlin, privacy is "sacrosanct," the private sphere "inviolable."[3] Berlin's language is heightened, but his reasons are depressed. Left alone, we are not obliged to attain the moral status of autonomy in matters of ethics or faith, or to realize our potential for enlightenment. Nor does liberty set us the romantic task of authenticity, or imaginative creativity, or cultivating intense feelings within an intimate circle of friends. Private liberty can mean unimpeded avowal of religious and moral conscience or unimpeded expressivism, but for Berlin it does not have to be an "opportunity concept," which makes being free a matter of what we can do.[4] It can mean freedom not to avow, or do, anything. Berlin's negative liberty has little appeal for rational, autonomous Lockean individuals or for their assertive romantic counterparts. It speaks most forcefully to fearful, exquisitely self-conscious selves who feel fatally diminished by external demands, especially coercive official ones.

Some accounts of the accommodation between liberalism and romanticism judge this division of labor and spheres compromising to liberalism and inherently unstable. Shrill and anxious liberals warn that romanticism is so seductive it fatally undermines the public discipline of legalism, or capitalism, altogether. We are liable to spin off and away into mysticism, eroticism, or the wilds of artistic imagination. Romanticized private life leads to radical detachment, on this view, to the pose of unhappiness and antipolitical retreat.[5] In fact, liberty does create enclaves for withdrawal and for even the darkest sorts of expression in private life. But the plain fact is that in this century the worst assaults on legalism and economic liberty have been the result of organized violence and not spontaneity, of grimly unromantic longings, not romantic ones.

For many theorists today, the most striking limitation of the conventional accommodation is not that it is unstable or subversive but that it is unsatisfyingly dry and pragmatic. Romanticism appears as just one life-style among others; it is tolerated, like "spilt religion," but carefully contained. Political theorists attuned to romantic inclinations judge this arrangement uninspired. Like Charles Taylor, they disparage "a 'Romantik' of private life, which is meant to fit into a smoothly running consumer society."[6] Individuality and expressivism are what every feature of political arrangements should be for—public, private, and the vast realm of the social as well.

Contemporary communitarians and individualists who share romantic discontents are less interested in defining the public-private divide than in giving each an infusion of affect and aesthetic delight. Typically, communitarians focus on renewed public life where people are gripped by feelings of commitment and relate to one another as friends rather than adversaries. Still, the implication is that every dimension of existence (even the self itself) should be transformed. Communitarians are slow to ask where powerful emotional commitments should be constrained in the interest of fairness and where they can be safely expressed, but this is more likely the result of disinterest in the institutional mechanisms of limited government than wholesale opposition to them. Overtly hostile to some elements of liberalism, neither communitarians nor individualists have actually proposed erasing the boundary between public and private life. They appear to take its existence for granted.

This distinguishes communitarian theorists from radical critics of negative liberty and separate spheres. Michel Foucault aggressively denies that public authority is a unique source of surveillance and control. The technology of subjection is everywhere in modern states, and his devaluation of formal limits on officials follows directly from the curious belief that institutional differences are illusory.[7] Indeed, the most subtle disciplinary contrivance is the idea of subjectivity. What we take to be the self is really an effect of power. So is the dream of freedom and self-determination in private life. They are all figments of "governmentality." The task of social theory, for Foucault, is to gain "strategic knowledge" of the forces of normalization (presumably with a view to anarchic insurrection). In contrast, neither communitarians nor individualists see liberal democracy as just another case of overweening power. Nor do they aim at aloofness and disengagement. The communitarian ambition for the reformation of both political theory and political life is deeper immersion and more intense connection, not liberation.

Recent Expressions of Romantic Aversion

Viewing contemporary communitarian and individualist theory as expressions of romantic aversion to liberalism is only one of several approaches.[8] It is useful because it underscores a powerful motivating force behind much contemporary theory and reminds us that common impulses and a common diagnosis can have widely divergent implications for political action and thought. Moreover, when communitarianism is approached from the perspective of its romantic roots, we see that both at the level of ontology and of political prescription its opposition to liberalism is compromised. Finally, it draws attention to the strange tendency of both communitarians and individualists to float high above the motley surface of pluralist society, thus missing the very element of liberalism that makes romantic reconciliation possible.

In the case of individualist theory there are distinguished antecedents for overcoming aversion to the banality of liberalism and its ethos of commercialism and cold impersonality. Reconciliation involves recasting liberal democracy dramatically, so that its proper, legalistic face recedes and a picture of democracy as an invitation to exhibitionism and striving emerges. Democracy becomes an invitation, in Thoreau's words, to "give a strong dose of myself." Conventional institutions such as electoral politics, markets, and the division of labor are enchanted. They appear as sublime spectacles of variety and self-display, as they did to Walt Whitman. The familiar is made new by "freshness of sensation, moments of illumination."[9]

Today this business of redescribing liberal democracy in radically individualist terms has been taken up by George Kateb. No one is more sensitive to the drive for self-assertion and self-reliance, the way the individualist feels incomparable and identifies expressiveness with the demonstration of some exemplary personal difference. One consequence is a reflexive opposition to authority and to every form of docility and invisibility. Kateb prefers to call this resistance democratic rather than liberal (in part to indicate that, in contrast to its privileged counterparts in European culture, American individualism is inclusive, and in larger part to attach to democracy an idealism about individuality that goes beyond the individualism of rights). Still, he shows clearly that individuality is consistent with and could not exist without the institutionalized limits on government associated with liberalism, chief among them "a system of rights housed in democratic political institutions."[10] In a similar vein, William Connolly envisions a strain of democracy that makes room for turbulence, recalcitrance, and exhibition of "otherness." He would "infuse 'instrumentalities' with space for the open self," creating an order "that can afford to let some forms of conduct be."[11] This is the best we can do, he thinks, once we recognize that every social form realizes some things in the self by subordinating others. Like Kateb, Connolly wants to see a shift from the democratic definition of ends to an ironic stance toward all communal ends. His attempt in *Politics and Ambiguity* is to underscore the ingredients of democratic practice that resist commonality. But unlike Kateb, he is unaccountably reluctant to appeal directly to historic liberal institutions, personal rights among them, to insure "slack."

Kateb does not stop with this portrait of liberal democracy as a scene of self-expression and antiauthoritarian self-defense. He is confident that democratic individualists are responsive to others, benignly accepting, ultimately generous and just—at least in the new stage of character he envisions as a possibility. I am less confident. Perhaps, as Kateb believes, individualists do not suffer the ordinary egoism of material self-interest. Clearly, though, they have their own mode of self-absorption and irresponsibility. Misanthropy on the part of radical individualists is not a lapse; it is, as Kateb acknowledges, the secret worm that gnaws at the Emersonians. It comes with the sense of being incomparable. "Casting one's whole influence" has an elitist ethos, a masculine and combative ethos, embodied not only in the alien Stirner but also close to home in the unlovable Thoreau—which is why I prefer to call this variation of individualism "heroic."

The individualist picture of connection to others, when one exists, is not of justice or principled mutual respect. It is a vision of an unplanned complementarity of excellences. Only an exotic picture of infinite difference, successive scenes of spontaneous interaction, is attractive; Walt Whitman's America shares more with the aesthetic sublime than with any institutional arrangement. Kateb gives sound reasons why individualists ought to be committed to liberal democracy and why democratic structures produce individualists in the first place. But he also recognizes that, from the individualist's perspective, institutions often lose their solidity. They dissolve into the charm of contrasts, into Whitman's "independent separatism." The individualist's reconciliation to liberal democracy is always tenuous because it depends on a state of heightened receptivity and aesthetic appreciation that is fleeting and cannot be maintained. When individualists are forced to grapple with principles and involve themselves in everyday practices, the glow of infinite variety disappears. Not surprisingly, heroic individualism rarely escapes its anarchic, isolationist logic.

Kateb is right, though, that the logic of self-assertion and resistance makes the enemies of liberal democracy the individualist's enemies, and that today these seem to include communitarians. Yet romantic longing is at work in contemporary communitarian thought, too. When communitarians invoke the ideal of a self capable of affect, empathy, and depth over against a person capable of bearing rights and pursuing advantages, or when they promote a contextualist methodology that attends to what is unique and expressive in our public culture over against what is universally justifiable, their work is more resonant of romanticism than of Aristotle or any identifiable tradition of democratic thought.

What is less clear is the consequence this has for liberalism. We know what communitarians find loathsome: preoccupation with rights, most of all, and a dreary, adversarial system of justice; also, rampant commercialism and arid utilitarianism. Their aversions are plain. But they are disinclined to propose alternatives. Community is more often an invocation than a reference to specific political forms. It is not just that the parameters of community are vague, its character at the most general level is undefined.

Does community signify corporate pluralism, where ethnic, religious, or cultural groups have formal political standing and territorial claims? That is the most likely referent, given communitarians' disgruntlement with liberal cosmopolitanism and their interest in the kind of collective identity that cannot be taken up and shed like membership in a voluntary association. It is the meaning of community that comes first to mind in light of the worldwide, postimperial experience of retribalization; and it has been the most common source of political convulsion, official violence, and deliberate cruelty of groups to one another in the second half of this century, too. "With all the beauty goes all the blood."[12] In the United States in the 1960s some blacks provided a taste of militant cultural assertion and its separatist tendencies. In fact, corporate pluralism is probably not what contemporary communitarians prefer. When they aggregate examples of parochial separatism—tribes, Puritan communities, Medieval Jewish ghettos—their intention seems to be to show that a sharply bounded social identity is possible, not to prescribe one. They appeal to this sort of communal self-definition to illustrate moral and psychological propositions about "belonging," not political ones.

Even so, using parochial group identity—whether to illustrate a preferred moral psychology or to indicate that the fundamental starting point of social analysis is not individualism (certainly not "atomistic individualism")—is troubling. Even if they do not advocate some version of corporate pluralism—even if they are determinedly postliberal—approving references to collective identity suggests that communitarians have chosen to ignore the fact that "belonging" is not always positive and that the desire of members to remain entwined or to escape (through assimilation or some other means) depends in part on the group's particular political, social, and economic circumstances.

We know too much about negative identity and its effects on self-esteem, its outcome in shame and submission or in self-destructive violence, to find these appeals to belonging in the abstract attractive.

When it comes to statements of political preference, most communitarians seem to have in mind a political order as inclusive as present-day liberal democracy. Here too the parameters are unclear: whether community is actual or promised (or "latent"); whether it is based on the stern stuff of civic virtue or on "the social face of love."[13] Among proponents of republicanism, it is unclear whether participatory community refers to neighborhoods and local control or extends to the state as a whole, or some unspecified division of powers between them. In light of the unstemmed profusion of examples of community that have made their appearance in recent political thought, it is ironic that one is missing altogether: the short-lived experimental community that sprouts up regularly in American culture in response to feelings of personal disconnection and whose whole purpose is to consciously embody some notion of collective identity based on a common good.

Political theory is very often stronger at criticism than at suggestions for reform, so what is more surprising is that communitarians are typically shy about indicating just what liberal institutions, if any, they would dispense with or curtail.[14] They exhibit their aversions, impatiently attack, and then pull back. It is almost impossible to get at the nature and limits of communitarian antiliberalism from what is said directly. A better approach is indirect, by looking at communitarians' characteristic methods of argument and at the arguments they do *not* employ. From this it emerges that their antiliberalism is ambivalent, as it must be since romantic aversions to liberalism simply do not translate into any of the conventional political alternatives.

Until recently, critics of atomistic individualism and legal formalism typically appealed to the idea of alienation. An essential part of the Marxian critical apparatus, alienation is not the exclusive property of the left; it is a moral reproach adopted by nostalgic conservatives as well. But alienation is absent from the communitarian vocabulary precisely because it means falling off from some original or possible unity. Communitarians do not propose a philosophy of essential unity—and not because they are incapable of providing one. They seem to accept that being strangers does not necessarily signify estrangement. Nor do they consider any of the available psychological theories that gives identification with some greater whole central place—as security against primitive anxiety, say—again, not because they are unfamiliar with psychoanalytic explanations of the drive to group identity. Alienation is a useful concept for political theorists who are comfortable, as contemporary communitarians are not, with the idea of original or essential unity and with some holistic alternative to liberalism stronger than the current, modest notion of "shared values."

The alternative approach many communitarian theorists employ is to discover (or articulate) a latent tradition of shared meanings beneath the surface fragmentation of liberalism. It is hard to tell what tradition means here, besides the obvious fact that every language or system of cultural meanings has developed over time; they are not things we personally invent or apply to conditions that are wholly new.[15] And despite the fact that communitarians juxtapose concrete traditions to universalist liberal principles, nothing in the idea of a tradition of shared meanings or values is logically antiliberal. The "assumed givens" of moral and political life that suffuse our political culture and that are found "inside us" could plausibly include norms of toleration, or habitual respect for rights and commitment to the justifications for them.

Uncovering hidden or forgotten elements of the past is a classic device for delegitimating what exists, but communitarians shy away from the full critical import of the thought that there is a disjuncture between latent and surface understanding. As it is used today the implications of discovery are benign. Communitarians discuss discovering a "latent" tradition of shared meanings in such a way as to suggest that nothing uncovered is likely to be incompatible with the public values of liberalism. The whole approach is reassuring. Insofar as what is latent is never altogether alien to us, and insofar as we can painlessly reclaim what we have forgotten or repressed, then bringing a latent tradition to light should not be wildly disruptive or weirdly dissonant with the conscious, liberal aspects of public culture and identity. Communitarian discoverers of latent shared meaning do not seem to worry (or to hope, as Foucault might) that repression serves a crucial need and that what is unconscious is repressed because it is dark, dirty, or dangerous.

The most interesting thing about the methodology of discovering latent shared meanings has not been any substantive find made so far, but the political import of the method itself. Its implicit politics emerge if we see discovery in contrast to radical utopian design on the one hand and to traditionalism on the other. Antiutopian, discovery avoids the deliberate invention of new values. Antitraditional, discovery does not look for prejudice, favor dumb habit, or think that age confers legitimacy. These contrasts are significant because radical utopianism and traditionalism are important sources of anti-liberalism and of justifications for censorial authority. Communitarians are careful not to invoke either, and they separate themselves in this way from historic antiliberalism of the left and right.

The injuries communitarians do inflict openly on liberalism are passive: withholding the title public morality form the discipline of impartiality and the title virtue from personal habits of being law-abiding and respectful toward others; ignoring the origin of rights (termed "instrumental") in some form of idealism about enlighten-ment or independence or in some vision of natural harmony. But withholding and ignoring are mild abuses; they hardly figure in the battery of attacks launched by unambivalent antiliberals in the past.

Still, George Kateb worries that the logical consequence of com-munitarian arguments is to give prestige to political life, thereby encouraging statist threats to individualism. Taken by itself, the most common line of argument does appear to point in that direction. Starting from the idea of the desirability of a "thick" self, the next step is to say that "thick" selves are situated in or constituted by their moral and cultural environments; then, in a final move, communi-tarians claim that "thickness" (identity, really) is inseparable from belonging to a community—meaning not simply a tradition of shared meanings but a political community where these elements of identity are consciously shared and enforced. Even if these steps added up to a compelling argument (and they do not, the largest unsubstantiated leap being from step two to three; there is no reason why a thick self could not develop in a pluralist medium), analysis of the logical con-sequences of this line of thought misses the psychological disparity between contemporary communitarianism and conventional propo-nents of statism. Again, it misses communitarianism's romantic roots.

For the communitarian purpose in opposing community to atom-istic individualism is not the traditional one of transcending the self through identification with a group or nation. On the contrary, the object is to recover strong expressive selves, to make "thin" selves "thick." The political arguments we expect to find in theories of community—such as that "belonging" serves political cohesion or that cohesion has some independent value—are missing, which is why contemporary communitarians have so little to say to (or to take from) either socialists or communal anarchists for whom community is a substantive ideal. This is not surprising. The principal communitarian charges, certainly the most frequent ones, are romantic. The argument is not that liberalism is so lacking in a public ethos that it is unviable, unable to produce collective action where necessary. The argument is not even that liberalism is unjust. Ethical indignance is eclipsed by revulsion at the fact that liberalism is impersonal and emotionally barren, or unlovely, or insufficiently "gripping." Liberalism produces "thin" selves, pathetic narcissists without purpose or center. In fact, the much-discussed moral capacity to identify with others in a common enterprise is only part of what the self is said to lack, and it is not communitarians' sole concern. A much more expansive notion of selfhood is at stake. It includes the capacity for articulating other purposes besides communal ones and, perhaps most important, the capacity for forming intense personal attachments, friendship and love, where men and women are transparent to one another.[16] Community is designed to repair decentered, disempowered, narcissistic selves diagnosed as incapable of sustaining either a public or private life.[17]

Preoccupation with the self has resulted in a careless tendency among communitarian theorists to swing between two conflicting formulations of formative connections. One pictures the self embedded in community, the other community "penetrating" the self. The two are logically distinct. Their psychological implications are dramatically different. And embeddedness has cozy political implications, while the idea of a self constituted by communal forces can point, as it does for Foucault, to severe social conditioning and control that is all the more efficient if it operates through self-discipline. In treating these formulations as if they were interchangeable, political theorists exhibit a stunning disregard for the actual dynamics of self-formation. "Embeddedness" is a static condition which, if it points to process at all, suggests older theories of socialization; the idea of the constituted self opens out to a more sophisticated developmental view—to processes of internalization, for example, of which identification is just one. Apparently these differences pale beside the constructive resonance they have in common. Both the embedded and the constituted self evoke formative attachments, which is enough to make them equally useful to theorists whose concern is the reparation of weak, empty, detached, and unexpressive selves. In either case, community is therapy.

The trouble is not that a therapeutic politics is necessarily manipulative or condescending. (It is not.) The trouble is, this therapy is misconceived. Communitarians are motivated by romantic longings and invoke them at every step, but they misapprehend their nature and force. The romantic self is inseparable from complexity and fluidity; the will to preserve a sense of infinite possibility is its essence. Communitarian prescriptions, whether embeddedness in community or penetration by community, are regressive. At best they speak to a single aspect of romantic longing; they are simplistic. And this absence of psychological realism is inseparable from the tendency to float above the messy reality of pluralism and to overlook its centrality to self-development. For the formation and preservation of identity through communal membership is not the only alternative to disassociation and the weak self.

When it comes to neglecting pluralism, communitarians and heroic individualists converge: individualists by imagining an imperial self that *is* a whole world, and communitarians by imagining they can discover a unified political world within the firmly constituted self. Pluralism gives the lie to both. It brings a measure of sociological realism to bear against both. And it points to a surer path home from romantic aversion. For if liberalism provokes romantic reaction, it also has a powerful claim on romantic sensibilities. Pluralism is the heart of liberalism, and the antidote to common aversions.

Pluralism and the Psychology of Self-Defense

Historically pluralism—the existence of diverse centers of social influence and political power—has always been at the heart of liberalism. It is the political condition for limiting government and insuring personal freedom, and the occasion for doing so. Madison saw pluralism as the best protection against accumulated power. Pluralism means the dispersion of power. It necessitates bargaining and negotiating and inhibits the formation of permanent political majorities. By multiplying the kinds and degrees of social influence and control, it mitigates some of the humiliating and corrupting effects of inequality. The political advantages of pluralist checks on power are fully acknowledged in liberal thought—at least they are when theorists have absolutism in mind or totalitarian leveling.

For the past two decades or so, this understanding has been submerged beneath a mountain of normative and analytical claims for pluralist politics as a way of making public policy. Political scientists dispute whether countervailing political forces are self-regulating, whether officials are "captured" by special interests, whether information is increased through pluralist bargaining or whether political outcomes are irrational, whether "potential groups" really can organize, and so on. By now pluralism has been discredited as an adequate description of contemporary politics and as a sufficient guarantee of fair political outcomes. Still, in its original meaning it continues to provide a good measure of distortions in the distribution of power, and it remains the chief deterrent against its accumulation.[18]

Other perspectives that recognize pluralism as the heart of liberalism have come to the fore meanwhile, looking beyond social structures to the actual experience of diversity. The experience of pluralism figures prominently in discussions of moral agency, since, in the absence of a genuinely open pluralist society, autonomy and choice are empty. And the experience of pluralism is essential to what is most positive in the romantic perception of liberalism. It appears as the condition for preserving the sense of individuality, spontaneity, and infinite possibility. The personal use of diversity requires of course that pluralism be liberal. What is essential is not only the fact of social differentiation but also making the experience of diversity real by enabling people to enter and exit associations and spheres. This, in turn, requires open groups which are denied guaranteed populations, with the result that a wide range of rights and claims are individual and not attached to collective identity. Liberal pluralism has two aspects, then: social structure and personal movement, the dispersion of power and "shifting involvements," to borrow Albert Hirschmann's dynamic phrase.[19]

For some, any picture of the personal use of shifting involvements brings to mind the bright, euphoric experimentation of the 1960s, with its promise of liberation and self-realization. It evokes a positive romanticism—Humboldt's cultivation of "beautiful souls," Schiller's play, or the quest for authenticity or erotic excitement. But a generation emerged from the period of the 1960s chastened. Its hopes for individuality and spontaneity are less perfectionist and fantastic than soberly self-protective. It sees pluralism and shifting involvements less as a maximal facilitating condition than as a necessity for self-defense. From a chastened romantic perspective, pluralism is self-protection. It is protection against dreaded identification with one role and confinement to one place, against tedium, satiation, definition, and ennui. The exploitation of pluralism is motivated by distress: by the suffering of selves that are too much constituted by attachments or by the paralysis and self-loathing associated with suffocating closeness and exhaustion of possibility.

Dread of finitude and definition is a common enough condition, some say characteristic pathology, of contemporary American culture. It is neither exotic nor rare. It is not confined to the confined. Nor is it the exclusive property of adolescence. Romantic longings persist throughout life. Psychologists now describe middle age as a life stage with its own dramas of hope, crises of identity, and attempted transformations. Francis Fitzgerald has described retirement communities as the inventions of people exploring old age as if it were a new frontier.[20] And dread of definition—along with its accompaniment, fear of a lack of distinctiveness—may be especially acute for selves that feel weak, whose hope from shifting involvements among plural spheres is less to fulfill potential than to ward off one-sidedness and preserve some sense of potentiality. Exuberant romanticism, the stuff of Werther, Adolfe, or Julien Sorel, is always unsatisfied because no activity, relationship, or feeling corresponds to the sweet dream of a limitless self with infinitely expansive powers. Not even the experience of pluralism can ward off its inevitable frustration. In contrast, defensive romanticism is threatened by identifying actions and associations because they illuminate a weak, uncertain self. This is the dark side of the romantic sensibility, which recognizes in pluralism insurance against painful finitude or one-sidedness.

"Embeddedness" and "belonging" have their origin, and doubtless their appeal, as attempts to respond sympathetically to this psychology of uncertainty, limitation, and longing. But community is not the appropriate response. Where it exists at all, the hunger for communally structured life is felt only by some sensibilities, and by them only sometimes; and even then desire may not attach to historically shaped political communities. It is the experience of pluralism and not the communitarian grip of civic culture (nor the heroic individualist's ephemeral aesthetic state) that effectively limits vulnerability, so that personal failure and humiliation in one arena are more apt to be contained there. The most powerful romantic self-defense is shifting involvements among pluralist spheres.

In his account of shifting involvements, Hirschmann concentrated on a single pendular movement between the pole of altruistic political involvement and the pole of private economic life. He pointed to painful satiation as the motive that explains our inability to sustain political fervor (whether revolutionary mobilization or participation in some active "issue public"), so that we return our attention from public to private concerns. We know that the experience of pluralism involves a far greater diversity of spheres, and that shifting involvements reflects a greater range of motivation than Hirschmann described. We shift involvements, moving from home to work (if we have employment outside the home), and in response to the pragmatic imperatives of interest and opinion. To this extent shifting involvements is in part a structually imposed necessity wherever there is social differentiation. But we also shift involvements in response to complicated, often unconscious personal inclinations to identify with or escape from one or another kind of authority or empathy, solidarity or solitude.[21]

The everyday experience of shifting involvements as self-defense is familiar. Formal contractual dealings with others is relief from overheated personal relations (as everyone knows who has gratefully returned to business as usual after a family seder.) Excited membership in a voluntary association is relief from the stern calculations required by managing our budgets, or our careers. The cost, when shifting involvements is impossible, is also familiar: for example, to women conscripted into the position of caretaker by a culture that makes them exclusively responsible for children. The inhibitions on their lives are unremitting. Total absorption in a single role eclipses any individual purpose. The situation of many women reinforces the perception of pluralism as our defense not only against public authority but also against all the private despotisms that make personal expansiveness unthinkable.

The best entree to the two faces of liberal pluralism—diverse spheres and the personal dynamics of shifting involvements—probably is via the literature of escape. Fictional or autobiographical, the story is the same: emergence from some group tradition in which the subject does not feel at home, despite insistent ascriptions of "belonging" by other members of the group and by outsiders. The story may be one of successful assimilation, but just as often the narrative's message is the limits of social mobility or disappointment with the dominant culture; the subtheme is loss of innocence or identity, confirming communitarian diagnoses of atomism and anomie. A recent account tells the story from a different angle. Richard Rodriguez's *Hunger of Memory* does not subscribe to the dichotomy of belonging versus independence-isolation, nor does it give an accounting of gains and losses. Instead, it describes the inevitableness of complexity and its consequences for one personality. The autobiography is an extended appreciation of the complementarity between personal longing and shifting involvements among separate spheres.

Rodriguez is educated out of his California, Spanish-speaking family into the public world of academic culture. His story of learning the English language and losing fluency in Spanish in part is a metaphor for maturation in general and for the move away from intimacy at home. But Rodriguez is not nostalgic. This story should not be sentimentalized. Rodriguez's personal history of warm and intimate family voices is not rare, but neither is brutality at home or perpetual, mutual misunderstanding. Cold-eyed, Rodriguez describes his experience of religious community. He finds certain changes in the Catholic liturgy regrettable, like folk singing and altars draped in appliquéd banners with the slogan, "God is Love." But his attitude toward changes in the English mass is more complicated. On the shift from the priest's "Credo" to the congregation's "we believe," he writes: "By translating credo into the English first person plural . . . the Church no longer reminds the listener that he is alone. 'We believe,' the congregation is encouraged to say, celebrating community—but only that fact . . . This assurance is necessary because, in a sense, it is no longer true." Catholics no longer live in a Catholic world, and Rodriguez warns against attempts to recover it by confining onself to some religious enclave. Even worse is the pretense that public life can be made intimate in compensation. He warns sharply against the seductions of political communities that use "family words" like friends, comrades, or brothers.[22]

For Rodriguez the result is not alienation. He makes other attachments, real and ideal. They are partial and limited, and some of them can be described as self-created—all of which communitarians resist. But falling off from original unity, whether family or some more inclusive collective identity, does not mean atomism or total disconnection. Rodriguez captures what it feels like to live out Georg Simmel's thought that devoting "only the substantively relevant parts of their personalities" to bonds with some whole is differentiation, not detachment. Simmel insists on the necessary connection between the experience of social differentiation and individuality: "it is precisely through the *alternation* of sensations, thoughts, and activities that personality documents itself." For Simmel, the very definition of individuality is "specificity of needs whose correlate is availability of the largest possible circle of possible selections."[23] As if to echo this thought, Rodriguez calls his education "the achievement of desire." He does not mean the satisfaction of desire but "the ability to shape into desire what would otherwise have remained indefinite meaningless longing."[24] *Hunger of Memory* traces the author's sober reconciliation to shifting involvements among plural spheres.

Nothing in this acknowledgment of the personal significance of pluralism suggests a resolution of political issues such as bilingualism, nor does it suggest that shifting involvements eliminates the uneasiness of marginality. What it offers is a psychologically sophisticated view of one common experience of liberal pluralism. External variety is often characterized as fragmentation, its reflection in identity as dissonance. But from the romantic perspective, pluralism has a unique coherence: it mirrors the familiar sense of a luxuriously complex self that resists finitude and definition.[25] Certainly, Rodriguez's account recommends the substitution of a plurality of concrete relations and spheres for "community" in Taylor's assertion that community is constitutive of the individual. It works against the usefulness of choosing between atomistic-holistic models for structuring possibilities for the self or society. If ontologic models of the self go a long way toward defining choices, as Taylor suggests, that is all the more reason to be dissatisfied with dichotomies that do not correspond well either to experience or to sophisticated philosophical psychology.[26]

Theorists of the self reject existential views of pure self-creation and Kantian attributions of autonomy, proposing instead that the self is embedded or constituted, intersubjective, or, in hostile versions, that the self is an effect of power. If political theorists are determined to take some view of the self as the ultimate starting point for social explanation, and even more if they are determined to translate some view of the self into judgments about political arrangements (as both communitarians and individualists plainly are) they need to take a strong dose of social and psychological realism.[27] At least they do if, like communitarians, they characterize themselves as contextualists concerned to represent us realistically to ourselves. The romantic sensibility, especially seen defending itself by means of the experience of pluralism, provides a corrective. Together, romanticism and pluralism point beyond the unexceptional observation that "the self is embedded in a social context" to the more complicated dynamics of self-fashioning and self-expression within an open multiplicity of contexts.

Only an aesthetic vision, a novel most likely, could bring us close to every contingency of personal experience, especially formative ones. Political theorists are not psychoanalysts, either, and the exhaustive, idiosyncratic details of relations and responses are not available to them. Even so, this is the direction political theory must take if it is to say anything very interesting about the vicissitudes of the self. And even if political theorists go back to bracketing the self and stick to more conventional moral and political assessments of liberalism, romantic aversions and affinities will still be of interest. The reasons are clear. The distinctive romantic dread of definition and attraction to diversity brings pluralism to mind at a time when political theorists are inclined to pay it less attention than ever before. It gives pluralism fresh justification as a special kind of self-defense. And it enlists powerful inclinations in its support.

The Permanent Structure of
Antiliberal Thought

STEPHEN HOLMES

Of all the strands of European social theory, few have proven so enticing and, above all, so enduring as antiliberalism. The political arm of the Counter-Enlightenment, as it might be called, has enjoyed a long and, by most standards, immensely successful career. It drew inspiration—and borrowed indignation—from Rousseau; the list of its nineteenth-century adherents, from Joseph de Maistre to Friedrich Nietzsche, could not have been more illustrious; on the Continent, during the 1920s and 1930s, it achieved something close to cultural dominance; and it continues to spawn articulate and influential proponents even today.

This unbroken continuity deserves stressing because contemporary antiliberals, such as Alasdair MacIntyre, Roberto Unger, and Michael Sandel, frequently neglect it.[1] They typically furnish a stylized, even sanitized, genealogy for their central ideas. MacIntyre, for instance, gladly invokes Aristotle. But he makes no mention of the bitter attacks on liberal theory and institutions that have loomed so large in nineteenth- and twentieth-century political thought. This omission is no accident. For one thing, antiliberals like to present themselves as iconoclasts. For another, every antiliberal argument influential today was vigorously advanced in the writings of European fascists. Brilliant but retrospectively discredited theorists, such as Giovanni Gentile and Carl Schmitt, violently assailed the liberal tradition.[2] They excoriated liberalism for its atomistic individualism,[3] its myth of the presocial individual, its scanting of the organic, its indifference to community, its denial that man belongs to a larger whole, its belief in the primacy of rights, its flight from "the political," its uncritical embrace of economic categories, its moral skepticism (or even nihilism), its decision to give abstract procedures and rules priority over substantive values and commitments, and its hypocritical reliance on the sham of judicial neutrality.[4] These are much the same arguments one hears today.

By mentioning the fascist interlude in the history of antiliberalism, I do not mean to convict today's antiliberals of harboring dangerous thoughts. (They benefit from historical circumstances that make them politically harmless.) I want to draw attention, instead, to the fundamentally ahistorical character of their thinking. Antiliberals talk endlessly about rootedness and tradition, but they nonchalantly disregard their own intellectual descent. They could easily distinguish themselves from their most unsavory precursors, I suppose. Yet they make no effort to do so—leaving readers perplexed. They blithely deplore what they consider the liberal individual's lack of "constitutive attachments,"[5] for example, but they never mention that this complaint was long the centerpiece of anti-Semitic propaganda, of political attacks on "uprooted" and cosmopolitan Jews.[6] They apparently want to rehabilitate fascist rhetoric without fascist connotations. Their failure to consider the grim history of antiliberalism is therefore a serious mistake. Silence about disagreeable antecedents makes it difficult to provide a balanced and fair assessment of their thought.

By depicting liberal morality as in "a state of grave disorder," MacIntyre casts himself in a clinical role.[7] He appears as a doctor of disorder, a therapist for sick theories and hapless societies infected by unwholesome ideas. Because antiliberals are focused so single-mindedly on the ailments before them, in fact, they almost always neglect themselves. I intend to compensate for this self-neglect—to right the balance, return the favor, and supply for them what they have bountifully provided for liberal thought: a diagnosis of antiliberalism's own inner pathologies. The appropriateness of a diagnostic approach is suggested by, among other things, their implausible assumption that, in the century of Hitler and Stalin, liberalism remains the Great Enemy of mankind.

Antiliberalism is more a mind-set than a theory. It is more a "culture" or cluster of shared prejudices than a closely argued system of thought. For an analysis of the most popular contemporary American versions of this omnipresent and inveterate outlook, questions of intellectual influence are relatively unimportant. I will focus, instead, on recurrent patterns—on the basic conceptual confusions and historical distortions that invariably becloud the antiliberal mind. I shall try to catalogue and dissect the enduring fallacies of antiliberalism. Economy of presentation requires the construction of an ideal type.[8] No single theorist, not even MacIntyre, is a perfect antiliberal. Liberalism's cleverest critics often qualify their attacks, making important concessions to the enemy. Many of them supplement their criticisms of liberal thinkers with criticisms of rival antiliberal thinkers as well. Despite these complexities, antiliberalism retains the shape of a coherent attitude, if not of a cogent doctrine. Above all, an identical set of mistakes and misdescriptions surfaces, with astonishing regularity, in almost every antiliberal work.

After a fairly exhaustive survey, I have managed to identify twenty fundamental fallacies or intellectual failings of antiliberalism: six theoretical confusions and fourteen historical errors. These fallacies have been a permanent feature of Western political theory since the French Revolution. No criticism or exposé will make them disappear. We may shame them into hiding temporarily, but they will soon resurface in a slightly altered guise. The best we can aspire to achieve is not a cure but a list of symptoms. Such an identity kit may nevertheless be of some value. Those who want to think seriously about the problems and deficiencies of the liberal tradition risk being pointlessly sidetracked by antiliberalism's confused and confusing barrage of charges. A survey of the misunderstandings and blunders of our most prominent antiliberals should, however briefly, help keep spurious accusations at bay.

Theoretical Weaknesses

The antiliberal mentality is plagued by various conceptual confusions. (1) Antiliberals typically invoke an indescribable community, employing a double standard to evaluate liberal and nonliberal social orders and conveniently eluding criticism of their own political ideals. (2) They treat "the social" as a moral category, drawing controversial assumptions from noncontroversial assumptions by a conceptual sleight-of-hand. (3) They assume that when a person transcends self-interest, he is necessarily behaving in a morally admirable way. (4) They oscillate deviously between community as an alternative to liberal rights and community as a mere supplement. (5) They fall into a self-contradiction when they criticize both liberal theory and liberal society. And (6) they erroneously conclude, from the premise that ideas shape behavior, that a critique of ideas will dramatically reshape behavior.

The Phantom Community. No society is as liberal as liberals would like. None fully realizes the principles and aspirations of liberalism. Thus, liberals regularly criticize societies that are liberal in principle but illiberal in practice—those that fail, for example, to protect rights and satisfy basic needs. Antiliberals lodge a different complaint. They blame "liberal society" not for failing to achieve liberal goals but for aiming so low. The "crisis" of our society is not that we have achieved justice only imperfectly, but that we have become fixated on such a colorless ideal. We cannot be satisfied, for example, with an expansion of welfare rights; something more should be achieved by the state. Politics must aim higher, at something more uplifting than justice— more inspiring, more comforting, more spiritual, more erotic.

That something is *community*. According to Roberto Unger, and this is a remark to be fished from almost any antiliberal text, "the political doctrine of liberalism does not acknowledge communal values."[9] This liberal failure is not surprising, because modern society as a whole is characterized by "the disintegration of community."[10] MacIntyre agrees that the "notion of the political community as a common project is alien to the modern liberal individualist world."[11] Under the influence of liberalism, from Sheldon Wolin's perspective, "the sense of community" has been "lost," and we all have begun to inhabit a "society of disconnected particulars."[12] For Sandel, citizens of a liberal state are doomed to the miserable isolation of "strangers."[13] And summarizing his reading of antiliberal literature, Robert Paul Wolff accurately writes: "The severest criticisms of liberal society, both from the left and the right, focus on the absence of community in even the most efficient and affluent liberal capitalist state . . . What is it that conservatives and radicals alike miss in liberal society? . . . *the social values of community*."[14] Liberalism is dissatisfying because it fails to provide what we yearn for most: fraternity, solidarity, harmony, and, most magically, community. Antiliberals invest this word with redemptive significance. When we hear it, all our critical faculties are meant to fall asleep. In the vocabulary of antiliberals "community" is used as an anesthetic, an amnesiac, an aphrodisiac. Unger actually calls it, apparently without irony, "the political equivalent of love."[15] There is nothing it will not do for you once you expose yourself to its redeeming powers.

But what is community? What does it look like? What are *its* problems? Antiliberals are divided on these questions. Some locate community in the past, others espy it in the future. The former write deprivation history, wringing their hands about the world we have lost. Their trademark is that melancholy cluster of words: "decay," "breakdown," "decline," "erosion," "impoverishment," and "eclipse."[16] The latter compose promissory history, in which anticipation and hope provide consolation for the dreariness or the meaninglessness of the present. For all their differences, commemorative and expectant communitarians share many singular habits of mind. While antiliberals of either stripe repeatedly inform us that we have mislaid or not yet discovered community, neither tells us anything specific about the community we lack. And this is not an incidental feature of antiliberalism; it is an essential one. Antiliberals rhapsodize about neighborhoods, churches, school boards, and so forth; but they never provide sufficient detail about the institutions they favor to allow us to compare the advantages and disadvantages of illiberal community with the vices and virtues of the liberal societies we know.[17]

All political arrangements involve the use of physical force. Thus, at a minimum, antiliberals should be specific about the conditions under which, in their ideal order, sanctions would be applied. Does moral revulsion at "radical separation" among citizens require making divorce and emigration illegal? What does a commitment to "solidarity" imply about the authority of majorities over dissident minorities? Should children of Jehovah's Witnesses be compelled to submit to the community-binding powers of the Pledge of Allegiance? Would present-day antiliberals advocate making *incivisme* into a punishable crime—as it was in France during the Terror? Presumably they would not. But they are reluctant to say so openly, perhaps to avoid being observed defending civil liberties and individual rights.

The Myth of "the Social." On the face of it, the category "social" should refer to the entire gamut of human motives, actions, and institutions. "Social" is (or should be) a descriptive term. To say that an action or motive is "social" is not to imply that it is necessarily good. Although some "social purposes" are morally praiseworthy, others (such as racial purity) are morally repugnant.[18] That an aspiration is "shared" does not imply that it is intrinsically admirable. Conversely, immoral behavior is not defined by any lack of a social dimension. No asocial atom would strive to humiliate others publicly or consume the envy of inferiors. The blood feud is not an absence of sociality but a form of sociality. The relation between master and slave is no less "social" (though it is less desirable) than the relation between intimate friends.

Antiliberals, however, transcend such common sense. They surreptitiously smuggle moral approval into ostensibly descriptive categories such as "group loyalty," "collective aims," "constitutive attachments," and "social bonds." Wolin, along the same lines, seems to apply the label "the political" solely to political activity that he admires. It is as if "the dental" referred exclusively to healthy teeth. Unfortunately, as history reveals, collective action can be monstrous and "group aims" may include genocide. And the personal identity of a racist or religious bigot may be—indeed, it is—"socially constituted" without being morally laudable.

In plain words, "the social nature of man" is too trite to count as an insight. The social constitution of the individual is worthless as an argument either for or against existing institutional arrangements. If *all* individuals are socially constituted, then the social self cannot serve as a critical standard to praise some societies and revile others. Faulty logic alone invests such a banality with important political consequences.[19] From the uncontroversial premise that "man is a social animal," antiliberals draw the highly controversial conclusion that a warm and solidaristic social order is morally obligatory. But the inference is bogus. They deduce a value from a fact only by sliding surreptitiously from a generic (and morally neutral) concept to a specific (and morally loaded) concept of "the social." The assurance of antiliberals that certain social relations are superior to others cannot be derived from their trivial observation that individuals acquire fundamental characteristics through socialization.

The seventeenth-century founders of liberalism, we are told, foolishly believed that "men are self-sufficient outside society."[20] Because "man is a social animal," liberalism is theoretically false and politically bankrupt.[21] What concerns me at this point is not the inaccuracy of such an argument but its ineptness. Antiliberals typically boast that they have transcended the fact-value distinction by invoking characteristically human potentials. Man alone is naturally endowed with capacities that can be exercised only in society.[22] Therefore, man is "obliged to belong" to society.[23] People are morally required to sustain the conditions without which they cannot realize their inborn potentials.

The weakness of this reasoning lies in the tacit assumption that the characteristically human capacities that cannot be exercised except in society are necessarily praiseworthy. What MacIntyre, Taylor, and others forget is that society is a dangerous place in which to grow up. It is only through intense social interaction that human beings acquire their worst follies and fanaticisms. The human capacity for intolerance or racism would never flourish in presocial isolation.[24] To repeat: the fact that human potentials develop only in social settings is morally neutral. In itself, it has no implications at all for what people are morally obliged to do.[25]

Either/Or. The third basic infirmity of antiliberal thought is an addiction to simplifying dichotomies, notably to the contrasts of private interest versus public virtue and base individualism versus noble community. These alternatives are unsatisfactory, first of all, because they obscure the possibility of private virtue. They also suggest that individualism is necessarily antisocial. This fails to account for the fact that individualism can involve a heightened concern for others as individuals, rather than as members of ascriptive groups.[26] The greatest threat to social cohesion, moreover, arises not from individualism but from collective passions, ideological conflict, and inherited rivalries between hostile factions.[27] In factional settings, solidarity is a problem not a solution.[28]

Antiliberals invariably suggest that when people overcome their self-interest, they are necessarily acting in an admirable and public-spirited way. They assume, in other words, that the selfless–selfish scheme maps smoothly onto the good-bad scheme. But this leaves out of account the prominent place of selfless cruelty in human affairs. It is much easier to be cruel if you act for the sake of others or for a cause than if you act for your own sake. Those who have homosexuals shot in the name of the Islamic Revolution are morally abhorrent, but they cannot be accused of antisocial individualism or base self-interest. And there would be no terrorism or ethnic warfare without selfless devotion to social groupings. The bloody events we read about every day contain a pertinent refutation of one of the crucial premises of antiliberalism. Those who overcome self-interest are *not* automatically benevolent or humane.

To and Fro. While trumpeting their own audacity, antiliberals are not quite exempt from ordinary inhibitions. Striving to catch our attention, they routinely present their indescribable community as an alternative to liberal society. Once they succeed in attracting a sufficient number of critical onlookers, however, they tend to retreat to the more modest position that such community is merely a supplement to liberal society. The first claim is absurd and the second is trivial. The double strategy of thrust and parry, however, should not be underestimated. It has rhetorical advantages. The built-in option between two claims—one newsworthy but implausible and the other convincing but bland—gives antiliberalism enormous resilience and a capacity for survival. By artfully shifting weight from one foot to another, antiliberals can claim both originality and sobriety, taking maximum advantage of whatever audience is at hand. The naive are promised something extraordinary and the doubters are appeased.

But these gains are purchased by the sacrifice of stylistic unity. Unlike the bold fascist tracts of the 1920s and 1930s, contemporary antiliberal works are typically marred by a schizophrenic tone. A high-pitched jeremiad is disconcertingly followed by a tiptoed retreat. After fiercely attacking liberalism, antiliberals inevitably flip-flop into last-minute concessions, erasing their initial protests, assuring us that they can continue to benefit, without hypocrisy, from the principles and the institutions that they otherwise heroically oppose.[29]

The Shifting Target. Antiliberals tend to oscillate woozily between criticism of liberal theory and criticism of liberal society.[30] Sometimes they say that liberalism is simply wrong: liberals are making a factual mistake when they suggest that individuals are preexistent atomic units, and that all social relations are as instrumental as voluntary contracts struck in the market. These "typically liberal" claims are false, runs the argument, because individuals are socially constituted, because wholes are prior to parts, and because what they like to call "constitutive" social relations exist. At other times, however, antiliberals advance a contrary line of argument. Liberalism, they mournfully confess, is descriptively correct: modern society has become atomized, social bonds have snapped, instrumental relations are universal, and group membership has become optional, that is, derivative from human wills and subservient to private interests. Mirroring that bleak truth, liberal theory is doomed to be a dismal but not inaccurate science.

This waffle is disorienting, but characteristic. (MacIntyre both denies that Aristotle's theory of the social self applies to "atomized" modern societies and insists that it does apply, although neo-Aristotelians alone have grasped the elusive fact. Sandel confusingly asserts that our lives are bad because they *enact* a theory that *misdescribes* our lives.[31]) It is obviously contradictory to say that liberal individuals do not exist and that the ones who exist are excruciatingly unhappy. Yet this entertaining contradiction is something like the official handshake of the antiliberal movement. On the one hand, social bonds exist even though liberals do not see them. On the other hand, social bonds do not exist, and liberals who report their nonexistence must suffer the fate of all those who bring the bad news—that is, they must be condemned for failing to denounce what they have discovered.

Theory as Therapy. Not surprisingly, some antiliberals feels uneasy about zigzagging between such patently incompatible claims. To reconcile the existence of liberal individuals with their nonexistence, they note that a person's self-understanding decisively affects his behavior. If a person thinks he is a croque-monsieur, this will not make him into a croque-monsieur, but it will cause him to act in unusual ways. Analogously, if he thinks he is an atomistic individual, this will not turn him into an atomistic individual; but it will lead him to behave oddly, as a liberal citizen, as an economic man. In other words: liberal ideology is simultaneously false *and* true. Our theory guides and hides our practice. Our impoverished language of radical individualism both distorts our behavior and denies us "access" to our communal selves.[32] Members of liberal societies have come to believe that individuals exist prior to and independently of social attachments and that all social relations resemble contracts in a market. Strictly speaking, this self-understanding is erroneous: some noninstrumental and constitutive social relations still or already exist. But liberal ideology is also correct: our moral and affective bonds are buried, either forgotten or never given a chance to flower. Because, we read over and over again, liberals disparage "the social," they not only misdescribe human action but also allow the best part of life to wither on the vine. By redescribing human existence accurately, as thoroughly dependent on a nourishing social milieu, antiliberals can make it worthwhile once again—or perhaps for the first time.

Antiliberals conceive of themselves, then, not only as diagnosticians, but also as midwives. They promise to unearth the buried treasure, to make explicit the implicit, to release the warm human potential half-frozen beneath the ice of liberal ideology. They advocate a transformative politics that is reassuringly benign. Merely by correcting the delusions of liberal theory, the hermeneutical sage will accomplish the reform of liberal society. He will "improve" us against our will, but therapeutically, not coercively—helping us to become explicitly what we already are latently. He will articulate the shared understandings that the rest of us have half-forgotten, thereby abolishing loneliness and rendering our lives, at last, joyfully communal.[33]

But intellectual criticism and social transformation cannot be so effortlessly combined. A theoretical cause in the past does not guarantee a theoretical cure in the present, because earlier ideas may have set irreversible social processes in motion. (Antiliberals never provide a causal account of how a philosopher-instigated transfiguration of humanity and society might actually come about.) In any case, the belief that a criticism of theory, by itself, entails a remaking of society speaks volumes about the self-image of antiliberals. The professional myth-demolisher is not just another desk-bound professor. He is, at least potentially, the founder of a beautiful new (or old?) world of togetherness and belonging.

Historical Distortions

Within antiliberal works, these six basic conceptual confusions, evasions, or errors are invariably supplemented by an array of historical mistakes. For one thing, antiliberals typically identify liberalism with "modernity," as if there were no significant illiberal strands in modern culture and no significant illiberal movements within modern politics. They uniformly underestimate the fragility and beleagueredness of the liberal tradition. Their polemical attitude leads them into serious distortions of classical texts as well. Consider MacIntyre's intemperate attack on David Hume—a fair and representative example. As the mouthpiece for a property-obsessed culture, we read, Hume violently repudiated the traditional natural-law teaching, affirmed by Thomas Aquinas, that theft is permitted in case of dire necessity.[34] Turning his back on starving children, except for some casual remarks about charity, he rejected immemorial taboos against excessive inequalities of wealth. That this shrill denunciation is misleading is the least that might be said. Hume accepted inequality of property because, on considering the conditions for a productive agricultural economy, he concluded that a free market in grain could better satisfy the needs of the poor than any other system. Moreover, the *Enquiries* contain one of the clearest eighteenth-century restatements of the traditional doctrine that all property rights lapse in case of dire necessity.[35]

We can demonstrate the inaccuracy of the portrait antiliberals draw of liberalism in this manner, simply by pointing to doctrines clearly advanced in a series of indisputably liberal works. We do not have to provide an alternative portrait of liberalism ourselves—however desirable that might be.[36] In what follows I have proceeded in a fairly nominalist manner, applying "liberal" to a select number of major modern theorists. When I write of "liberalism," I do not mean a vague Zeitgeist or the outlook of modern man but a clearly identifiable cluster of political principles and positions defended by, among others, Milton, Spinoza, Locke, Montesquieu, Hume, Voltaire, Smith, Kant, Madison, and J. S. Mill. (The foremost contemporary heir to this loose "tradition" is John Rawls.) Although they differed in many important respects, these theorists shared a good deal in common. Most of them were anticlerical and antimilitaristic. Most favored religious toleration, an independent judiciary, abolition of torture, liberty of thought and expression, and government by public discussion among elected and accountable representatives. And most tended to have a relatively welcoming attitude toward commercial society. "Liberalism" is as good a term as any for this shared body of political purpose and moral principle.

But what about the "typically liberal" doctrines ridiculed by contemporary antiliberals? Not a single one was espoused by *any* major liberal thinker.[37] Indeed, the huge discrepancy between the legends promulgated by antiliberals and the positions actually defended by liberal theorists is what originally suggested a need for this anatomy of antiliberalism. There is room for legitimate disagreement about how a concept such as "liberalism" should be handled. But one thing is certain: no description of liberalism can be accurate if, like the storybook account popularized by antiliberals, it applies to *none* of the representative thinkers I have listed.

Antiliberals routinely distort liberal texts by reading them apolitically, by taking them out of their historical context and ignoring their political and polemical aims. In most cases, as a result, we can correct antiliberal falsifications by showing that liberalism was a political platform, not a philosophy of man.[38] Here, then, are the fourteen most common misrepresentations perpetrated and popularized by today's antiliberals.

The Myth of the Presocial Individual. The most pernicious liberal myth, according to the majority of antiliberals, is the fiction of the presocial individual. Seventeenth- and eighteenth-century liberals purportedly conceived of society as a voluntary compact between preexistent persons. They assumed that a socially uninfluenced individual could, before learning a language or being socialized into a culture, identify his pregiven needs and negotiate contracts to ensure their satisfaction.[39] As all antiliberals dispassionately explain, such robinsonades are highly implausible. Social relations are not secondary and optional, but primary and necessary. Since presocial individuals do not exist, Locke was simply dreaming.

The most annoying insinuation of antiliberal writers is that the great European liberals were not only unintelligent but also completely incapable of common sense. Taylor does not exactly assert that Locke believed an individual could develop his ability to speak English in the absence of social interaction with English-speakers. But what else does his analysis of "atomistic" social theory imply? To put his sort of accusation in perspective, we should recall that Weber, Durkheim, and Simmel—to mention only the weightiest of modern sociologists—devoted their careers to studying the *social basis* of modern individualism. Significantly, those who actually knew something about the social constitution of the individual never imagined that their findings would in any way revolutionize the self-understanding of liberal citizens or bring liberal polities crashing down.

As Hume's example shows, commitment to liberal institutions is wholly independent of a naive attitude toward the myth of a social contract.[40] But not even the liberals who consistently invoked the state of nature were so unrealistic as to deny the social nature of man. Locke, for one, never suggested that fully formed adults entered the world without any need for primary socialization.[41] The social contract myth should be read politically, not descriptively. An emphasis on the voluntariness of social "bonds" was meant to discredit a specific set of involuntary relations characteristic of traditional European societies. To "atomize" human self-understanding was to attack "organic" chains of dependence and subordination as well as to undermine dangerous clan and sectarian groupings. Significantly, inhabitants of the state of nature gave little thought to God.[42] Theorists struggling to justify the basic institutions of religiously divided societies were thus naturally attracted to the social contract myth.

Implicitly, all liberal writers acknowledged the social constitution of the individual. The fundamental human passions of pride and envy, for example, are discussed at length in almost every liberal work. Such passions obviously presuppose social awareness and are incompatible with the mutual indifference of windowless monads. Like all political programs, liberalism was "antisocial" in a trivial sense: it proposed that certain widely accepted social institutions be abolished and replaced by others. Liberalism can only be considered antisocial in a more serious sense if society itself is identified with its hierarchical, parochial, and oppressive subforms. Antiliberals typically argue that "eighteenth-century rationalism tried to envision humanity stripped of such supposed inessential attributes as cultural, ethnic, and class particularities."[43] This claim admittedly contains a faint and distorted echo of the truth. But the accusation that liberals believed the self to be factually "disencumbered" of such particularities is baseless. Liberal institutions may ask a judge to *ignore* the race or religion of a defendant before the bench. But the attempt to desensitize legal institutions to ethnic traits does not imply (how could it?) that being black or Catholic has no importance for a person's life. The liberal conception of the person as neither black nor white, neither Catholic nor Jew, has an obvious political function. It was never intended to deny the obvious reality of primordial attachments.[44]

In the same unfriendly spirit, antiliberals frequently identify liberal individualism with epistemological solipsism. Wolin writes: "The basic [liberal] assertion, that each was the best judge of his own interests and hence no outside agency could properly dictate his happiness, rested squarely on the belief that no individual could truly understand another."[45] That liberals had a somewhat more nuanced view is easy to prove. For one thing, they all subscribed to the legal principle that "no man should be judge in his own case," suggesting the political irrelevance of solipsism.[46] Liberals did make certain descriptive claims, for example, that a privy councilor probably knew less about a peasant's interest than did the peasant himself. But their basic point—again—was political or normative, and not descriptive at all. The claim that others can sometimes know what is good for us better than we know it ourselves may be dangerous even when it is not always false. No matter how well-founded in some cases, it cannot be safely elevated into a maxim of government. In sum, to deny that others can define our profoundest interests is not to affirm the ultimate privacy of self-knowledge. It is simply to remove a certain perilous strategy of justification from the arsenal of public officials.

Hostility toward the "Common Good." Liberals, we are repeatedly told, deny the existence of any "genuine shared common good."[47] This accusation too is largely unfounded. It flies in the face, for example, of Locke's assertion that "the public good is the rule and measure of all lawmaking." Locke worried, it is true, that the government's appeal to the common good might be "a specious show of deceitful words," that is, a lie useful for the wielders of power. But would liberals have denounced "the pretense of public good" and the "pretense of care for the public weal" if they had not believed that such a common good existed and was being violated by abusers of authority?[48]

In general, liberal ambivalence toward the common good cannot be understood without recalling how that concept had been traditionally misused. In the *Politics,* Aristotle distinguished the master from the slave by contending that the master has privileged insight into the common good.[49] With his own unaided vision, a slave cannot grasp the rational principle upon which joint advantage depends; he must be instructed and coerced by his superiors. The common good can only be known directly by a few—the wise, the virtuous, and the holy. Far from being innocent, the idea of the common good was traditionally implicated in the justification of privilege, hierarchy, and deference. This political background goes far toward explaining the deflationary approach liberals took toward the rhetoric of the common good.

Liberals wholeheartedly endorsed the common good of collective welfare. They distrusted the idea of the common good to the extent that "the good" was identified with certain dangerous and oppressive values. Religious orthodoxy was a "common good" liberals hoped to live without. If religion is set aside, the most obvious thing citizens share is a desire for military success. As antimilitarists as well as anticlerics, liberals often distrusted the idea of the common good because of its traditional associations with dynastic war and persecution. Sometimes the idea of the common good also contained an implicit or explicit denial that different opinions about the common good had a legitimate place within the state. Tolerance for honest differences about the nature of the common good implies the political unreliability or inadequacy of *virtue.* In a pluralistic society, willingness to subordinate private interest to what one considers "the" common good, does not, by itself, solve our most urgent political controversies and problems.

Hostility toward Politics. It is misleading to suggest that liberals were fundamentally antistatist, hostile to both political authority and political participation. This common antiliberal thesis is implausible on its face because antistatism was the ideology of ecclesiastics (and anticlericalism was a crucial element in liberal thinking).[50] In fact, all liberals subscribed to Montesquieu's assertion that "without government, no society can subsist."[51] An important chapter in the *Wealth of Nations* shows that the emergence of individual freedom was inextricably connected to the process of state-building and the strengthening of centralized institutions.[52] The first chapter of Mill's *Considerations of Representative Government* and the last chapter of his *Principles of Political Economy* are both devoted to extensive discussions of the positive contribution of state power to liberal freedom. In truth, liberals opposed arbitrary authority, but not authority in general.

Similarly, they opposed obligatory participation, but not participation in general.[53] To violate rights in a liberal society is to defy the authority of the state. This alone suggests that political power and individual liberty are not necessarily antithetical from a liberal point of view.[54]

The Sacrifice of the Public to the Private. The commonplace that liberals wanted the private sector to expand and the public sphere to contract is also patently one-sided.[55] No liberal ever expressed sympathy for private courts, private taxation, private armies, or the private right to declare war. As etymology reveals, the liberal attack on inherited privilege was actually an attack on "private" laws. Dueling was a voluntary exchange between consenting adults; but liberals never hesitated, in this case, to enforce state prohibitions against individual choice. Earlier, kings could sell political rights to the nobility in exchange for money or service. Liberals did not conceive of citizenship in this privatistic way, but rather as a potentially universal right, certainly not as a transferable piece of property.[56] (Eventually all liberal societies instituted a powerful taboo against the buying and selling of votes.)

A good case could be made, on the other hand, for the primacy of publicity in liberal thought. By "publicity" I mean, first of all, the principle that criminal trials, legislative sessions, and government budgets should be open to public inspection. Montesquieu mounted a fierce attack on secret accusations, unsigned denunciations of fellow courtiers delivered by stealth to the king.[57] Accusations, liberals standardly argued, must be made publicly, with full opportunity for explanation and rebuttal. But they conceived of publicity as a stimulant as well as a depressant. Besides curbing abuses and corruption, it could supply new suggestions, counterarguments, and useful information. If policies are set publicly and public criticism is encouraged, a government can avoid self-contradictory legislation, discern problems before they get out of hand, and correct its own mistakes. Liberals conceived the central institution of liberal politics to be the opposition—not least of all because the back-and-forth of public disagreement was thought to sharpen the minds of all parties and produce decisions more intelligent than any proposals presented at the outset.[58]

The Primacy of Economic Man. According to antiliberal mythology, "most liberals followed the view that man affirmed his existence through economic activity." The primary concern of liberal reformers, we read, was to assure freedom for economic exchange. "Liberalism . . . began as a doctrine for liberating economic egoism." R. H. Tawney, who pined for "the social harmonies of a vanished age," claimed that liberals supported religious toleration only because it was good for trade.[59] Liberal man is an economic animal.

The desire for religious freedom was no mere by-product of the desire for economic freedom. Similarly, the liberal campaign against judicial cruelty, discussed by Judith Shklar in Chapter 1 of this volume, cannot be reduced to a bourgeois strategy for maximizing profits. The attempt to free science from ecclesiastical interference was another liberal cause that by no means derived from the spirit of capitalism. For Locke, toleration (within politically defined limits) came first. And the unlimited accumulation of knowledge was considerably more important to him than the unlimited accumulation of property.

It is true that liberals tended to have a welcoming attitude toward commercial society. They did not think that commerce was the worse thing one person could do to another. (Anyone who views commerce this way seriously underestimates mankind's capacity for cruelty.) While antiliberals endlessly berate liberals for "instrumental thinking," they never mention liberalism's obviously instrumental attitude toward market relations and economic growth. Montesquieu, for example, argued that "commerce cures destructive prejudices."[60] Trade teaches people that agreement about rules is compatible with disagreement about the meaning of life. A life of business devalues wild impulsiveness, instills habits of foresight and methodical calculation, and undermines the economic interests and values of the aristocracy. Because it brings citizens into everyday contact with foreigners, commerce also destroys parochialism and promotes tolerance for diversity.

There is probably no better illustration of the completely instrumental attitude liberals displayed toward commercialism than the following passage from Voltaire's *Philosophical Letters:* "Enter the Exchange of London, that place more respectable than many a court, and you will see there agents from all nations assembled for the utility of mankind. There the Jew, the Mohammedan, and the Christian deal with one another as if they were of the same religion, and give the name of infidel only to those who go bankrupt."[61] The sociological insight underlying this passage is marvelously simple. In sect-riven societies, social cooperation requires an element of mutual indifference. If I consider murdering you because of your religious beliefs, our ability to cooperate or learn from one another will be ruinously small. Liberals valued commerce not only because it allowed individuals to satisfy their interests, but also because it was a social coolant. Commerce deeroticizes social bonds. Arm's-length transactions in the marketplace give members of hostile groupings an apprenticeship in coexistence, preparing the ground for cooperation of a noneconomic sort.

The Subjectivity of Values. For MacIntyre, one of liberalism's most destructive ideas is that "the desires of every individual are equally to be taken into account in deciding what is right to do."[62] From the assumption that values are purely subjective, we are told, liberals concluded that all human desires were of equal worth.[63] How accurate is this claim? It is true that liberals wanted to decentralize the authority to define personal happiness, dispersing it into the hands of unsupervised individuals.[64] Mill also deliberately tried to redescribe religious commitments as subjective preferences on the grounds that people would be unwilling to persecute others for a "mere" point of view, while atrocities might always be justified by invoking supposedly objective values.[65]

But liberal skepticism was primarily political, not moral. (Antiliberals slide over this distinction because they systematically ignore questions of legal compulsion.) Liberals assumed that public officials cannot always be trusted to codify and enforce the distinction between the moral and immoral. From this premise, however, we cannot logically conclude that liberals denied the reality or importance of a substantive moral-immoral distinction. The opening sentence of Locke's *Treatise,* asserting that slavery is a "vile and miserable" condition, suggests a commitment to a nonarbitrary distinction between good and bad. And the entire myth of the social contract rests on a substantive principle of fairness that cannot be reduced to a maxim of prudence. The individual is morally required to give up his own right to enforce the law of nature if everyone else does so too. From a self-interested standpoint, it would be preferable to benefit from the self-restraint of others while benefiting from one's own lack of self-restraint. But that kind of arrangement is explicitly ruled out by the self-exemption taboo at the heart of liberal morality. The rule that you cannot make an exception of yourself is not a subjective preference. It is not a value which we can choose or not, as we please. The self-exception taboo is a standard by which liberal citizens are required to judge and curb their own first-order desires.

The real starting point for liberal morality was not the subjectivity of values, but the historical intractability of moral conflict.[66] Antiliberals like to align themselves with morality itself against the supposed value-neutrality they ascribed to liberals.[67] The "morality" they extol, however, remains conveniently void of content. Their pose as advocates of social harmony would be threatened if they admitted that they were contemplating the victory of one specific morality, be it radical or conservative, over its rivals.

The Thinness of "Rights." According to MacIntyre, rights do not exist, "and belief in them is one with belief in unicorns and witches." While liberals deplore our failure to enforce rights, antiliberals lament our obsessive concern for rights—for these "fictions" that are designed only to foster untrammeled egoism.[68] Antiliberals scorn rights for several reasons. They sometimes paint the protection of rights as an alternative to the exercise of capacities and as an obstacle to meaningful involvement with fellow citizens.[69] These are implausible contrasts. Some rights, such as the right to vote and freedom of speech and the press, are designed to make possible the exercise of important human capacities.[70] Freedom of religion protects group activities as well as private conscience. In any case, allowing the police to abuse the citizenry is not likely to maximize civic involvement. Even Rousseau recognized that citizens will avoid the public square if government officials can violate private lives at will.[71] In general, rights are valued as preconditions for all manner of worthwhile human endeavor. (Obligatory and full-time civic involvement, on the other hand, would definitely condemn many valuable human potentials to go to waste.) But antiliberals, echoing a folly of the young Marx, continue to assert that rights destroy community and drive citizens into mean-spirited isolation.[72]

Another complaint about rights is their abstractness.[73] By the abstractness of rights, antiliberals mean chiefly this: if I am concerned solely about your rights, I will treat you like a generic person, not as a unique individual caught up in a tight web of social relations. This complaint about the unrealism of liberalism's "disencumbered self" was classically expressed in Maistre's attack on the Declaration of the Rights of Man: "there is no such thing as *man* in the world. In my lifetime I have seen Frenchmen, Italians, Russians, etc. . . . But as for *man,* I declare that I have never in my life met him; if he exists, he is unknown to me."[74] The abstractness of rights, however, is a necessary condition for their universality. This universality, in turn, is based upon an ethical commitment to the equal treatment of persons, a commitment that liberalism does not view as an arbitrary or subjective preference. In criminal law, moreover, abstractness has significant advantages. It allows us to respect Charles Manson's rights even though we obviously cannot respect him as a person.

The Sham of Neutrality. On this question antiliberals frequently cobble together two contradictory claims. They argue that liberal neutrality toward conceptions of the good life is impossible: liberal regimes favor some alternatives and disadvantage others. Then they add, inconsistently, that liberal neutrality is pernicious, an ignominious collapse into wishy-washiness, fence-sitting, and moral disorientation. Liberals fail to be morally neutral (they take a stand), and they fail to be morally engaged (they do not take a stand).[75] Antiliberals reconcile these two seemingly inconsistent claims in the usual way: liberal regimes are bad because they fail to understand their non-neutrality and thus fail to enforce it vigorously enough. They fail to *understand* themselves and thus fail to *be* themselves in a healthy sense. But this acrobatic afterthought does not lead antiliberals any closer to common sense. Yes, perfect neutrality is impossible; but relative neutrality is well within human powers. The umpire at a baseball game, to take a trivial example, is not perfectly neutral: he enforces the rules of baseball, not of badminton or golf. But would anyone want to claim that he cannot be impartial between rival teams? A Protestant celebrating the promulgation of the Edict of Nantes would not have been impressed by a "proof" that neutrality is philosophically impossible.[76]

Attacks on the idea of neutrality contain a sordid message. They imply that one form of "intolerance" is worth another. There is no difference between my imposing my beliefs on others by force and a democratic government's forcibly preventing me from imposing my beliefs on others by force. We may not want to say that the latter is perfectly "neutral." But then we will simply have to find some other word to capture the important distinction at stake.

The Discarding of Self-Restraint. Both Tawney and Leo Strauss associate liberal principles with the loosing of acquisitive instincts onto the world.[77] The abolition of the usury taboo symbolized the collapse of archaic ethical inhibitions on the possessive individual. Joseph Schumpeter answered this sort of claim with admirable succinctness: "Precapitalist man is in fact no less 'grabbing' than capitalist man. Peasant serfs for instance or warrior lords assert their self-interest with a brutal energy all their own."[78] The usury taboo itself had been an instrument of greed, allowing princes to confiscate the wealth of Jews whenever it proved convenient.[79]

More generally, liberalism did not involve an imprudent uncorking of base passions or a collapse of self-restraint. Oddly enough, Nietzsche, who attacked liberalism from the opposite direction, seems to have been right on this matter. He abhorred liberalism because of the straitjacket it imposed upon the individual's will to power. He denounced liberalism for having erected "restraint from mutual injury" into the fundamental moral principle of modern society.[80] In his typical anemic way, Locke had written that "no one ought to harm another in his life, health, liberty, or possessions."[81] Liberalism asked people to give up one of their most ardent desires: the yearning to inflict physical pain on people they hate—a yearning independent of any calculation of personal advantage. But to refrain from harming others is to stifle the spontaneous expression of human instinct. Life is essentially a matter of rapaciousness, violence, and the victory of the strong over the weak. Thus, liberalism is a clever but craven repudiation of human vitality.[82] Though morally perverse, Nietzsche's emphasis on liberal self-restraint is intellectually preferable to the fiction of liberal restraintlessness propagated by conservative-minded antiliberals.[83] Finally, in a comparative, and still Nietzschean, vein, we should recall that preliberal politics was not exactly untainted by the basest of human passions.

Instrumental Reason. Martin Heidegger's influence on contemporary American antiliberals, though subterranean and indirect, is all-pervasive. Hannah Arendt and Strauss made a decisive contribution here, adapting Heidegger's harsh diagnosis of modernity to the mental horizon of their new American audience. Having immigrated to this country, they could not plausibly say that the "decline" of modern times resulted from a forgetfulness of Being. That would have been wholly unintelligible to their culturally backward readers. They responded to this marketing problem by Americanizing Heidegger's basic idea. Decadent modernity, they said, resulted from a forgetfulness of *x*—of the Greek polis, on the one hand, of classical natural law, on the other. Marcuse, Adorno, and fellow members of the Frankfurt school, for their part, helped popularize the Heideggerian idea that "modern man" has lost his reverence for nature and adopted a basically instrumental attitude toward the world. A penchant for instrumental thinking is the principal sign of our fallen condition.[84] Habituated to thinking instrumentally about nature, we tend to think instrumentally about each other as well. That is obviously what MacIntyre has in mind when he denounces the "dominance of the manipulative mode in our culture."[85]

The association of liberalism with the glorification of instrumental or manipulative relations is bizarre from several points of view. Slavery, the most instrumental of all human relations, was neither invented by liberal societies nor condoned by liberal principles. Locke's entire theory was based on a denial that "we were made for one another's uses." No reader of Montesquieu's *Persian Letters* would gather that liberals admired instrumental relations. Smith argued explicitly that you cannot treat people like "pieces upon a chess-board." Similarly, Kant's injunction to view others always also as ends in themselves never caused him to repudiate liberal institutions. According to Mill too, "no men are mere instruments or materials in the hands of their rulers."[86] It is not easy to reconcile attacks on liberal rights and liberal skepticism with a sincere abhorrence of manipulation. Rights, for one thing, were designed to prevent unwanted and oppressive manipulation. Similarly, skepticism about "mankind's true good" was meant to inhibit attempts of superiors to manage and control their inferiors.

A Static View of Preferences. Liberal writers are said to have had no idea of the social processes through which individual preferences are shaped and reshaped.[87] Since the French Revolution, it is true, liberals have tended to distrust self-appointed moral legislators bent on "improving" citizens against their will. Transformative politics is not always benign. But the charge of liberal naivete about this matter is without foundation. Liberal emphasis on the *cordializing* effects of commerce, already mentioned, is a case in point. The liberal virtues extolled by Kant are obviously acquired by training not by birth or religious inspiration. And consider one of Madison's main arguments for an extended republic. If all citizens find themselves aligned with electoral minorities on some issues, their characters and aspirations will be changed for the better. Civilized into the virtues of tolerance and forbearance, they are less likely, when they happen to be in the majority, to advance extreme demands or behave in bullying ways. The socially uninfluenced individual also makes no appearance in *The Wealth of Nations*. Instead, Smith is consistently concerned with the social causes of emergence of different types of personality. A philosopher differs from a street porter chiefly because he was socialized in a different milieu. Similarly, having grown up in a bustling environment, a city-dweller has a different "temper and disposition" than those raised in the countryside. One of Europe's main contributions to the prosperity of the colonies was the moral character it bequeathed to the colonists.[88] In other words, the common notion that liberals completely ignored elementary processes of character formation and preference transformation bespeaks considerable inattention to what liberal writers actually wrote.

Man as a Pleasure-Pain Machine. Another page in the antiliberal storybook explains that liberalism gave government "the commission to increase pleasure and decrease pain."[89] To indict liberalism for having debased mankind, antiliberals frequently contrast the liberal concern for "mere life" with the Aristotelian concern for "the good life."[90] Some antiliberals (echoing Arendt) like to assert that liberalism lowered the goals to be pursued by human beings. Base-minded theorists convinced citizens to turn away from noble aspirations such as honor and focus instead on ignoble concerns such as survival.[91] In this way, liberals demeaned their fellow men—perhaps reducing them to the moral status of dogs. This claim raises many questions. We could inquire, for example, if it applies to Kant. But we should also ask if the desire to live is really "low." And how about the desire for our children to live?

The state-society distinction, in any case, provides another important rejoinder to complaints about the "lowering" of human aspirations. Liberal theorists may have refused to idealize the goals of the state, but that does not imply that they debased the aspirations of society as a whole. The political goals of peace, security, welfare, and justice were the preconditions for the pursuit of other goals in various nonpolitical but nevertheless social domains. On the basis of a politically achieved order, individuals or subgroups could pursue any number of loftier aims: knowledge, bliss, friendship, salvation, oneness with nature, or personal development. Antiliberals, in fact, trip over their own feet when they *both* accuse liberals of having transformed the state into a mere instrument of individuals *and* adduce the lower goals of the state as evidence that liberals have lowered the goals of individuals. Liberal citizens have an instrumental relation toward the state. Thus, when they lowered the goals of politics, they did not lower the goals of human life.

Antiliberals speak glowingly about willingness to die for one's country. Historically, a martial ethos has been the most effective way to discipline citizens and lead them "up" from individualism. Confrontations with a deadly enemy certainly help reinforce communal bonds.[92] This is the context in which MacIntyre mentions "the honorable resort to war."[93] But the desire to die for one's group has always been subordinate to the desire to kill for one's group. (Killing is a more sportive way to "soar above mere life" than being killed.) At any rate, liberals who identified good and bad with bodily pleasure and pain were, to a large extent, engaged in an antimilitaristic polemic, an attack on the shin-guard ethics of the battlefield.[94] As a descriptive matter, liberals recognized that experiences of pleasure and pain often depended on opinion.[95] They certainly knew that human beings tend to feel pleasure at the death of their enemies and pain at the death of their friends—although such delights and agonies are not strictly physical in origin.

Overconfidence in Reason. Antiliberals often suggest that modern science is basically immoral, even though it helps 99 percent of the human race alive.[96] Science is denigrated as objectifying and cold. It is accused of having denuded nature of moral purpose, thereby leaving practical reason dangerously unmoored. By inculcating an instrumental attitude toward the world, apparently, it encourages us to view each other as objects ripe for manipulation. Conservative-minded antiliberals add that science is a prime example of human arrogance—as if our feeble minds could solve all problems without the aid of religion! Liberals are denounced for converting Reason into a God and expecting it to answer all their prayers.

In point of fact, the Enlightenment was a limits-of-reason tradition. Arrogance is more justly ascribed to religious authorities presuming to tell individuals how to save their souls than to doctors experimenting with inoculations against smallpox. The main theme of a liberal work such as Voltaire's *Philosophical Dictionary* is the inability of reason to answer certain large questions. The nature of matter and the soul are inscrutable to the human mind. Scholastic attempts to penetrate to the essence of things failed because they overtaxed human cognitive capacities.[97]

Maistre and Louis de Bonald, however, were effective propagandists. They successfully promulgated the myth of a direct causal link between the activity of the eighteenth-century philosophes and the Reign of Terror.[98] Once this idea of a "dialectic of Enlightenment" was launched, it was able to sustain itself by an air of paradoxical profundity. As an heir to this nineteenth-century Catholic tradition, Unger can write coolly that "legalism and terrorism, the commitment to rules and the seduction of violence, are rival brothers, but brothers nonetheless."[99] This assertion of an underlying kinship between rationality and brutality takes many forms. Michel Foucault's suggestion that the physical and psychological mistreatment of the mentally ill was a logical consequence of the modern idea of reason is only the most notorious example of this amazingly common claim.[100] On the American scene, arguments for a "dialectic of Enlightenment" take many forms. According to one version, progress leads to specialization; specialization leads to a neglect of fundamentals; a neglect of fundamentals leads to an erosion of civilization, and thus to an end of progress. Another version runs: liberalism destroys religion, chan-neling man's innate idealism into political utopianism, that is, into the kind of revolutionary violence which destroys liberal institu-tions.[101]

How should we respond to these claims? Is it true that when we take the Enlightenment tradition too far something terrible will occur? This conclusion is not quite so obvious as antiliberals pretend. First of all, French liberal writing in the 1790s had little trouble criticizing Robespierre with purely Enlightenment categories: he was a secular priest, a fanatic, a zealot, an enthusiast. Moreover, the leading Jac-obins exhibited few signs of excessive rationality. Viewed clearly, the counterrevolutionary assimilation of freedom and terror, of reason and barbarism, amounts to a rather crude *post hoc, ergo propter hoc* fallacy. Although the Terror came after the Enlightenment, it had other causes than the Enlightenment's success. It may even have re-sulted from the failure of the Enlightenment to take root.

And consider the assertion that religious skepticism destroys social trust. During the Middle Ages, when people really "believed," they nevertheless went on rampages. It is thus impossible to map the faith-doubt scheme neatly onto the moderation-immoderation scheme. Few people, in any case, have ever met a dangerous skeptic.[102] Most of us (most of the time) are incapable of withholding judgment. Psychologically, skepticism is such a difficult attitude to maintain that mass skepticism can never be a major social problem. Blind credulity will always remain more dangerous to mankind than doubt.

Antonym Substitution. Antiliberals do not just decontextualize liberal thought. They also provide a false context of their own making, one that lends a very different meaning to the principles being attacked. A characteristic feature of antiliberal thought is the fallacy of antonym substitution. Theorists with a bias against liberal thought regularly distort the significance of central liberal ideas by replacing the counter-concepts that originally bestowed political significance on the prin-ciples in question with antonyms either ignored or explicitly rejected by liberals themselves. The liberal idea of competition, for example, is routinely subjected to a denigrating contrast with brotherly love. The principal antonym of competition, however, was not love but monopoly. And monopoly has nothing to do with love—as anyone knows who has studied, say, the relation of the higher clergy to the peasantry in the old regime. By antonym substitution, antiliberals have concealed the moral and political motivation for the original liberal embrace of the principle of competition. By such a conceptual sleight-of-hand, one might say, the nineteenth century made the eighteenth century unintelligible.

Other examples of antonym substitution are legion and well worth pondering. Antiliberals misleadingly counterpose skepticism to moral wisdom. The original antonyms of liberal doubt, however, were false certainty and enthusiasm. Private property is unfavorably compared to charity; while liberals saw it as an alternative to princely confiscation. Instrumental attitudes, as I said, are disparagingly contrasted with moral attitudes; but they seem more attractive when opposed, as they were in the seventeenth and eighteenth centuries, to wastefulness and status display. Similarly, rights are prejudicially contrasted with duties, an opposition that makes the former seem mean-spirited and selfish. The original opposites of rights, however, were tyranny, slavery, and cruelty. Why the liberal crusade against oppression should be considered selfish has never been clear.[103]

In an attempt to discredit liberal theory, antiliberals unfairly contrast the adjustment of interests to rational consensus. Such a contrast makes it mysterious why anyone of good will could ever have advocated the former alternative. The original antonym of interest-based compromise, however, was not rational agreement but civil war. Viewed as an alternative to ideal-driven slaughter, interest-driven accommodation seems much less ignoble than antiliberals would have us believe. That is precisely how it seemed, to European liberals in the seventeenth and the eighteenth centuries.

Antiliberals expose the purportedly liberal maxim "I can do whatever I want" as nihilistic self-indulgence by contrasting it misleadingly with the reassuring precept "I shall do whatever morality requires." But the original antonym of "I will do what I want" was "I must do whatever my master or my social rank demands." Antiliberals contrast liberal freedom with authority in general. But liberals were hostile only to arbitrary authority. Rule-governed authority they assumed to be essential for the creation and maintenance of a just social order. Finally, as I also mentioned, antiliberals always contrast liberal individualism with community *tout court*. Individualism was never counterposed to all forms of community, however, only to stifling and authoritarian kinds—sects, clans, caste systems, and parochial village life. Far from being anticommunal, liberals strove to create a specific kind of community, a community in which citizens enjoyed the cooperation and mutuality made possible by a system of liberal rights.[104]

By antonym substitution, antiliberals make it difficult to understand why intelligent and reform-minded theorists embraced the doctrines they did. By decontextualizing liberalism, they deradicalize it and obscure its original appeal. The most noteworthy victims of antonym substitution have probably been the categories of self-interest and self-preservation. To discredit these concepts, antiliberals contrast them with benevolent concern for others, public-spiritedness, and devotion to moral ideals. Almost universally neglected are the antonyms which suggest themselves to common sense: self-hatred, self-destruction, self-mortification, self-effacement, and a failure to take an interest in oneself. These too are "habits of the heart." Subject to a combined assault by religious, authoritarian, romantic, militaristic, and socialist traditions, the concept of self-interest acquired, by the end of the nineteenth century, a totally unmerited infamy. Most outlandishly, self-interest is now routinely depicted as the opposite of the public interest, as if doing something for yourself were necessarily a failure of patriotism or a betrayal of one's fellow man.

Despite the prevailing mythology, no liberal ever affirmed self-interest as an *alternative* to the public interest. All liberals expressed deep concern about "sinister interests." They prized self-interest only so long as it was regulated by a norm of justice and, even then, only because—as Albert Hirschman has shown—they conceived it as a practical alternative to various malevolent passions and conceits as well as to the fraudulent display of benevolent motives.[105] To understand the relatively friendly attitude liberals displayed toward self-interest, we need only contemplate the original and provocative antonyms of the idea: privilege, paternalism, blood revenge, envy, military glory, religious zealotry, the grandeur of the state, and self-effacing obedience to God's inscrutable will.[106]

Conclusion

Antiliberals characteristically commit other mistakes that I have left undiscussed. Think only of the odd view that liberalism somehow heightened personal anxiety. According to Wolin, "anxious man emerges as the creation of liberalism."[107] Actually, tolerance for public disagreement and political contestation suggests that liberal societies are relatively free from primal anxiety. But the twenty fallacies I have set forth here seem to be the most common and important antiliberal errors.

In an abstract diagnosis of this sort, of course, there lurks the danger of caricature. If you are friendly to antiliberalism, you will doubtless say that I have focused solely on one side of antiliberal thought, wresting it out of context and exaggerating its importance to discredit the tradition as a whole. Even those who feel treated unfairly, however, should welcome reflections such as these. If I have cast light only on a single tendency or strand—rather than, as I claim, the enduring core—of antiliberalism, the exercise could still prove useful. At the very least it will provide antiliberals with a checklist of possible misinterpretations. In that case, they can begin to help the rest of us, their curious but baffled readers, understand what they "really" want to say.

Notes

One. The Liberalism of Fear

I would like to thank my friend George Kateb for good advice and encouragement in writing this paper.

1. J. W. Allen, *A History of Political Thought in the Sixteenth Century* (London: Methuen, 1941), pp. 89–97, 370–377. Quentin Skinner, *The Foundations of Political Thought,* 2 vols. (Cambridge: Cambridge University Press, 1978), II, 241–254.
2. See Judith Shklar, *Ordinary Vices* (Cambridge, Mass.: Harvard University Press, 1984).
3. See, for instance, Laurence Berns, "Thomas Hobbes," in Leo Strauss and Joseph Cropsey, eds., *A History of Political Philosophy* (Chicago: Rand McNally, 1972), pp. 370–394. C. B. Macpherson, *The Political Theory of Possessive Individualism* (Oxford: Clarendon, 1962). These interpretations depend on seeing Locke as very similar to Hobbes, as Leo Strauss did in *Natural Right and History* (Chicago: University of Chicago Press, 1953), pp. 202–251.
4. Alexander Hamilton et al., *The Federalist Papers,* ed. Clinton Rossiter (New York: New American Library, 1961), nos. 10, 51.
5. Georges Duby, *The Chivalrous Society,* trans. Cynthia Postan (Berkeley: University of California Press, 1977), pp. 81–87.
6. Ralph Waldo Emerson, "The Conservative," *Essays and Lectures,* ed. Joel Porte (New York: Library of America, 1983), p. 173.
7. Edward Peters, *Torture* (Oxford: Basil Blackwell, 1985), pp. 103–140.
8. Isaiah Berlin, "Introduction" and "Two Concepts of Liberty," *Four Essays on Liberty* (Oxford: Oxford University Press, 1982), pp. xxxvii–lxiii, 118–172. Isaiah Berlin, "The Originality of Machiavelli," *Against the Current* (New York: Viking, 1980), pp. 25–79.

9. *The Metaphysical Elements of Justice,* ed. and trans. John Ladd (Indianapolis: Bobbs-Merrill, 1965).

10. For the best account of the notion of instrumental rationality and its implications, see Seyla Behabib, *Critique, Norm and Utopia* (New York: Columbia University Press, 1986).

11. George Kateb, "Remarks on the Procedures of Constitutional Democracy," *Nomos,* xx, *Constitutionalism,* ed. J. Roland Pennock and John Chapman, pp. 215–237.

12. Michael L. Walzer, *Spheres of Justice* (New York: Basic Books, 1983), pp. 26–28, 312–316.

13. See Thomas Nagel, *The View from Nowhere* (Oxford: Oxford University Press, 1986), for the philosophical panorama from that nonposition.

14. This is a critical response to Michael Walzer, "The Moral Standing of States," in Charles R. Beitz et al., eds., *International Ethics: A Philosophy and Public Affairs Reader* (Princeton: Princeton University Press, 1985), pp. 217–238.

15. Nancy L. Rosenblum, *Another Liberalism* (Cambridge, Mass.: Harvard University Press, 1987), for romantic liberalism, and Michael J. Sandel, *Liberalism and the Limits of Justice* (Cambridge: Cambridge University Press, 1982), for communitarianism, respectively.

16. Charles Taylor, "The Nature and Scope of Distributive Justice," in Frank S. Lucash, ed., *Justice and Equality Here and Now* (Ithaca, N.Y.: Cornell University Press, 1986), pp. 34–67.

17. Alan Ritter, *Anarchism* (Cambridge: Cambridge University Press, 1980).

Two. Humanist Liberalism

I would like to thank Jeffrey Abramson, Robert Keohane, Cass Sunstein, and especially Nancy Rosenblum for their helpful comments on the work out of which this chapter developed.

1. See, for example, Teresa Brennan and Carole Pateman, " 'Mere Auxiliaries to the Commonwealth': Women and the Origins of Liberalism," *Political Studies* 27 (1979): 183–200; Jean Bethke Elshtain, *Public Man, Private Woman* (Princeton: Princeton University Press, 1981), esp. chap. 3; Genevieve Lloyd, *The Man of Reason* (Minneapolis: University of Minnesota Press, 1984), esp. chap. 5; Susan Moller Okin, "Women and the Making of the Sentimental Family," *Philosophy and Public Affairs* 11 (1982): 65–88; Carole Pateman, "Feminist Critiques of the Public/Private Dichotomy," in Stanley Benn and Gerald Gaus, eds., *Public and Private in Social Life* (London: Croom Helm, 1983), pp. 281–303.

2. I discuss this issue at greater length and give some examples of false gender neutrality in contemporary political theories in Susan Moller Okin, "Gender, the Public and the Private," in David Held, ed., *Political Theory Today* (Oxford: Polity, forthcoming); also in *Justice, Gender and the Family* (New York: Basic Books, 1989).

3. For example, Zillah R. Eisenstein, *The Radical Future of Liberal Feminism* (New York: Longman, 1980); Alison M. Jaggar, *Feminist Politics and Human Nature* (Totowa, N.J.: Rowman and Allanheld, 1983), esp. chap. 7.

4. For discussions of the importance of this fact to liberalism, see John Rawls, "Kantian Constructivism in Moral Theory," *The Journal of Philosophy* 77 (1980): 515–572, esp. 517–519, and "Justice as Fairness: Political not Metaphysical," *Philosophy and Public Affairs* 14 (1985): 223–251; also Charles E. Larmore, *Patterns of Moral Complexity* (Cambridge: Cambridge University Press, 1987), esp. chaps. 3, 4.

5. For arguments for such a position, see, for example, Michael Walzer's *Spheres of Justice* (New York: Basic Books, 1983). Though Walzer is sometimes classified as a communitarian because of his emphasis on "shared understandings" as the necessary foundations for a theory of justice, he is, on balance, more accurately described as a liberal socialist. Philip Green, in *Retrieving Democracy* (Totowa, N.J.: Rowman and Allanheld, 1985), also bases his egalitarian democracy on a combination of liberal and socialist traditions and agenda. Rawls, though typically regarded as a defender of welfare-state capitalism, both specifically says that "a liberal socialist regime can . . . answer to the two principles of justice," and, when envisaging the private property alternative, aims toward a regime, "in which land and capital are widely though not presumably equally held" (*A Theory of Justice* [Cambridge, Mass.: Harvard University Press, 1971], p. 280). See Richard Krouse and Michael McPherson, "Capitalism, 'Property-Owning Democracy,' and the Welfare State," in Amy Gutmann, ed., *Democracy and the Welfare State* (Princeton: Princeton University Press, 1988). Many varieties of liberalism, especially the libertarianism of Robert Nozick, *Anarchy, State and Utopia* (New York: Basic Books, 1974), are completely antipathetic to socialism.

6. Thomas Hobbes, "Philosophical Rudiments Concerning Government and Society," in Sir William Molesworth, ed., *The English Works of Thomas Hobbes,* 11 vols. (London: John Bohn, 166), II, 109. Though Hobbes was no liberal in his conclusions, advocating an absolute rather than restrained state, many of his most important ideas—including original individual equality and freedom—became central tenets of liberal theory.

7. Nancy Chodorow, *The Reproduction of Mothering* (Berkeley: University of California Press, 1974), and "Family Structure and Feminine Personality," in Michelle Rosaldo and Louise Lamphere, eds., *Woman, Culture, and Society* (Stanford: Stanford University Press, 1974). See also Dorothy Dinnerstein, *The Mermaid and the Minotaur* (New York: Harper and Row, 1977).

8. See, for example, Kenneth M. Davidson, Ruth Bader Ginsburg, and Herma Hill Kay, *Sex-Based Discrimination* (St. Paul, Minn.: West, 1974; also 1978 supplement by Wendy Williams); Carol Smart, *The Ties that Bind: Law, Marriage and the Reproduction of Patriarchal Relations* (London: Routledge and Kegan Paul, 1984).

9. For example, Linda J. Nicholson, *Gender and History* (New York: Columbia

University Press, 1986); Joan W. Scott, "Gender: A Useful Category of Historical Analysis," *American Historical Review* 91 (December 1986): 1053–1075.

10. Herma Hill Kay, "Equality and Difference: A Perspective on No-fault Divorce and its Aftermath," *University of Cincinnati Law Review* 56 (1987): 1–90; James B. McLindon, "Separate but Unequal: The Economic Disaster of Divorce for Women and Children," *Family Law Quarterly* 21 (Fall 1987): 351–409; Susan Moller Okin, *Justice, Gender and the Family,* chap. 7; Lenore J. Weitzman, *The Divorce Revolution: The Unexpected Social and Economic Consequences for Women and Children in America* (New York: Free Press, 1985); Heather Ruth Wishik, "Economics of Divorce: An Exploratory Study," *Family Law Quarterly* 20 (Spring 1986): 79–107.

11. For a recent and succinct analysis of this situation, see Barbara Bergmann, *The Economic Emergence of Women* (New York: Basic Books, 1986), esp. chaps. 9–11. For a summary of findings of more recent research, see "Women: Out of the House, But Not Out of the Kitchen," *New York Times,* Feb. 24, 1988, p. A1.

12. "Women in the Law Say Path Is Limited by 'Mommy Track,' " *New York Times,* Aug. 8, 1988, p. A1; "Curbs for Minors Seeking Abortion Upheld on Appeal," *New York Times,* Aug. 9, 1988, p. A1.

13. There is a high incidence of recruitment of judges from those who have risen to partnership in the most prestigious law firms. Others are often drawn from the equally highly competitive field of academic law, which also places its greatest demands—those of the tenure hurdle—on lawyers in the child-rearing years, and therefore discriminates against those who participate in parenting.

14. David Ellwood, *Poor Support: Poverty in the American Family* (New York: Basic Books, 1988), p. 133. Sixty-two percent of the women cited household or family responsibilities as their reason for either working only part-time or not having a job. Only 5 percent of the men cited such reasons for not working full-time. (The standard definition of year-round, full-time work is 35 hours per week for 50 weeks, including vacations.)

15. Walzer, *Spheres of Justice,* p. 304 (italics in original). Compare Benjamin Barber, *Strong Democracy* (Berkeley: University of California Press, 1984), pp. 173–178. Though he starts with the statement that "at the heart of strong democracy is talk," Barber's discussion is unusual in its emphasis that listening is just as important a part of "talk" as speaking, and that the "potential for empathy and affective expression" is as crucial to it as is eloquence or creativity. Thus his approach is less biased in favor of traditionally masculine and away from traditionally feminine qualities than is usual in such discussions of political speech.

16. "On Authority: or, Why Women are not Entitled to Speak," in J. Roland Pennock and John W. Chapman, eds., *Authority Revisited* (New York and London: New York University Press, 1987).

17. I experienced a particularly graphic example of this a number of years ago when a male colleague started to scream at me in a meeting for no discernible

reason. When, after some time, the chairman attempted to intervene, the enraged man turned to him, only to explode: "I can't help it. She reminds me of my mother!"

18. John Locke, *A Letter Concerning Toleration* (Indianapolis: Bobbs Merrill, 1950), pp. 28–29.

19. I discuss this at greater length in Okin, "Gender, the Public and the Private." See also Martha Minow, "We the Family: Constitutional Right and American Families," *The American Journal of History* 74 (1987): 959–983; Nikolas Rose, "Beyond the Public/Private Division: Law, Power and the Family," *Journal of Law and Society* 14 (1987): 61–76.

20. Rawls, *Theory of Justice*, p. 71.

21. Ibid., pp. 128–129, 300–301, 462–472, 490–491, 511–512. It seems significant that in "The Basic Structure as Subject," *American Philosophical Quarterly* 14 (1977): 159–165, Rawls does *not* specify the family as part of the basic structure of society, though his statements about the importance of this structure for how individuals "get to be what they are" (p. 160) are at least as strong as those in *A Theory of Justice*. For commentary on Rawls's treatment of the family, see Jane English, "Justice Between Generations," *Philosophical Studies* 31 (1977): 1–104; Karen Green, "Rawls, Women and the Priority of Liberty," *Australasian Journal of Philosophy*, supp. to 64 (June 1986): 26–36; Deborah Kearns, "A Theory of Justice—and Love: Rawls on the Family," *Politics* (Journal of the Australasian Political Studies Association), 18 (1983): 36–42; Susan Moller Okin, "Justice and Gender," *Philosophy and Public Affairs* 16 (1987): 42–72, and "Reason and Feeling in Thinking about Justice," *Ethics* 99 (1989): 229–249.

22. Rawls, *Theory of Justice*, pp. 463, 490.

23. Bruce Ackerman, *Social Justice in the Liberal State* (New Haven: Yale University Press, 1980), Ronald Dworkin, *Taking Rights Seriously* (Cambridge, Mass.: Harvard University Press, 1977), William Galston, *Justice and the Human Good* (Chicago: University of Chicago Press, 1980), Robert Nozick, *Anarchy, State and Utopia* (New York: Basic Books, 1974).

24. Walzer, *Spheres of Justice*; Okin, "Justice v. Gender."

25. Alasdair MacIntyre, *After Virtue* (Notre Dame: University of Notre Dame Press, 1981), chap. 12, pp. 222–226, 201.

26. Alasdair MacIntyre, *Whose Justice? Which Rationality?* (Notre Dame: University of Notre Dame Press, 1988), pp. 10, 105, 401–403.

27. Ibid., p. 326. I expand on these points in *Justice, Gender and the Family*.

28. Even feminists who are attracted by the communitarian notion of the constituted self sometimes do not mention this. For some who *do*, see Seyla Benhabib and Drucilla Cornell, "Introduction: Beyond the Politics of Gender," in *Feminism as Critique* (Minneapolis: University of Minnesota Press, 1987), pp. 12–13, and Marilyn Friedman, "Feminism and Modern Friendship: Dislocating the Community," *Ethics* 99 (1989): 275–290.

29. Rawls, *Theory of Justice*, pp. 126–130.

30. Michael J. Sandel, *Liberalism and the Limits of Justice* (Cambridge: Cambridge University Press, 1982), p. 23.

31. Ibid., pp. 30–31.

32. Sandel, *Liberalism and the Limits of Justice,* p. 31, quoting David Hume, *An Enquiry Concerning the Principles of Morals* (La Salle, Ill.: Open Court, 1966), pp. 17–18.

33. Larmore, *Patterns of Moral Complexity,* pp. 121–130, esp. 126.

34. Will Kymlicka, "Liberalism and Communitarianism," *Canadian Journal of Philosophy* 18 (1988), pp. 181–204, at p. 190 (italics in original).

35. Larmore, *Patterns of Moral Complexity,* p. 123. It is not clear to me how Larmore reconciles this anti-Kantian position with his earlier discussion of the need in "rational dialogue" to be able to retreat to neutral ground. There he says: "abstracting from a controversial belief does not imply that one believes it any the less, that one has had reason to become skeptical toward it. One can remain as convinced of its truth as before, but for the purposes of the conversation one sets it aside" (p. 53). This suggests, as a critic of Sandel's conception of the self might, that we may be tied to our ends and attachments in living the good life, but still able to abstract from them for the purpose of thinking about justice. Sandel, by contrast, takes the view that certain beliefs may be so constitutive of our identity that we are unable without violating our selves to set them aside for any purpose.

36. Ibid., esp. chaps. 3, 4.

37. Larmore says: "The public has to do with what belongs within the political system, whereas the private covers whatever belongs outside it" (ibid., p. 42). For evidence of Rawls's more explicit recent adherence to the dichotomy, he cites Rawls's "Kantian Constructivism in Moral Theory" and "Justice as Fairness: Political not Metaphysical." See also John Rawls, "The Priority of Right and Ideas of the Good," *Philosophy and Public Affairs* 17 (1988), where Rawls explicitly endorses Larmore's reliance on the distinction between the political and the nonpolitical, and his reading of Rawls's theory as a theory of *political* justice (for example, pp. 253–254, n. 2). Rawls discusses some ambiguities of and difficulties with the requirement that the state be "neutral" (pp. 260–264).

38. Larmore, *Patterns of Moral Complexity,* p. 106 (italics mine).

39. Rawls, "Justice as Fairness," p. 245, n. 27, and "Priority of Right," p. 263.

40. See Susan Kingsley Kent, *Sex and Suffrage in England: 1850–1914* (Princeton: Princeton University Press, 1987), and Mary L. Shanley, *Feminism, Marriage and the Law in Victorian England* (Princeton: Princeton University Press, forthcoming).

41. Larmore specifies that a political decision "can count as neutral only if it can be justified without appealing to the presumed intrinsic superiority of any particular conception of the good life" (*Patterns of Moral Complexity,* p. 44).

42. In October 1988 the U.S. Congress failed to pass a bill mandating large-scale employers to provide unpaid parental leave for their employees. This leaves the United States with the dubious distinction of being the only Western-industrialized country other than South Africa without such a policy.

Three. *Liberal Democracy and the Costs of Consent*

1. This is a now familiar criticism put forward in its classical form by Comte, Marx, and the nineteenth-century sociological tradition, and given modern philosophical expression by Charles Taylor, Michael Walzer, William Sullivan, Alasdair MacIntyre, and many others—for example, Michael Sandel, who in his critique of Rawls's liberal conception of the self writes: "But a self so thoroughly independent as [Rawls's] rules out any conception of the good (or the bad) . . . It rules out the possibility of any attachment (or obsession) able to reach beyond our values and sentiments to engage our identity itself. It rules out the possibility of a public life . . . And it rules out the possibility that common purposes and ends could inspire more or less expansive self-understandings and so define a community." Michael J. Sandel, *Liberalism and the Limits of Justice* (Cambridge: Cambridge University Press, 1982), p. 62.
2. "Despotism may govern without faith, but liberty cannot. Religion is much more necessary in the republic . . . than in the monarchy . . . it is more needed in democratic republics than in any others. How is it possible that society should escape destruction if the moral tie is relaxed?" Alexis de Tocqueville, *Democracy in America,* ed. Phillips Bradley, 2 vols. (New York: Vintage, 1960), II, 318.
3. William E. Connolly, *Politics and Ambiguity* (Madison: University of Wisconsin Press, 1987), p. 3.
4. Thus, when in *State and Revolution,* Lenin (what irony!) writes that "while the state exists there is no freedom. When there is freedom there will be no state," he is speaking quintessentially liberal language.
5. Liberals rightly pall at the idea of Hobbes as a liberal predecessor because his fear of anarchy leads him to embrace an authoritarian conception of the state incompatible with limited government. Yet inasmuch as the state serves a liberty the natural condition imperils, Hobbes does share a crucial liberal premise: that the legitimating political principle is in the service of individual self-preservation, which is the sine qua non of liberty. For a recent, subtly argued construction of Hobbes as a defender of the individual and his fragile body, see George Kateb, "Hobbes and the Irrationality of Politics," paper presented to the American Political Science Association convention, September 1988.
6. Jean-Jacques Rousseau, *The Social Contract,* bk. I, chap. 6.
7. Will Kymlicka defends liberals against communitarian charges that their conception of the individual is abstract and atomistic. But, in addition to turning every liberal from Rawls to Dworkin and Nozick into John Stuart Mill, he misses the essence of the criticism, which is not simply that liberals neglect community or the constraints of encumbered selves, but that they consistently treat both as secondary to and logically and morally dependent on prior conceptions of unencumbered individuals. See Will Kymlicka, "Liberalism and Comunitarianism," *Canadian Journal of Philosophy* 18 (June 1988): 181–204.
8. See Marshall Berman's splendid essay on modernity and disorder, which

uses Marx's phrase in its title: *All That Is Solid Melts Into Air* (New York: Simon and Schuster, 1982).

9. Judith Shklar's Chapter 1 in this volume is representative. Both Richard Flathman and, from a very different point of view, George Kateb champion freedom without entering into a full discussion of its costs to community and identity, although Kateb acknowledges the debt liberty owes to citizenship in "The Moral Distinctiveness of Representative Democracy," *Ethics* 91 (April 1981): 357–374.

10. This argument was first advanced after World War II by Theodor Adorno and his colleagues in *The Authoritarian Personality* (New York: Harper, 1950), and by psychologists such as Erich Fromm, Robert Jay Lifton, and Viktor Frankl.

11. Sandel, *Liberalism and the Limits of Justice,* p. 54.

12. John Rawls, *A Theory of Justice* (Cambridge, Mass.: Harvard University Press, 1971). As I have argued elsewhere (*The Conquest of Politics* [Princeton: Princeton University Press, 1988], pp. 54–55)—Kymlicka, "Liberalism and Communitarianism" notwithstanding—Rawls's logical prioritization of liberty entails a psychological and political prioritization that defeats the attempt at mediation.

13. Robert Nozick is the most vociferous recent advocate of this brand of strong liberalism. See his *Anarchy, the State and Utopia* (New York: Basic Books, 1974).

14. C. B. Macpherson's account of possessive individualism (in *The Political Theory of Possessive Individualism* [Oxford: Oxford University Press, 1961]), may not always be creditable as intellectual history, but it remains a persuasive vision of the liberal democratic conception of the self, and how the self-possessing individual becomes the acquisitive (property-owning) individual.

15. The social contract theorists tried to have it both ways, surrounding their ruminations about the possible historicity of the social contract with caveats about the hypothetical character of the state of nature. Rousseau is typical here, offering an anthropology of natural man in the *Second Discourse* that he studiously avoids in *The Social Contract,* where he makes it clear not only that the state of nature is hypothetical, but that man's actual condition is one of dependency (man is "everywhere in chains").

16. See Shklar's powerful defense of the liberalism of fear in Chapter 1.

17. The familiar portrait of man's life in the state of nature in *Leviathan,* chap. 13.

18. "Liberty, or freedom, signifieth, properly, the absence of opposition; by opposition, I mean external impediments of motion . . . a freeman, is he, that in those things, which by his strength and wit he is able to do, is not hindered to do what he has a will to." *Leviathan,* chap. 21.

19. The lexical ordering of the principles of justice "means that a departure from the institutions of equal liberty required by the first principle cannot be justified by, or compensated for, by greater social and economic advantages" (Rawls, *Theory of Justice,* p. 61).

20. Benjamin R. Barber, *Strong Democracy: Participatory Politics for a New Age*, (Berkeley: University of California Press, 1984).

21. Reversing the polarity and giving community the priority that, for liberal individualists, the individual enjoys, only reverses the imbalance and creates a different set of problems well known to critics of communitarian (totalitarian) collectivism. Most recent communitarians respect the dialectical interplay of individual and community, however, and do not dispute the ultimate concern for individuals. The question is not the normative priority of the individual, but how the individual is morally and politically constituted. This is the essence of Michael Sandel's critique in *Liberalism and the Limits of Justice*, and is a position that Rawls himself moves toward in his recent work (see note 23).

22. The collaborative character of participatory politics does not, as liberal critics sometimes seem to suppose, require that conflict be wished away or denied. On the contrary, as Rousseau observed, without conflict there would be no politics and thus no need for government at all (the anarchist premise, which is closer to libertarian liberalism than democratic communitarianism). Connolly typically exaggerates the democratic penchant for conflict-free harmony; see also note 27.

23. Philosophers have come to appreciate that the rigid conception of the person demanded by the fiction of the legal person or the free agent needs to be supplemented by a richer conception of the moral and social person. This is particularly apparent in John Rawls's recent work, which, as it pushes a morally constructed person toward its center, distances itself from hypothetical persons bent into abstract Archimedean positions. See, for example, "Kantian Constructivism in Moral Theory" (The Dewey Lectures), *Journal of Philosophy* 77 (September 1980): 515–573; and "Justice as Fairness: Political Not Metaphysical," *Philosophy and Public Affairs* 14 (Summer 1985): 223–251.

24. "There can be no right without a consciousness of common interest on the part of members of a society . . . Without this recognition or claim to recognition there can be no right" (T. H. Green, *Lectures on the Principles of Political Obligation* [London: Longmans, 1941], p. 48).

25. "No society can make a perpetual constitution, or even a perpetual law. The earth belongs always to the living generation . . . every constitution then, and every law, naturally expires at the end of 19 years," Thomas Jefferson, Letter to Madison, 1789. Jefferson and John Stuart Mill share with libertarians like Nozick an affection for perpetual consent, but whereas for the libertarians this suggests private consent to public acts, to Jefferson and Mill it suggests the importance of active citizenship and ongoing participation.

26. This line of criticism has an impressive pedigree. In *Political Parties* (Glencoe: University of Illinois Press, 1915), Robert Michaels turns Rousseau's disdain for representation into a profound critique of the party system.

27. "We need a theory and practice of democracy," writes Connolly, "that appreciates [the] element of disharmony. One that understands harmoni-

zation to be normalization." *Politics and Ambiguity*, p. 8. "Normalization" as used here is highly pejorative, suggesting the kinds of leveling, routinization, and noncoercive repression *(gleichschaltung)* long associated with both democratic conformism (in Tocqueville's critique) and bourgeois liberalism (in Foucault's critique). But the harmony that issues from the interplay of democratic wills has the richness of a seven-tone chord and is neither unitary nor repressive.

28. See Benjamin R. Barber, "Political Judgment: Philosophy as Practice," *The Conquest of Politics* (Princeton: Princeton University Press, 1988), where I have tried to spell out a political theory of judgment in greater detail.

Four. Undemocratic Education

1. Many of the arguments in this chapter are more fully developed in Amy Gutmann, *Democratic Education* (Princeton: Princeton University Press, 1987).
2. This is a nonironic interpretation of *The Republic*. My aim is not to offer an interpretation that is faithful to Plato's intentions or to the full range of his arguments, but rather to use the *Republic* to illuminate the premises of a common political understanding of education.
3. *The Republic*, bk. IX, 590d (italics mine).
4. Ibid., bk. VII, 541a.
5. Ibid., bk. IX, 592a.
6. The phrase comes from David B. Tyack, *The One Best System: A History of American Urban Education* (Cambridge, Mass.: Harvard University Press, 1974).
7. *Crito*, in *The Last Days of Socrates*, trans. Hugh Tredennick (Harmondsworth: Penguin, 1970), pp. 90–91 (50b–51c).
8. Charles Fried, *Right and Wrong* (Cambridge, Mass.: Harvard University Press, 1978), p. 152.
9. The usage of liberal here is loose because there are many liberal theories that do not rest upon neutrality in this sense. On a broader understanding of liberalism, which includes theories that do not rest upon neutrality among good lives, democratic education qualifies as liberal.
10. John Stuart Mill, *On Liberty*, chap. 5, para. 13.
11. Bruce Ackerman, *Social Justice in the Liberal State* (New York and London: Yale University Press, 1980), pp. 141–148. Ackerman applies the principle of liberal neutrality to all educators, parents as well as professional teachers.
12. Ibid., p. 139.
13. Nor does anyone have a right to act on the belief that *any* conception of the good life is better than any other. The claim that some conceptions of the good are better (or worse) than others is suspect on these liberal grounds even when it is not self-serving.
14. Rogers M. Smith develops this Lockean understanding in *Liberalism and American Constitutional Law* (Cambridge, Mass.: Harvard University Press,

1985). See also Nathan Tarcov's complementary interpretation of *Locke's Education for Liberty* (Chicago: University of Chicago Press, 1984).

15. William Galston, "Liberal Virtues," *American Political Science Review* 82 (December 1988: 1287).

16. Saying that the alternative should not tyrannize over common sense does not mean that it should not criticize common sense. Philosophy gives common sense its due by recognizing that first principles are impossible to prove, that they must be judged in significant part by their practical implications, and that this judgment entails the use of common sense ("practical judgment" is the stricter term). This process of achieving what John Rawls has called "reflective equilibrium," a process of philosophical reasoning that is not uniquely tied to Rawls's theory, leaves ample room for criticizing common (and uncommon) sense.

17. Immanuel Kant, *Kant on Education (Ueber Padogogik),* trans. Annette Churton (Boston: D. C. Heath, 1900), p. 17.

18. Ping-Ti Ho, *The Ladder of Success in Imperial China: Aspects of Social Mobility, 1368–1911* (New York: Columbia University Press, 1962), p. 262.

19. Bob Mozert et al. v. Hawkins County Public Schools et al., U.S. District Court for the Eastern District of Tennessee, Northeastern Division, no. CIV-2-83-401 (Oct. 24, 1986), p. 12.

20. Mill, *On Liberty,* chap. 5, para. 14.

21. The right is limited not by virtue of being weak, but by virtue of leaving room for other educational authorities.

22. The testimony of two witnesses for the plaintiffs, cited in the decision of the United States Court of Appeals (Sixth Circuit) that reversed the decision of the District Court and remanded with directions to dismiss the complaint (827 F. 2d. 1058 [6th Cir. 1987] at 1062).

23. Alan L. Feld, Michael O'Hare, and J. Mark Davidson Schuster, *Patrons Despite Themselves: Taxpayers and Arts Policy* (New York: New York University Press, 1983), p. 215. For ways in which information concerning private donations could be made more accessible to the public, see pp. 215–216.

24. For some of the unethical practices made easy by our present indirect subsidy system, see ibid., pp. 169–77.

25. For a summary of the historical record, see Dick Netzer, *The Subsidized Muse: Public Support for Arts in the United States* (Cambridge: Cambridge University Press, 1978).

26. T. M. Scanlon, "Symposium on the Public Benefits of the Arts and Humanities," *Art and the Law* 9 (1985): 170.

27. Quoted in "J.-J. Rousseau, Citizen of Geneva to Monsieur D'Alembert," in Jean Jacques Rousseau, *Politics and the Arts,* trans. Allan Bloom (Ithaca, N.Y.: Cornell University Press, 1973), p. 4.

28. See Thomas Nagel, "Symposium on the Public Benefits of the Arts and Humanities," *Art and the Law* 9 (1985): 237.

29. Richard Rorty and Michael Walzer explicitly defend this priority principle.

See Rorty, "The Priority of Democracy to Philosophy," in Merrill D. Peterson and Robert C. Vaughan, eds., *The Virginia Statute for Religious Freedom: Its Evolution and Consequences in American History* (New York: Cambridge University Press, forthcoming); and Walzer, "Philosophy and Democracy," *Political Theory* 9 (August 1981): 384–394.

Five. Civic Education in the Liberal State

1. See Robert K. Fullinwider, "Civic Education and Traditional American Values," *QQ* 6 (Summer 1986): 5–8.
2. Albert Hirschman, *The Passions and the Interests* (Princeton: Princeton University Press, 1977).
3. Immanuel Kant, "Perpetual Peace," in Lewis White Beck, ed., *Kant on History* (Indianapolis: Bobbs-Merrill, 1963), pp. 111–112.
4. See especially Rogers Smith, *Liberalism and American Constitutional Law* (Cambridge, Mass.: Harvard University Press, 1985); Nathan Tarcov, *Locke's Education for Liberty* (Chicago: University of Chicago Press, 1984); Harvey Mansfield, Jr., "Constitutional Government: The Soul of Modern Democracy, *The Public Interest* 86 (Winter 1987): 53–64.
5. James Q. Wilson, "The Rediscovery of Character: Private Virtue and Public Policy," *The Public Interest* 81 (Fall 1985): 3–16.
6. Charles Glenn, Jr., *The Myth of the Common School* (Amherst: University of Massachusetts Press, 1988).
7. "Education for Democracy: A Statement of Principles," (Washington, D.C.: American Federation of Teachers, 1987), p. 8.
8. This paragraph summarizes the central argument of my "Liberal Virtues," *American Political Science Review* 82 (December 1988): 1277–1290.
9. Amy Gutmann, *Democratic Education* (Princeton: Princeton University Press, 1987), p. 39.
10. Ibid., pp. 44–46.
11. Alphaeus Mason, ed., *Free Government in the Making*, 3rd ed. (New York: Oxford University Press, 1965), p. 385.
12. See William Galston, "Public Morality and Religion in the Liberal State," *PS* 19 (Fall 1986): 807–824.
13. Gutmann, *Democratic Education*, pp. 30–31.
14. For a very different way of drawing this line, see Bruce Ackerman, *Social Justice in the Liberal State* (New Haven: Yale University Press, 1980), chap. 5.

Six. Class Conflict and Constitutionalism in J. S. Mill's Thought

1. John Stuart Mill, *Autobiography* (New York: New American Library, 1965), pp. 121–122.
2. *The Collected Works of John Stuart Mill*, ed. John M. Robson, 25 vols. (Toronto: University of Toronto Press, 1965–1986), 10, 88, 90, 92 ("Bentham"); 23, 471–472.

3. Mill, *Autobiography*, p. 125; *Works*, 13, 434; 20, 182–184; 23, 403.

4. "The new political philosophy of the present generation in France" which is "scattered among many minds . . . may be pronounced greatly in advance of all the other political philosophies which [have] yet existed," Mill, *Works*, 20, 184; cf. 20, 182–183, 313; 13, 458.

5. Mill, *Autobiography*, p. 124; *Works*, 10, 154 ("Coleridge"); 18, 127 ("Civilization"); 19, 380, 423 *(Considerations on Representative Government)*.

6. Mill, *Works*, 20, 183–184.

7. Mill, *Works*, 8, 906 *(A System of Logic)*. "The State of every part of the social whole at any time, is intimately connected with the contemporaneous state of all others . . . In constructing, therefore, a theory of society, all the different aspects of the social organization must be taken into consideration at once," *Works*, 10, 308 *(Auguste Comte and Positivism)*; 18, 18 ("Rationale of Representation"); 23, 693; John Stuart Mill, *Principles of Political Economy*, 7th ed. (Clifton, N.J.: Augustus M. Kelley, 1973), p. 695.

8. "I understand by Sociology not a particular *class* of subjects included *within* politics, but a vast field *including* it—the whole field of enquiry and speculation respecting human society and its arrangements, of which the forms of government, and the principles of the conduct of governments are but a part," Mill, *Works*, 14, 68.

9. Mill, *Works*, 4, 320. The "change in the premises of my political philosophy" made it a more complex and "many-sided" political theory *(Autobiography*, pp. 123, 125, 129).

10. Mill, *Works*, 8, 911–912 *(Logic)*.

11. Ibid., 8, 875; 21, 224.

12. Mill, *Works*, 10, 89–92 ("Bentham"), 307 *(Comte)*. Man, that "complex and manifold being, whose properties are not independent of circumstance, and immovable from age to age . . . but, are infinitely various, indefinitely modifiable by art or accident," *Works*, 21, 241; cf. ibid., 21, 277 *(The Subjection of Women)*; *Autobiography*, p. 193.

13. Mill, *Works*, 20, 184–185.

14. Mill, *Autobiography*, p. 124.

15. Mill, *Works*, 10, 308 *(Comte)*; 8, 930 *(Logic)*; 20, 262.

16. Mill, *Autobiography*, p. 129.

17. Mill, *Works*, 20, 187.

18. Mill, *Works*, 10, 323 *(Comte)*; *Autobiography*, p. 124.

19. Mill, *Works*, 23, 404.

20. Mill, *Works*, 7, 370–378; 8, 883 *(Logic)*; 10, 326 *(Comte)*; *Autobiography*, pp. 122–123, 171.

21. Mill, *Works*, 7, 329 *(Logic)*.

22. Ibid., 7, 444–445; 8, 869–870, 898 *(Logic)*; 4, 337; *Autobiography*, pp. 122–123, 171.

23. Mill, *Works*, 7, 594; 8, 847–848, 861 *(Logic)*; 4, 336–337; 15, 846; 16, 1241; 21, 237.

24. Mill, *Works*, 7, 519; 8, 791 *(Logic)*; 19, 396, 398 *(Considerations)*.

25. Mill, *Works,* 10, 387.

26. Mill, *Works,* 18, 57 ("DeTocqueville on Democracy in America, 1"), 157 ("DeTocqueville on Democracy in America, 11"); 20, 184; *Autobiography,* p. 143. The task of the political theorist is to offer an "enlightened estimate of tendencies and consequences," *Works,* 21, 275 *(Subjection).*

27. Mill, *Works,* 7, 603; 8, 875, 890 *(Logic).*

28. Mill, *Works,*, 8, 898 *(Logic).*

29. Ibid., 8, 912; 4, 320.

30. Mill, *Works,* 10, 326 *(Comte).*

31. Ibid., 10, 99 ("Bentham").

32. Ibid., 10, 109–110 ("Bentham").

33. Mill, *Works,* 6, 102.

34. Mill, *Works,* 16, 1385; 18, 182 ("DeTocqueville, 11"); 19, 448 *(Considerations); Political Economy,* pp. 752, 761, 763.

35. Mill, *Works,* 18, 28 ("Rationale"), 202 ("DeTocqueville, 11"); 5, 707 *(Chapters on Socialism);* 19, 354 ("Recent Writers on Reform"), 445 *(Considerations); Political Economy,* 754.

36. Mill, *Works,* 19, 505 *(Considerations).*

37. Mill, *Works,* 18, 221 *(On Liberty);* cf. ibid., 18, 71 ("DeTocqueville, 1"); 19, 650.

38. Mill, *Works,* 18, 197 ("DeTocqueville, 11").

39. Mill, *Works,* 6, 469 ("Reorganization of the Reform Party").

40. Mill, *Works,* 18, 200 "DeTocqueville, 11").

41. Ibid., 18, 172.

42. Mill, *Works,* 5, 762.

43. Mill, *Works,* 4, 369 ("The Claims of Labor"); 6, 478 ("Reorganization").

44. Mill, *Works,* 6, 485 ("Reorganization").

45. Mill, *Works,* 379 ("Claims").

46. Mill, *Works,* 6, 479 ("Reorganization").

47. Mill, *Works,* 4, 380 ("Claims"); *Political Economy,* pp. 761, 763.

48. Mill, *Political Economy,* p. 756.

49. Mill, *Works,* 16, 1014.

50. Ibid., 16, 1103. "The contrariety of interests between person and person, class and class, which pervades the present constitution of society," *Works,* 5, 725 *(Socialism).*

51. Mill, *Works,* 5, 650, 666; 15, 749; 16, 1442; 19, 591 ("Centralization").

52. Mill, *Works,* 17, 1837–1838.

53. Mill, *Works,* 5, 707–708 *(Socialism).*

54. Mill, *Works,* 4, 293; 18, 28 ("Rationale"); *Political Economy,* pp. 419, 460, 693–694, 710–711, 719–720.

55. Mill, *Works,* 5, 656–657.

56. Ibid., 5, 634.

57. The formation of trade unions and bargaining for wages became matters of "prudence and social duty," *Works,* 5, 646–647, 662.

58. Ibid., 5, 634.

59. Mill, *Works,* 15, 749.

60. Mill, *Works*, 5, 660; *Political Economy*, p. 934.
61. That Mill *can* be interpreted in this way, I do not deny. He clearly recognizes that there are two conflicting theories of justice at the core of the conflict between workers and capitalists (*Works*, 5, 650), and he does argue that this conflict must be decided on the grounds of social utility (ibid., 5, 655). What then? Even if both sides accepted this proposition, we still do not know *which* side of the dispute is in accordance with social utility, nor do we know how this determination is to be made. The same difficulty characterizes Mill's essay on *Utilitarianism,* where he observes that there are conflicting theories of justice associated with various kinds of social inequalities (*Works*, 10, 244 ["Utilitarianism"]), or different theories of punishment (ibid., 10, 252), or, as in the example above, different theories as to how profits ought to be distributed (ibid., 10, 253–254). In none of these instances does Mill offer a specific illustration as to how the general principle of utility enables us to decide which of the contending theories of justice is the correct one on utilitarian grounds. Mill's philosophical mistake, if it can be called that, is his apparent assumption that a controversy between plausible theories of justice could be resolved if only one uncovered "the principles which lie under justice and are the source of its authority," that is, general utility (ibid., 10, 252), whereas, if the latter principle is incorporated into each of the contending theories of justice as part of its argument for "justice," as is commonly the case, it is obvious that the controversy is not one step closer to a solution than it was before. So much for Mill the philosopher. The alternative, I am suggesting, is to rely upon the specific judgment (or rather, an interpretation of the specific judgment) of Mill the social observer that, for example, cooperative socialism *is* more in accordance with social utility than the private ownership of the means of production, although the intermediate philosophical steps by which Mill arrives at this conclusion remain unclear. (Cf. *Works*, 15, 749.) This last point must not be exaggerated, however, since Mill did rest his conviction upon what he perceived to be a developing tendency in society toward cooperation. The "practical principle" of cooperation, he wrote, is "progressively widening . . . as society advances." Cooperative socialism was one manifestation of this broad and "progressive change" in social relations. It is in this context, in accordance with his social science methodology, that Mill the political theorist believes that the system of wage labor will be replaced by cooperative socialism (*Works*, 5, 442, 707 [*Socialism*]; *Political Economy*, pp. 698–699, 763–764, 772–773, 789–792).
62. Mill, *Works*, 5, 665.
63. "The power of striking tends to bring about something approximating to what I consider the only right organization of labor, the association of the workpeople with the employers by a participation of profits," Mill, *Works*, 15, 735; *Political Economy*, p. 938.
64. Mill, *Works*, 5, 665; 10, 341 *(Comte)*.
65. Mill, *Works*, 5, 442, 666; 20, 352; *Autobiography*, p. 168.
66. Mill, *Works*, 15, 857, 859.

67. Mill, *Works*, 16, 1439; cf. ibid., 16, 1103; 4, 382 ("Claims"); *Political Economy*, pp. 773, 789.
68. Mill, *Works*, 5, 738 *(Socialism)*; *Political Economy*, pp. 203–204, 772–773.
69. Speaking of cooperative socialism, Mill wrote that "it is scarcely possible to rate too highly this material benefit, which yet is as nothing compared with the moral revolution in society that would accompany it," *Political Economy*, p. 789; cf. *Works*, 5, 442; 15, 546, 813; 17, 1535.
70. Mill, *Works*, 5, 551. "A just principle should be carried out so far as it can go, that is, to the point at which it is stopped by insurmountable obstacles," *Works*, 5, 573. "The first object in every practical discussion should be to know what perfection is," *Political Economy*, p. 804.
71. Mill, *Works*, 19, 475 *(Considerations)*.
72. Mill, *Works*, 5, 444. "No rational person will maintain it to be abstractedly just, that a small minority of mankind should be born to the enjoyment of all the external advantages which life can give, without earning them by any merit or acquiring them by any exertion of their own, while the immense majority are condemned from their birth, to a life of never-ending, never-intermitting toil, required by a bare, and in general a precarious, subsistence. It is impossible to contend that this is in itself just. It is possible to contend that it is expedient," *Works*, 20, 351.
73. Mill, *Works*, 5, 444; 14, 85, 87.
74. The economic institutions of society, Mill wrote, may be grounded either on the principle of private property or on the communal ownership of property. The former principle states "that what any individuals have caused by their own labor, and what the law permits them to be given to them by others, they are allowed to dispose of at pleasure, for their own use." This view of property, he declares, is "far inferior to the law of community"—common ownership. The only reason for not adopting the latter is that "mankind are not prepared for it"; that is, through the overcoming of practical obstacles through education (*Works*, 14, 50; cf. ibid., 14, 85, 87). Cooperative socialism represents "the nearest approach to social justice, and the most beneficial ordering of industrial affairs for the universal good, which it is possible at present to foresee," *Political Economy*, p. 792; cf. *Autobiography*, p. 168. Speaking of Harriet Taylor's ideas, which he claimed to share, Mill wrote that her "final aim" was "a state of society entirely communist in practice and spirit," embodying a standard of "perfect distributive justice" *(Works*, 15, 601).
75. Mill, *Works*, 10, 341 *(Comte)*. "The very idea of distributive justice, or of any proportionality between success and merit, or between success and exertion, is in the present state of society so manifestly chimerical as to be relegated to the regions of romance, *Works*, 5, 714 *(Socialism)*.
76. Mill, *Works*, 18, 184–185 ("DeTocqueville, 11"). "For my own part, not believing in universal selfishness, I have no difficulty in admitting that Communism would even now be practical among the *elite* of mankind, and may become so among the rest." 19, 405 *(Considerations)*; cf. *Autobiography*, pp. 168–169.

77. Mill, *Works,* 19, 444 *(Considerations);* cf. ibid., 19, 411–412; *Political Economy,* p. 206.

78. Mill, *Autobiography,* pp. 168–169. "The selfish type of character formed by the present standard of morality, and fostered by the existing social institutions," *Political Economy,* p. 212. The fact that because of their alienation from political and social life the working class had not been corrupted, relatively speaking, by the selfish habits engendered by the social institutions of Victorian England was for Mill one of the most positive features of transferring political power into their hands (*Works,* 15, 840; 16, 1103, 1209; 17, 1870).

79. Mill, *Works,* 20, 354; 10, 109–110 ("Bentham"). Accepting "the mass of physical and moral evils which . . . directly grow out of the facts of competition and individual property" does not mean that some of these evils cannot be removed, nor does it involve a denial that the system as a whole may persist "for a considerable time to come," *Works,* 5, 442, 728 *(Socialism),* 736, 750; *Political Economy,* p. 217.

80. Mill, *Works,* 6, 207.

81. Mill, *Works,* 25, 1106.

82. Mill, *Works,* 19, 588 ("Centralization").

83. Ibid., 19, 446, 448, 505 *(Considerations);* 18, 196 ("DeTocqueville, 11").

84. Mill, *Works,* 19, 448, 470 *(Considerations);* 16, 1385. This proviso, it should be noted, already projects Mill's argument in the *Considerations* into the hypothetical and ideal future in relation to the existing institutions in his society.

85. Mill, *Works,* 19, 447, 467 *(Considerations).*

86. "If ever democratic institutions are to be obtained quietly, a great change in the sentiments of the two great classes towards one another must precede" that event, *Works,* 6, 448; cf. 18, p. 182 ("DeTocqueville, 11"). The end of class conflict represented for Mill "the best aspirations of the democratic spirit," *Political Economy,* p. 791; cf. p. 752.

87. Mill, *Works,* 19, 447 *(Considerations);* 16, 1014.

88. Mill, *Works,* 19, 479, 498 *(Considerations).*

89. Mill, *Works,* 25, 1106; 19, 433 *(Considerations).*

90. Mill, *Works,* 19, 350 ("Recent Writers"), 405 *(Considerations);* 16, 1452; 17, 1759.

91. "I dislike all merely class representation, and I still more disapprove of all class subordination," Mill, *Works,* 16, 1252. "It is not for the sake of class interests" as such that I support working-class representation, Mill wrote, but because the working class should not "be without what every other class has—representatives in Parliament who can speak from their own knowledge of the wants, the grievances, and the modes of thought and feeling of their class," *Works,* 16, 1485; cf. ibid., 16, 1130; 18, 43–45 ("Rationale").

92. Mill, *Autobiography,* p. 215; *Works,* 16, 1452, 1534.

93. Mill, *Works,* 17, 1759; 19, 432, 457–458 *(Considerations).*

94. Mill, *Works,* 18, 252–254 *(Liberty).* Mill's argument that "in politics" there

is a division between opinions favorable "to property and to equality, to cooperation and to competition . . . to sociality and individuality" restates the point he makes elsewhere in his writings that these beliefs express competing and class-based principles of justice.

95. Mill, *Works*, 19, 459 *(Considerations);* 10, 108 ("Bentham"), 134 ("Coleridge"); 20, 270, 506.

96. Mill, *Works*, 20, 269, 358–359; 10, 122 ("Coleridge").

97. Mill, *Works*, 18, 198, 200 ("DeTocqueville, 11"); 10, 108 ("Bentham"); 25, 1106.

98. Mill, *Works*, 18, 88 ("DeTocqueville, 1"), 268–269 *(Liberty);* 15, 588, 765; 20, 359.

99. Mill, *Works*, 19, 459 *(Considerations)*. Nevertheless, even after writing the *Considerations,* Mill thought it "essential that the principle of superior education is entitled to superior political might should be in some way constitutionally recognized," *Works*, 15, 843. The question is, in what way? Mill had no wish to create "an intellectual aristocracy," nor did he favor a second House in Parliament composed of an intellectual elite, *Works*, 15, 631; *Works*, 19, 513–519 *(Considerations)*. By 1865, I believe Mill had given up the idea of plural voting (see note 100 below), and the best that can be said is that he held very high—I would say wildly exaggerated—expectations that Hare's electoral scheme would produce an intelligentsia among elected representatives which would wield this "superior political might," *Works*, 19, 453–456 *(Considerations)*.

100. It is precisely at this point that commentators frequently overlook or set aside Mill's understanding of the structure of his society in favor of attributing to him a general philosophical commitment to elitism. Mill conceded that plural voting was probably too closely associated with property qualifications, which he opposed, and would have to be given up, *Works*, 16, 998; cf. 15, 905; *Autobiography,* pp. 183–184. Even education was not "a complete guarantee against being swayed by class interests," *Works*, 15, 608. Hence, while Hare's plan of personal representation would allow some individuals of national reputation to overcome the constraints of "local influence," it would not set aside the structural influence of class interests in constitutional government, *Works*, 15, 653–654; 19, 460 *(Considerations)*.

101. Speaking of "party creeds," which, for most people, "run hand in hand with their interests or with their class feelings," Mill observes that reason is a powerful weapon when it is used to defend "their own side of the question" by "the best and wisest persons" who share that party and/or class perspective. But, he adds, "we expect few conversions by the mere force of reason, from one creed to the other." With a few exceptions, reason simply determines "what *sort*" of a partisan position a person adopts, *Works*, 6, 469 ("Reorganization"). Still, "a minority" or "the best members of both classes" might be able to "lay aside their class preferences, and pursue jointly the path traced by the common interest," *Works*, 19, 447, 498 *(Considerations);* 16, 1014, 1032.

102. The reason for this is simply that most forms of socialism in the nineteenth

century—and all the forms that Mill endorsed—adhered to the principle of equality for women.

103. Mill, *Political Economy*, pp. 210–211; *Autobiography*, p. 168; *Works*, 5, 745–746 *(Socialism)*; 19, 396 *(Considerations)*.

104. Mill, *Works*, 14, 294; 18, 261 *(Liberty)*; *Autobiography*, p. 156. Mill preferred Fourier's system both because it did give greater weight to individuality and because it presented the fewest number of practical obstacles to its realization, *Works*, 5, 748 *(Socialism)*; *Works*, 14, 34; *Political Economy*, pp. 213–216.

105. Mill, *Autobiography*, p. 181; *Works*, 18, 227, 274–275, 286–287 *(Liberty)*.

106. Mill, *Works*, 18, 306 *(Liberty)*. In the *Considerations*, the example Mill gives is that of a despot operating within "the rules and restraints of constitutional government," which include a free press, the management of local interests, and an elected legislature, *Works*, 19, 402.

107. Mill, *Works*, 19, 385, 396 *(Considerations)*.

108. Mill, *Political Economy*, pp. 211, 948–950; *Autobiography*, p.143; *Works*, 19, 400–401, 410 *(Considerations)*.

109. Mill, *Political Economy*, p. 211.

110. Mill, *Works*, 18, 293 *(Liberty)*.

111. Ibid., 18, 305–306. Mill asserts that "there is a circle around every individual human being which no government . . . ought to be permitted to over-step." Yet, this area of liberty and individuality, he believes, can be defended "*whatever* theory we adopt respecting the foundation of the social union" (*Political Economy*, p. 943 [italics mine]). In other words, the preservation of individual liberty is, for Mill, both a question to be considered independently of the social relations of a capitalist or a socialist society, and an ideal that is compatible with either "foundation" of the social relations between individuals.

112. The foundation and essence of private property, according to Mill, "is the right of producers to what they themselves have produced," *Political Economy*, pp. 208–210, 218. Since these comments occur in the context of his description of an ideal system of private property, based upon "the principles on which the justification of private property rests," it is relevant to consider what that system looks like, especially since these remarks are invariably misinterpreted in the secondary literature on Mill. In the first place, a proper system of private property would never allow the private ownership of land. Secondly, there must be a broad "diffusion, instead of the concentration of wealth" in a few hands. Thirdly, there must be a close and permanently established link between personal exertion, that is, labor or personal sacrifice, and property. Notwithstanding the fact that none of these propositions, with the exception of the (unsuccessful) movement for the nationalization of land, were regarded by Mill as *empirical tendencies in his own society*, numerous commentators have blithely cited these remarks in order to portray Mill as a defender of private property as it presently exists! For other comments by Mill on the general relation between property and individual agency, see *Works*, 5, 450; 14, 51.

113. Mill, *Political Economy,* pp. 210, 373.
114. Mill, *Works,* 18, 307–308 *(Liberty);* 19, 421–422, 439–440 *(Considerations).*
115. Mill, *Works,* 18, 309–310 *(Liberty);* 19, 400–401, 436, 438, 440 *(Considerations); Political Economy,* p. 950.
116. Mill, *Works,* 19, 535 *(Considerations); Political Economy,* pp. 948–949.
117. Mill, *Works,* 19, 411–412, 469 *(Considerations); Political Economy,* p. 373.
118. Mill, *Political Economy,* pp. 204–205, 373.
119. Ibid., pp. 960–961. There are other practical reasons, such as not giving the government a monopoly of talent and intelligence, which Mill believes justifies not making joint-stock companies part of the government.
120. Ibid., p. 959; *Works,* 19, 436 *(Considerations).*
121. Mill, *Political Economy,* p. 773.
122. Mill, *Works,* 5, 434, 672, 690, 730 *(Socialism); Political Economy,* p. 143.

Seven. *Making Sense of Moral Conflict*

This chapter was written with Leszek Kolakowski and Allan Bloom in mind. I am grateful to G. A. Cohen for his incisive criticisms.

1. See discussion in Charles Larmore, *Patterns of Moral Complexity* (Cambridge: Cambridge University Press, 1987), pp. 10, 37–38, 159–160.
2. See Marco Orru, *Anomie: History and Meanings* (Boston: Allen and Unwin, 1987), p. 28. See also Martin Ostwald, *Nomos and the Beginnings of the Athenian Democracy* (Oxford: Clarendon, 1969).
3. Larmore, *Patterns,* p. 10.
4. Bernard Williams, "Conflicts of Values," *Moral Luck* (Cambridge: Cambridge University Press, 1981), p. 75.
5. J. P. Sartre, *L'Existentialisme est un humanisme* (Paris: Nagel, 1959), pp. 39–43.
6. Isaiah Berlin, *Four Essays on Liberty* (Oxford: Oxford University Press, 1969), pp. xlix–l.
7. Leszek Kolakowski, *Main Currents of Marxism,* 3 vols. (Oxford: Oxford University Press, 1978), III, 528.
8. Blaise Pascal, *Pensées,* V. 294.
9. Leszek Kolakowski, *Religion* (London: Fontana, 1982), pp. 187, 189.
10. Allan Bloom, *The Closing of the American Mind* (New York: Simon and Schuster, 1987), p. 39.
11. Kolakowski, *Religion,* p. 187.
12. See Michael Walzer, "Political Action: The Problem of Dirty Hands," *Philosophy and Public Affairs* 2 (Winter 1973): 175.
13. Niccolò Machiavelli, *Il Principe,* chap. xv.
14. Leon Trotsky, *Terrorism and Communism* (Ann Arbor: University of Michigan Press, 1951), p. 82.
15. Larmore, *Patterns,* p. 132.
16. Ibid., pp. 141, 143.

17. Notably by the Polish sociologist Maria Ossowska. The following books by her are available in English: *Social Determinants of Moral Ideas* (London: Routledge and Kegan Paul, 1971); *Bourgeois Morality,* trans. G. L. Campbell (London: Routledge and Kegan Paul, 1986), and *Moral Norms: A Tentative Systematisation,* trans. Irena Gulowska (Warsaw and Amsterdam: PWN, 1980).

18. Bernard Williams, *Ethics and the Limits of Philosophy* (London: Fontana, 1985), p. 160.

19. Cf. Ronald Dworkin, "Is There Really No Right Answer in Hard Cases," *A Matter of Principle* (Cambridge, Mass.: Harvard University Press, 1985).

20. Berlin, *Four Essays,* p. 1.

21. Williams, "Conflicts of Values," pp. 76, 77.

22. John Rawls, "Justice as Fairness: Political not Metaphysical," *Philosophy and Public Affairs* (Summer 1985): 225.

23. Thomas Nagel, "The Fragmentation of Value," *Mortal Questions* (Cambridge: Cambridge University Press, 1979), pp. 134, 138, 134.

24. Larmore, *Patterns,* p. 10. Larmore clearly uses a broader (and vaguer?) sense of "moral" than does Nagel. His "projects and friendships" would not, it seems, fall within Nagel's definition.

25. See Joseph Raz, *The Morality of Freedom* (Oxford: Oxford University Press, 1986), chap. 13.

26. David Hume, *Essays Moral and Political,* ed. T. H. Green and T. H. Grose (London, 1875), II, 68.

27. John Ladd, *The Structure of a Moral Code: A Philosophical Analysis of Ethical Discourse Applied to the Ethics of the Navaho Indians* (Cambridge, Mass.: Harvard University Press, 1957), p. 316. Cf. Richard Brandt, *Hopi Ethics* (Chicago: Chicago University Press, 1954). I have sought to address this problem in a forthcoming paper on the use of ethnocentricity.

28. R. Grandy, "Reference, Meaning and Truth," *Journal of Philosophy* 70 (1973): 445. See my concluding chapter, "Relativism in its Place," to Martin Hollis and Steven Lukes, eds., *Rationality and Relativism* (Oxford: Blackwells, 1982).

29. See Larmore, *Patterns,* chap. 6.

30. Kolakowski, *Religion,* p. 192.

31. See Steven Lukes, *Marxism and Morality* (Oxford: Oxford University Press, 1985).

32. Max Weber, *Politik als Beruf,* trans. in H. H. Gerth and C. W. Mills, eds., *From Max Weber* (London: Routledge and Kegan Paul, 1948). Leszek Kolakowski, "Ethics without a Moral Code," *Triquarterly* 22 (1971): esp. 72–74.

33. Max Weber, *Wissenschaft als Beruf* ("Science as Vocation") in Gerth and Mills, *From Max Weber,* pp. 148.

34. Bloom, *Closing of the American Mind,* pp. 143, 197, 201, 207, 219.

35. Alasdair MacIntyre, *After Virtue* (London: Duckworth, 1981), p. 111.

36. Jürgen Habermas, *Autonomy and Solidarity: Interviews,* ed. P. Dews (London: Verso, 1986), p. 206.

37. Jürgen Habermas, *Legitimation Crisis* (London: Heinemann, 1973), pp. 107, 111. See Steven Lukes, "Of Gods and Demons: Habermas and Practical Reason," in John Thompson and David Held, eds., *Habermas: Critical Debates* (London: Macmillan, 1982).

38. Bloom, *Closing of the American Mind*, p. 34.

39. Berlin, *Four Essays*, pp. lv–lvi. Berlin is rather tough on "single-minded monists," calling them "ruthless fanatics, men possessed by an all-embracing coherent vision," who "do not know the doubts and agonies of those who cannot wholly blind themselves to reality." I tend to agree with James Griffin, who, in a discussion of incommensurability, observes that computation on a single scale does not need a substantive "single central principle." He suggests plausibly that: "if we assembled all the deplorable fanatics that history has ever seen and asked them to divide into two lobbies, labelled 'monists' and 'pluralists,' my money would be on the pluralists' winning hands down." It is hard to think that a happy, productive life counts for nothing, but unfortunately it seems terribly easy to think that it counts for nothing up against what is seen as the "incommensurably higher"! (James Griffin, *Well-Being* [Oxford: Clarendon, 1987], p. 91). Liberalism is about fairness between conflicting moral and religious positions, but it is also about filtering out those that are incompatible with a liberal order and taming those that remain.

40. Rawls, "Justice as Fairness," pp. 248–249.

41. Bloom, *Closing of the American Mind*, p. 30.

42. John Rawls, "Kantian Constructivism in Moral Theory." The John Dewey Lectures, *Journal of Philosophy* 77 (September 1980): 542.

43. For a sophisticated argument that these exhaust the field, see Alasdair MacIntyre, *Whose Justice? Which Rationality?* (Notre Dame, Ind.: University of Notre Dame Press, 1988), for example, "There is no standing ground, no place for enquiry, no way to engage in the practice of advancing, evaluating, accepting, and rejecting reasoned argument apart from that which is provided by some particular tradition or other" (p. 350), and "Progress in rationality is achieved only from a point of view" (p. 144).

44. See Thomas Nagel, "Moral Conflict and Political Legitimacy," *Philosophy and Public Affairs* 16 (1987): 215–240.

Eight. Liberal Dialogue Versus A Critical Theory of Discursive Legitimation

I wish to thank Nancy Rosenblum for her helpful editorial suggestions on this chapter.

1. Immanuel Kant, *The Metaphysical Elements of Justice,* trans. John Ladd (New York: Bobbs-Merrill, 1965), p. 34. "Justice is therefore the aggregate of those conditions under which the will of one person can be joined with the will of another in accordance with a universal law of freedom."

2. Cf. John Rawls, "Kantian Constructivism in Moral Theory," The John Dewey Lectures, *Journal of Philosophy* 77 (September 1980): 515–572; "Jus-

tice as Fairness: Political, not Metaphysical," *Philosophy and Public Affairs* 14 (Summer, 1985): 223–251. In "The Idea of an Overlapping Consensus," *Oxford Journal of Legal Studies* 7 (1987): 1–25, Rawls has distanced himself from a liberalism based upon a comprehensive moral doctrine like that of Kant and John Stuart Mill. I am skeptical, however, that his theory of justice can function without such a strong moral basis.

3. Rawls's contribution to the "Liberalism and the Moral Life" conference "On the Idea of Free Public Reason" does not change my assessment. As far as I can tell, in this essay as well the emphasis is on the individual and not the dialogic use of reason.

4. See Karl-Otto Apel, "The A Priori of the Communication Community and the Foundations of Ethics: the Problem of a Rational Foundation of Ethics in the Scientific Age," in *Towards a Transformation of Philosophy,* trans. Glyn Adey and David Frisby (London: Routledge, Kegan and Paul, 1980), pp. 225–301; Jürgen Habermas first suggested this model in his essay "Wahrheitstheorien," in *Wirklichkeit und Reflexion,* ed. H. Fahrenbach (Pfüllingen: Neske, 1973), but significantly modified its elements in his most recent "Diskursethik: Notizen zu einem Begründungsprogramm," *Moralbewusstsein und kommunikatives Handelns* (Frankfurt: Suhrkamp, 1983), pp. 53–127 (an abridged English translation of this essay is forthcoming in Seyla Benhabib and Fred Dallmayr, eds., *The Communicative Ethics Controversy* (Cambridge, Mass.: MIT Press, 1989).

5. Immanuel Kant, "Perpetual Peace," *Kant's Political Writings,* ed. Hans Reiss (Cambridge: Cambridge University Press, 1983), p. 126.

6. Kant, "Perpetual Peace," p. 113.

7. Bruce Ackerman, *Social Justice in the Liberal State* (New Haven: Yale University Press, 1980).

8. Bruce Ackerman, "Why Dialogue?," *Journal of Philosophy* 86 (January 1989): 5–22.

9. Ackerman, *Social Justice in the Liberal State,* p. 4.

10. Ibid., p. 11.

11. "Why Dialogue?," p. 8.

12. Ibid., p. 9.

13. Ibid., pp. 16–17.

14. It is not inconceivable that there will be situations when restraining public dialogue in a polity may be morally desirable. The most frequently cited instances are national security considerations or what the tradition used to describe as *raisons d'état.* I am extremely skeptical even about such prima facie morally plausible cases which would lead to the imposition of gag rules in a society. Take the case of the suppression by the State Department and some media officials of the news of the extermination of the Jews and the building of concentration camps in Europe during the Second World War. In order not to create public pressure for the United States to enter the war, the U.S. government censored such news for a while. Is it so clear, however, which is the better argument in such an instance? Were the national security considerations of the United States at that point in time

so clearly superior to the moral claims of the European Jews to demand help and an end to their extermination from any source whatever? And may it not have been desirable on moral grounds for the American public to be informed right away and as fully as possible of these circumstances rather than under conditions of a carefully orchestrated war effort? Cf. David S. Wyman, *The Abandonment of the Jews* (New York: Pantheon, 1984). I believe that the moral burden of proof in such cases is almost always on the shoulders of the advocates of gag rules. However, every polity in which political discourse is an institution respects certain constraints on the use of free speech. Furthermore, individuals and associations may be guided by a certain sense of what is appropriate "public speech." A philosophical and moral theory of public dialogue that views this as a procedure for moral legitimation accepts constitutional guarantees to free speech as well as suggesting some norms of public dialogue. But insofar as it is also critical of existing relations, such a view may challenge both existing legal practices and cultural codes of speech from the standpoint of a moral norm.

15. For these criticisms, see "Why Dialogue?."

16. Compare, on the charge of "emptiness," Steven Lukes, "Of Gods and Demons: Habermas and Practical Reason," in *Habermas: Critical Debates,* ed. John B. Thompson and David Held (Cambridge, Mass.: MIT Press, 1982), pp. 136–140.

17. For my criticism of this strong justification, see Seyla Benhabib, *Critique, Norm and Utopia. A Study of the Foundations of Critical Theory* (New York: Columbia University Press, 1986), chap. 8. Charles Larmore has some interesting suggestions along similar lines in *Patterns of Moral Complexity* (Cambridge: Cambridge University Press, 1987), pp. 51–56. I disagree with Larmore that a "neutral justification of political neutrality" is possible. There is nothing neutral about the norm of "rational dialogue," which Larmore also endorses in the Habermasian model. I think there may be some confusion here between the political and the philosophical sense of neutrality. Philosophically, a norm of rational dialogue is based on strong assumptions, which we nonetheless think can be shown to be "reasonable" from a moral point of view. Politically, the norm of rational dialogue is neutral to the extent that it does allow a plurality of conceptions of the good to be pursued in a modern society, while clearly advocating, endorsing, or holding up as an ideal a way of life embodying the norm of egalitarian reciprocity. In this sense the discourse model is utopian, for it anticipates a future which we do not yet share. However, such a utopian and philosophically non-neutral position does not justify the violation of political neutrality, that is, the acceptance of all conceptions of the good that are willing to submit themselves to the test of discursive justification. Nor can we exclude even opponents of the norm of reciprocal equality from public dialogue as long as they wish to participate in it—or maybe even reject it altogether for themselves but allow it to continue for others. The search for a "neutral justification of neutrality" may well be the swan song of a certain brand of liberalism that, in an attempt to make its moral

standpoint less and less controversial, ends up hollowing out the political vision that makes liberalism so challenging as a theory of political institutions.

18. Habermas, "Diskursethik," p. 103 (my translation).
19. Jurgen Habermas, "Moralbewusstsein und kommunikatives Handeln," *Moralbewusstsein und kommunikatives Handeln* (Frankfurt: Suhrkamp, 1983), pp. 169–182.
20. Cf. Nancy Fraser, "Toward a Discourse Ethic of Solidarity," *Praxis International* 5 (January 1986): 425.

Nine. Cross-Purposes: The Liberal-Communitarian Debate

1. This chapter applies a distinction which has been defined and explored in depth by Mimi Bick in her dissertation for Oxford, "The Liberal-Communitarian Debate: A Defense of Holistic Individualism" (unpub. diss., Trinity, 1987). My discussion owes a great deal to her work.
2. I am here following Mimi Bick's terminology; "Liberal-Communitarian Debate," chap. 1.
3. Sen's definition, which appears in Amartya Sen, "Utilitarianism and Welfarism," *The Journal of Philosophy* 76 (1979): 463–489, runs: "Welfarism: The judgement of the relative goodness of states of affairs must be based exclusively on, and taken as an increasing function of, the respective collections of individual utilities in these states." I have discussed the atomist component of welfarism so defined in "Irreducibly Social Goods" (forthcoming).
4. See Ronald Dworkin, "Liberalism," in Stuart Hampshire, ed., *Public and Private Morality* (Cambridge: Cambridge University Press, 1978); and "What Liberalism Isn't," *The New York Review of Books* 20 (January 1983): 47–50.
5. Michael Sandel, *Liberalism and the Limits of Justice* (Cambridge: Cambridge University Press, 1982).
6. See, for instance Amy Gutmann, "Communitarian Critics of Liberalism," *Philosophy and Public Affairs* 14 (Summer 1985): 308–322. Brian Barry offers a particularly crass example of the confusion. See his review of Michael Sandel's *Liberalism,* in *Ethics* 94 (April 1984): 523–525.
7. See Sandel, *Liberalism,* p. 35.
8. Ibid., chap. 2.
9. John Rawls, *A Theory of Justice* (Cambridge, Mass.: Harvard University Press, 1971), p. 101.
10. See, for example, Michael Sandel, "Democrats and Community," *The New Republic,* Feb. 22, 1988, pp. 20–23.
11. Mimi Bick, "Liberal-Communitarian Debate," pp. 164–168, cites the case of Morelly as another example in this category.
12. See the debate between Amartya Sen, "Equality of What?" in *Choice, Welfare and Measurement* (Oxford: Blackwell, 1982), and "Capability and Well-Being," WIDER Research Paper (forthcoming); G. A. Cohen, "Equality

of What? On Welfare, Resources and Capabilities," WIDER Research Paper (forthcoming); Ronald Dworkin, "What is Equality?: Part 2. Equality of Resources," in *Philosophy and Public Affairs* 10 (1981): 283.

13. I have tried to sketch the common features that unite the theories of Dworkin, "Liberalism," "What Liberalism Isn't," and "What is Equality?"; Rawls, *Theory of Justice;* Nagel, "Moral Conflict and Political Legitimacy," *Philosophy and Public Affairs* 16 (Summer 1987): 215–240; and T. M. Scanlon, "Contractualism and Utilitarianism," in Amartya Sen and Bernard Williams, eds. *Utilitarianism and Beyond* (Cambridge: Cambridge University Press, 1982).

14. Montesquieu, *Esprit des Lois,* bk. IV, chap. 5.

15. See Stephen Schiffer's account of "mutual knowledge" in *Meaning* (Oxford: Oxford University Press, 1972), pp. 30 ff.

16. See Greg Urban, "Ceremonial Dialogues in South America," *American Anthropologist* 88 (1986): 371–386.

17. I have tried to argue this in Charles Taylor, "Theories of Meaning," *Human Agency and Language* (Cambridge: Cambridge University Press, 1985).

18. *Nicomachean Ethics,* 1167b3.

19. There is another version of the civic humanist tradition, and of what I later refer to as its republican thesis, which has been articulated by Quentin Skinner and attributed by him to Machiavelli. See Quentin Skinner, "The Idea of Negative Liberty: Philosophical and Historical Perspectives," in Richard Rorty, J. B. Schneewind, and Quentin Skinner, eds., *Philosophy in History* (Cambridge: Cambridge University Press, 1984). According to this, the appeal of the theory is purely to instrumental considerations. The only way to defend any of my freedoms is to sustain a regime of activity participation, because otherwise I shall be at the mercy of others who are far from having my interest at heart. On this version, we do without common goods altogether, and freedom is redefined as a convergent value. Skinner may be right about Machiavelli, though I am unconvinced. But this interpretation could not capture, for example, Montesquieu, Rousseau, Tocqueville, Mill (in *On Representative Government*), or Hannah Arendt. (Skinner does not claim that it does.) In that sense, the description that I am offering remains historically very relevant. The issue concerns which of these variants is relevant to today's politics. I am convinced that mine is.

20. For this revisionist, or elite, theory of democracy, see Joseph Schumpeter, *Capitalism, Socialism and Democracy,* 3rd ed. (New York: Harper, 1950).

21. The United States is peculiarly fortunate in that, from the very beginning, its patriotism welded together the sense of nationality with a liberal representative regime. For other Western nations these have been distinct, and even in tension. Think of France, where until recent decades a strong sense of national identity went along with a deep rift in the society, where an important segment rejected liberal democracy, even saw the greatness of France as entailing its rejection. The stability of contemporary Western democracies results from a fusion between national identity and free regimes

finally having been achieved, so that now Atlantic countries are proud to share a democratic civilization. But what happened at the beginning in the United States was achieved late and sometimes painfully in some other countries, for example, Germany or Spain—and perhaps now in Argentina? I have discussed this issue in "Alternative Futures," in Alan Cairns and Cynthia Williams, eds., *Constitutionalism, Citizenship and Society in Canada* (Toronto: University of Toronto Press, 1985).

22. Of course there *have* been challenges to the requirement to take the pledge of allegiance, and the issue of whether it should be imposed was the occasion of some fairly base demagoguery in the 1988 presidential election. But this punctual challenge to a particular ritual on, say, religious grounds, although it poses a dilemma for a republican regime, does not frontally attack the central beliefs and attitudes that patriotism lives by, as my constructed examples were meant to do.

23. See Hannah Arendt, *The Human Condition* (Chicago: University of Chicago Press, 1958), Robert Bellah et al., *Habits of the Heart* (Berkeley: University of California Press, 1985), and William Sullivan, *Reconstructing Public Philosophy* (Berkeley: University of California Press, 1982).

24. Aristotle, *Politics,* 1259b5.

25. See Michael Sandel, "The Procedural Republic and the Unencumbered Self," *Political Theory* 12 (February 1984): 81–96.

26. John Rawls seems to define the American liberal tradition pretty well exclusively in terms of the procedural ideal. See "Justice as Fairness: Political not Metaphysical," *Philosophy and Public Affairs* 14 (Summer 1985): 223–251. Michael Sandel takes issue with this view of American history, arguing for the recent hegemony of the procedural republic. See Sandel, "Procedural Republic," and also his forthcoming book. The issue is also hotly debated among American historians.

27. See Taylor, "Alternative Futures."

Ten. Democratic Individuality and the Meaning of Rights

1. George Kateb, "Democratic Individuality and the Claims of Politics," *Political Theory* 12 (August 1984): 331–360.

2. In A. S. P. Woodhouse, ed., *Puritanism and Liberty* (Chicago: University of Chicago Press, 1951), p. 53.

3. Henry Thoreau, *Walden and Other Writings* (New York: Modern Library, 1937), p. 70.

4. Luke 10:30–37.

5. Matthew 5:45.

6. Compare the discussion in Nancy Rosenblum, *Another Liberalism* (Cambridge, Mass.: Harvard University Press, 1987), pp. 103–124.

7. Ralph Waldo Emerson, "Politics," in *The Complete Essays and Other Writings* (New York: Modern Library, n.d.), p. 423.

8. Thoreau, "Civil Disobedience," *Walden,* p. 655.

9. "Thoreau," in Emerson, *Complete Essays,* p. 897.

10. Wallace Stevens, "Esthetique du Mal," *Collected Poems* (New York: Vintage, 1982), p. 320.
11. "Walden," in Thoreau, *Walden,* p. 292.
12. "Nature," in Emerson, *Complete Essays,* p. 3.
13. For example, Emerson's words about "crossing a bare common" in *Nature,* pp. 6–7.
14. *Nature,* in Emerson, *Complete Works,* p. 6.
15. "Art," in Emerson, *Complete Works,* p. 307. For a somewhat different tendency, see Emerson's essay, "Thoughts on Art," also published in 1841, in Stephen E. Whicher, Robert E. Spiller, and Wallace E. Williams, eds., *The Early Lectures of Ralph Waldo Emerson* (Cambridge, Mass.: Harvard University Press, 1964), II, 42–54. However, Emerson called this latter piece a "poor obsolete essay." See Robert E. Spiller and Wallace F. Williams, eds., *The Early Lectures of Ralph Waldo Emerson* (Cambridge, Mass.: Harvard University Press, 1972), III, 372.
16. William Hazlitt, "On Imitation," in David Bromwich, ed., *Romantic Critical Essays* (New York: Cambridge University Press, 1987), pp. 92–96.
17. Letter to Benjamin Bailey, 22 Nov. 1817, in Robert Gittings, ed., *Letters of John Keats* (New York: Oxford University Press, 1970), p. 37.
18. Letter to Tom Keats, 25–27 June 1818, in Gittings, *Letters of John Keats,* p. 103.
19. Walt Whitman, "Preface, 1855," *Leaves of Grass and Selected Prose,* ed. John Kouwenhoven (New York: Modern Library, 1950), p. 444.
20. Whitman, "Preface, 1855," p. 447.
21. Thoreau, *Walden,* p. 283.
22. *Henry James: Autobiography,* ed. Frederick W. Dupee (Princeton: Princeton University Press, 1983), p. 563.
23. See, for example, "The Subject and Power" in Hubert L. Dreyfus and Paul Rabinow, *Michel Foucault: Beyond Structuralism and Hermeneutics,* 2nd ed. (Chicago: University of Chicago Press, 1983), p. 216.
24. See, for example, Foucault's words in Noam Chomsky and Michel Foucault, "Human Nature: Justice versus Power," in Fons Elders, ed., *Reflexive Water* (London: Souvenir Press, 1974), pp. 149–151.
25. John Stuart Mill, "On Liberty," *The Philosophy of John Stuart Mill,* ed. Marshall Cohen (New York: Modern Library, 1961), p. 289.
26. For his great meditation on this theme, see D. H. Lawrence, *American Literature* (1923; New York: Penguin, 1977).
27. "Circles," in Emerson, *Complete Essays,* p. 282.

Eleven. Pluralism and Self-Defense

1. Nancy L. Rosenblum, *Another Liberalism* (Cambridge, Mass.: Harvard University Press, 1987).
2. Richard Rorty, "Habermas and Lyotard on Postmodernity," in Richard J. Bernstein, ed., *Habermas and Modernity* (Cambridge: Polity Press, 1985), pp. 174–175.

3. Isaiah Berlin, "Two Concepts of Liberty," *Four Essays On Liberty* (Oxford: Oxford University Press, 1969), pp. 161, 126–129, 171.

4. Charles Taylor, "What's Wrong with Negative Liberty," in Alan Ryan, ed., *The Idea of Freedom* (Oxford: Oxford University Press, 1979).

5. Daniel Bell, *The Cultural Contradictions of Capitalism* (New York: Basic Books, 1976).

6. Charles Taylor, "Language and Human Nature," *Human Agency and Language: Philosophical Papers 1* (Cambridge: Cambridge University Press, 1985), p. 247.

7. Michel Foucault, *Discipline and Punishment* (New York: Vintage, 1979).

8. This approach sets aside important aspects of contemporary political theory, including methodology and metatheoretical claims.

9. M. H. Abrams, *Natural Supernaturalism* (New York: Norton, 1971), p. 377.

10. George Kateb, "Democratic Individuality and the Claims of Politics," *Political Theory* 12 (August 1984): 331–360, and Chapter 10, "Democratic Individuality and the Meaning of Right." See in contrast my discussion of individuality in chaps. 1 and 5 of *Another Liberalism*.

11. William Connolly, *Politics and Ambiguity* (Madison: University of Wisconsin Press, 1987), pp. 96, 84n.

12. Harold Isaacs, *Idols of the Tribe* (New York: Harper and Row, 1975), p. 216.

13. Roberto Unger, *Law and Modern Society* (New York: Free Press, 1976), p. 206.

14. For example, Charles Taylor writes of the goal of identification with the will of a rational community. Later in the same paragraph he concedes the possibility that differences will be too great for people to coexist within a self-governing community, in which case the goal is to create more space to allow "otherness to be," Taylor, "Connolly, Foucault and Truth," *Political Theory* 13 (August 1985): 134. See too Taylor's discussion of the possibility, after all, of liberal patriotism and of a conception of the rule of right as an important shared good, in Chapter 9 of this volume. One exception is Michael Sandel's suggestion that communitarians would be more likely than liberals to allow a local community to ban pornographic bookstores; see Sandel, "Morality and the Liberal Ideal," *The New Republic*, May 7, 1984, p. 17.

15. Thomas Nagel, "Agreeing in Principle," *Times Literary Supplement,* July 8–14, 1988.

16. Taylor's formulation is inclusive: the personal capacities at issue include all those involved in "openness to certain matters of significance." He looks for nothing less than a new model of human maturity. See Taylor, "The Concept of a Person," *Human Agency,* p. 105.

17. Robert Bellah, et al., *Habits of the Heart* (Berkeley: University of California Press, 1985).

18. William Kornhauser, *The Politics of Mass Society* (Glencoe, Ill.: Free Press, 1959). For a thorough review of participatory criticisms of pluralism and a defense of "public pluralism" in which government has a part in both

organizing marginal elements from the bottom up and regulating the give-and-take of interests from the top down, see William Kelso, *American Democratic Theory: Pluralism and Its Critics* (Westport, Conn.: Greenwood, 1978).

19. Albert O. Hirschmann, *Shifting Involvements: Private Interest and Public Action* (Princeton: Princeton University Press, 1982).

20. Francis Fitzgerald, *Cities on a Hill* (New York: Simon and Schuster, 1981).

21. Nancy L. Rosenblum, "Studying Authority: Keeping Pluralism in Mind," in J. Roland Pennock and John Chapman, eds., *Authority Revisited: Nomos XXIX* (New York: New York University Press, 1987), pp. 102–130.

22. Richard Rodriguez, *Hunger of Memory* (New York: Bantam,1983), pp. 106, 35.

23. Georg Simmel, *On Individuality and Social Forms* (Chicago: University of Chicago Press, 1971), pp. 291, 293, 269.

24. Rodriguez, *Hunger*, p. 72.

25. There has been a recent surge of interest in internal and external complexity and the relation between them. Even more striking than theorists of moral complexity per se, in this regard, is Thomas Nagel, who sets his argument for an objective morality in the context of a philosophical psychology by which personalities do not have a unified standpoint on the world. Thomas Nagel, *The View from Nowhere* (Oxford: Oxford University Press, 1986).

26. Taylor, "Introduction," *Human Agency and Language,* p. 8. See the discussion of ontology-advocacy in this volume.

27. For a discussion of the lack of psychological sophistication in current political theory, see Nancy L. Rosenblum and Sherry Turkle, "Political Philosophy's Pyschologized Self," in Cheryl Welch and Murray Milgate, eds., *Critical Issues in Social Theory* (Boulder, Colo.: Westview, forthcoming).

Twelve. The Permanent Structure of Antiliberal Thought

1. The works I principally have in mind are Alasdair MacIntyre, *After Virtue,* 2nd ed. (Notre Dame, Ind.: University of Notre Dame Press, 1984), and *Whose Justice? Which Rationality?* (Notre Dame, Ind.: University of Notre Dame Press, 1988); Roberto Unger, *Knowledge and Politics* (New York: Free Press, 1975), and *Politics, A Work in Constructive Social Theory,* 3 vols. (Cambridge: Cambridge University Press, 1987); and Michael Sandel, *Liberalism and the Limits of Justice* (Cambridge: Cambridge University Press, 1982). Various kindred spirits will be cited later.

2. Carl Schmitt, *The Crisis of Parliamentary Democracy,* trans. Ellen Kennedy (1923–1926), (Cambridge, Mass.: MIT Press, 1985); *The Concept of the Political,* trans. George Schwab (1928–1932) (New Brunswick, N.J.: Rutgers University Press, 1976); *Römischer Katholizismus und politische Form* (1923) (Stuttgart: Klett-Cotta, 1984); *Verfassungslehre* (Berlin: Duncker & Humblot, 1928); and Giovanni Gentile, *Genesi e struttura della società* (Florence: Sansoni, 1946); *Che cosa é il fascismo* (Florence: Vallecchi, 1925).

3. Compare MacIntyre's assertion that liberals see "the social world as nothing but a meeting place for individual wills" (*After Virtue,* p. 25) with Gentile's

claim that "The error of the old liberalism [is] the atomistic conception of society, understood as the accidental grouping and encounter of abstract individuals" (*Genesi e struttura della società*, p. 65).

4. For some useful citations and an utterly implausible analysis, see Herbert Marcuse, "The Struggle against Liberalism in the Totalitarian View of the State," *Negations* (Boston: Beacon, 1968), pp. 3–42.
5. Sandel, *Liberalism and the Limits of Justice*, pp. 175–183.
6. Zeev Sternhell, *Neither Right nor Left: Fascist Ideology in France* (Berkeley: University of California Press, 1986).
7. MacIntyre, *After Virtue*, pp. 2, 256.
8. Readers sympathetic to antiliberalism will no doubt view my criticisms as oversimplifications. Are not the thinkers I describe as "antiliberal" much too diverse to be classified together as a single group espousing a single viewpoint? Some are religious while others are Marxist. Some pine for the loss of community, while others regret the eclipse of authority. Some are full-fledged enemies of liberalism, others, as I mention, are much less ardent in their hostility, and not a few incorporate important liberal ideas into their own thinking. So how can I justify using an omnibus term to lump together such a heterogeneous set of writers? Despite their important differences, I answer, today's antiliberals also share enough in common to justify a unified treatment. The range of perceptions and biases they share appears even more formidable when viewed against a background of what divides them.
9. Unger, *Knowledge and Politics*, p. 76.
10. Unger, *Law in Modern Society* (New York: Free Press, 1976), pp. 61–62.
11. MacIntyre, *After Virtue*, p. 156.
12. Sheldon Wolin, *Politics and Vision* (Boston: Little, Brown, 1960), p. 350; he also mentions, tantalizingly, a "community tinged with truth" (p. 294).
13. Sandel, *Liberalism and the Limits of Justice*, p. 183; cf. George Will, *Statecraft as Soulcraft* (New York: Simon and Schuster, 1983), p. 143.
14. Robert Paul Wolff, *The Poverty of Liberalism* (Boston: Beacon, 1968), pp. 183, 184.
15. Unger, *Knowledge and Politics*, p. 261.
16. There is nothing novel about critics for whom "disparagement of liberalism forms part of a general lamentation over the moral and spiritual degeneration of modern society," Francis Coker, "Some Present-Day Critics of Liberalism," *American Political Science Review* 47 (March 1953): 12.
17. In discussing the basis of their hopelessly vague "community" antiliberals frequently blur together the following three ideas: consensus, similarity, and mutual identification. Assenting to common beliefs, however, in no way implies membership in a common group. And there is a world of difference between a resemblance and a relationship.
18. Likewise, empathy with the victimized is laudable; but identification with the victimizer is not.
19. Bernard Yack provides a useful analysis of the confusions contained in the antiliberal postulate that some forms of social life are more social than others:

"Does Liberal Practice 'Live Down' to Liberal Theory: Liberalism and its Communitarian Critics," in Charles Reynolds, ed., *Community in America: The Challenge of 'Habits of the Heart'* (Berkeley: University of California Press, 1988), pp. 147–169.

20. Charles Taylor, "Atomism," *Philosophy and the Human Sciences* (Cambridge: Cambridge University Press, 1985), p. 200.

21. Ibid., p. 189. This "refutation" of liberalism may have been coined in 1796, when the Catholic reactionary Louis de Bonald wrote that "society constitutes man." Because people only acquire recognizably human needs through socialization and interaction, he argued, "man exists only through society" ("Théorie du pouvoir politique et religieux dans la société civile," *Oeuvres complètes,* 15 vols. [Paris: Migne, 1859], I, 123). The usual suggestion is that the social constitution of the individual logically entails that the edifice of liberal politics be razed and replaced by a system celebrating the supremacy of society over the individual.

22. Robert Bellah et al., *Habits of the Heart: Individualism and Commitment in American Life* (New York: Harper and Row, 1985), p. 144.

23. Taylor, "Atomism," pp. 198, 200.

24. Paraphrasing Sandel's lyrical conclusion: "we can know 'a bad' in common that we cannot know alone" (*Liberalism and the Limits of Justice,* p. 183).

25. A troubled child whose identity is "constituted" by socialization in an emotionally disturbed family does not seem to have the kind of "obligation to belong" that Taylor assumes. Because my identity is "constituted" by my enemies and even by the remote past, the entire assumption that causal influence entails moral duties seems bizarre, to say the least.

26. This is the fundamental theoretical insight of Lawrence Stone's controversial *The Family, Sex and Marriage in England, 1500–1800* (New York: Harper & Row, 1979).

27. More gently: "the real and recognized dilemma of modern liberalism . . . is not that people are naturally egoistical, but rather that they disagree about the nature of the good life" (Amy Gutmann, "Communitarian Critics of Liberalism," *Philosophy and Public Affairs* 14 [1985]: 317).

28. The possible tension between citizenship and communal attachments, ignored by antiliberals, is helpfully discussed in Clifford Geertz, "The Integrative Revolution: Primordial Sentiments and Civil Politics in the New States," *The Interpretation of Culture* (New York: Basic Books, 1973), pp. 255–310.

29. Taylor, "Atomism," p. 209; Will, *Statecraft as Soulcraft,* p. 80.

30. This point is stressed by Yack, "Does Liberal Practice 'Live Down' to Liberal Theory," and by Michael Walzer, "The Communitarian Critics of Liberalism," forthcoming in *Political Theory,* 1989.

31. Michael Sandel, "The Procedural Republic and the Unencumbered Self," *Political Theory* 12 (1984): 82.

32. This is the working premise of Bellah, *Habits of the Heart.*

33. The useful phrase "latent community" is suggested by Nancy Rosenblum,

"Moral Membership in a Postliberal State," *World Politics* 36 (July 1984): 589.

34. MacIntyre, *Whose Justice? Which Rationality?*, pp. 307–308.

35. David Hume, *Enquiries Concerning the Human Understanding* (Oxford: Clarendon, 1962), p. 186. MacIntyre levels the same charge against Blackstone. It too is easily refuted—in this case, by the section of subsistence rights at the beginning of the *Commentaries*.

36. Fortunately I do not need to justify applying a common label to a loose assemblage of thinkers who lived in different centuries and wrote in quite dissimilar national contexts. The enemies of liberalism have set the terms of the debate. They use the word "liberalism" as if it were historically noncontroversial; and they will no doubt continue to do so. I could of course engage them terminologically; but verbal prohibitions and instructions are pointless. Even if the word "liberalism" were intellectually useless—which it is not—it will not go away.

37. The evidence adduced here will be a sampling, not an exhaustive survey.

38. This is the essence of John Rawls's answer to the antiliberal attack on his work in "Justice as Fairness: Political Not Metaphysical," *Philosophy and Public Affairs* 14 (1985): 223–251.

39. For example, Bellah, *Habits of the Heart*, p. 143.

40. Hume, "Of the Original Contract," *Essays: Moral, Political and Literary*, pp. 465–487.

41. See *The Educational Writings of John Locke*, ed. James Axtell (Cambridge: Cambridge University Press, 1968).

42. Montesquieu, "De l'esprit des lois," *Oeuvres complètes*, 2 vols., II, 235 (I, 2).

43. Will, *Statecraft as Soulcraft*, p. 143; MacIntyre, *Whose Justice? Which Rationality?*, pp. 334–335.

44. In some circumstances, in fact, toleration and voluntariness can nourish such prepolitical "bonds."

45. Wolin, *Politics and Vision*, p. 341.

46. Locke, *Two Treatises of Government*, p. 316 (II, 2, 13); Madison, *The Federalist Papers*, No. 10, p. 79.

47. MacIntyre, *After Virtue*, p. 170.

48. John Locke, *A Letter Concerning Toleration* (Indianapolis, Ind.: Bobbs-Merrill, 1955), pp. 36, 50, 40, 16.

49. Aristotle, *Politics*, 1254b, 20–22.

50. Wolin, *Politics and Vision*, p. 317; Will, *Statecraft as Soulcraft*, p. 45.

51. Montesquieu, "De l'esprit des lois," 39, II, 237 (I, 3); "it is impossible for the human race to subsist, at least in any comfortable and secure state, without the protection of government" (Hume, "Of the Original Contract," *Essays*, p. 466).

52. Adam Smith, *Wealth of Nations*, (New York: Modern Library, 1937), book III, chap. 3.

53. Eighteenth-century arguments for the restricted suffrage are frequently mis-

interpreted in this regard. Montesquieu, for example, believed that the British were right to limit the franchise to the propertied classes because the poor would predictably sell their vote for a meal ("De l'esprit des lois," II, 400 [XI, 6]). The restricted suffrage was, among other things, a technique for limiting the influence of money in public life.

54. According to Hume, "liberty is the perfection of society; but still authority must be acknowledged essential to its very existence" ("Origin of Government," *Essays*, p. 41). This claim contrasts nicely with MacIntyre's nostalgic remark that liberal modernity is "a culture to which the notion of authority is alien and repugnant" (*After Virtue*, p. 42).

55. Wolin, *Politics and Vision*, p. 291; Will, *Statecraft as Soulcraft*, p. 21.

56. Guido de Ruggiero, *The History of European Liberalism* (Boston: Beacon, 1959), p. 2.

57. Montesquieu, "De l'esprit des lois," p. 317 (VI, 8).

58. The liberal idea that public disagreement produces intelligent decisions (George Sabine, "The Historical Position of Liberalism," *American Scholar* 10 [1940–41]: 49–58), first formulated in Milton's *Areopagitica,* should be contrasted with the romantic and antilibral notion that public participation produces beautiful citizens.

59. Wolin, *Politics and Vision*, p. 300. Will, *Statecraft as Soulcraft,* p. 89; the distinction between economic goals (such as monetary profit) and economic or calculative thinking (which may serve noneconomic goals) does not always register clearly with antiliberal writers. R. H. Tawney, *Religion and the Rise of Capitalism* (1927; Gloucester, Mass.: Peter Smith, 1962), pp. 57, 207.

60. Montesquieu, "De l'esprit des lois," II, 585.

61. Voltaire, "Lettres philosophiques," *Mélanges* (Paris: Pléiade, 1961), pp. 17–18; Voltaire modeled his argument here on a famous passage in Spinoza. While pouring scorn on "the avaricious . . . who think supreme salvation consists in filling their stomachs and gloating over their money-bags," Spinoza did not allow disdain for wealth to obscure his vision of the instrumental value of economic relations. Far from weakening the state, he argued, economic freedom increases the stability and power of a regime: "The city of Amsterdam reaps the fruit of this freedom in its own great prosperity and in the admiration of all other people. For in this most flourishing state, and most splendid city, men of every nation and religion live together in the greatest harmony, and ask no questions before trusting their goods to a fellow citizen, save whether he be rich or poor, and whether he generally acts honestly or the reverse. His religion and sect is considered of no importance" (*Theologico-Political Treatise* [New York: Dover, 1951], pp. 262, 254).

62. MacIntyre, *Whose Justice? Which Rationality?*, p. 98; it is worth comparing MacIntyre's attack on Weber (*After Virtue*, pp. 26–27, 114–115, 143–144) with Strauss's claim that Nazism was the logical culmination of Weber's value-pluralism (*Natural Right and History* [Chicago: University of Chicago Press, 1953], p. 42).

63. Unger, *Knowledge and Politics,* pp. 63–103; Taylor, "Atomism," p. 201; Wolin, *Politics and Vision,* p. 332; Will, *Statecraft as Soulcraft,* pp. 69, 90.

64. Shirley Letwin, *The Pursuit of Certainty* (Cambridge: Cambridge University Press, 1965), pp. 127–188.

65. Mill, "On Liberty," *Essays on Politics and Society,* ed. J. M. Robson (Toronto: University of Toronto Press, 1977), p. 230; according to one antiantiliberal, "Subjectivism . . . functions as a political sedative, robbing evaluative claims of their inflammatory edge" (Don Herzog, "As Many as Six Possible Things before Breakfast," *California Law Review* 75 [1987]: 613).

66. See Steven Lukes, "Making Sense of Moral Conflict," Chapter 7 in this volume.

67. According to MacIntyre, "Morality has to some large degree disappeared" (*After Virtue,* p. 22).

68. Ibid., pp. 69–70.

69. Taylor, "Atomism."

70. The right to a jury trial, incidentally, shows that liberal rights are not merely negative, not merely aimed at establishing *freedom from* state interference; they may also guarantee *access to* state institutions.

71. Rousseau, "Sur l'économie politique," *Oeuvres complètes* (Paris: Pléiade, 1964), III, 255–256.

72. Karl Marx, "On the Jewish Question," *The Marx-Engels Reader,* ed. Robert Tucker (New York: Norton, 1978), pp. 26–46.

73. Antiliberals lodge this complaint without mentioning a single specific liberal right. Taylor's assertion that liberals ignored the institutional preconditions for rights would seem foolish if he actually discussed the right to a jury trial or the right to vote.

74. Joseph de Maistre, *Considerations on France* (1797; Montreal: McGill-Queen's University Press, 1974), p. 97.

75. This putative contradiction is the theme of MacIntyre's chapter on "Liberalism Transformed into a Tradition," *Whose Justice? Which Rationality?,* pp. 326–348.

76. For a cogent defense of the liberal idea of neutrality, see Charles Larmore, *Patterns of Moral Complexity* (Cambridge: Cambridge University Press, 1987), pp. 40–68.

77. The personal ties between Tawney and Strauss are symptoms of a significant intellectual sympathy; see Ross Terrill, *R. H. Tawney and His Times* (Cambridge, Mass.: Harvard University Press, 1973), pp. 83–84.

78. Joseph Schumpeter, *Capitalism, Socialism, and Democracy* (New York: Harper and Row, 1950), p. 123.

79. Montesquieu, "De l'esprit des lois," II, 639 (XXI, 20).

80. Friedrich Nietzsche, "Jenseits von Gut und Böse," sec. 259, *Werke* (Darmstadt: Wissenschaftliche Buchgesellschaft, 1973), pp. 728–729.

81. Locke, *Two Treatises of Government,* p. 311 (II, 2, 6).

82. The paradoxical nature of this claim is worth stressing: liberalism is the quintessence of weakness, but it is also (lamentably) victorious. Note that Roberto Unger, in shifting from the antiliberalism of *Knowledge and Politics*

to the superliberalism of *Politics*, has merely exchanged a traditional Catholic for a Nietzschean criticism of liberal thought and institutions. His current position can be usefully compared to that of George Bataille, summarized and criticized persuasively in Jürgen Habermas, *The Philosophical Discourse of Modernity* (Cambridge, Mass.: MIT Press, 1987), pp. 211–237.

83. The myths of the state of nature and the social contract were monuments to the liberal belief in self-renunciation. To live civilly, individuals had to surrender their primordial right to act as executioners of the law of nature.

84. Wolff, *Poverty of Liberalism*, p. 172; Taylor, "Atomism," p. 210.

85. MacIntyre, *After Virtue*, 107. MacIntyre also believes that a shared commitment to instrumental reason helps explain the "deep cultural agreement" (ibid., p. 35) between capitalist and communist countries. His even-handed claim that "both ways of life are in the long run intolerable" recalls Heidegger's stupefying assertion that "America and Russia . . . are metaphysically the same" (*An Introduction to Metaphysics* [1935; New Haven: Yale University Press, 1959], p. 45).

86. Locke, *Two Treatises of Government*, p. 311 (II, 1.6). Adam Smith, *The Theory of Moral Sentiments* (Oxford: Oxford University Press, 1976), p. 234 (VI, ii, 2).

87. Taylor, "Atomism," p. 209.

88. Smith, *Wealth of Nations*, pp. 15, 384, 556. The best known illustration of Smith's pervasive concern for character formation occurs in his discussions of the division of labor (ibid., pp. 8–9, 735).

89. Will, *Statecraft as Soulcraft*, p. 72.

90. Taylor, "Atomism," p. 201.

91. This charge conflicts with the claim that liberals had *no* steady goals but were obsessed, instead, solely with the most efficient means to whatever ends happened to cross their minds.

92. Schmitt, *Concept of the Political*.

93. MacIntyre, *After Virtue*, p. 200.

94. They were engaged in an anticlerical polemic as well, aimed against the disregard, say, of physical health implied by the Christian single-mindedness about otherworldly salvation.

95. Andrzej Rapaczynski, *Nature and Politics: Liberalism in the Philosophies of Hobbes, Locke, and Rousseau* (Ithaca, N.Y.: Cornell University Press, 1987), pp. 150–170.

96. Wolin, *Politics and Vision*, pp. 316–317.

97. Locke, *Essay Concerning Human Understanding*, p. 120 (II, ii, 2).

98. According to Strauss, Rousseau had already argued that "enlightenment paves the way for despotism" ("On the Intention of Rousseau," *Hobbes and Rousseau*, ed. Maurice Cranston and Richard Peters [Garden City, N.J.: Doubleday Anchor, 1972], p. 267).

99. Unger, *Knowledge and Politics*, p. 75.

100. For two successful demolitions of this pattern of thought, see Luc Ferry and Alain Renault, *La pensée 68: Essai sur l'anti-humanisme contemporain* (Paris:

Gallimard, 1985), pp. 105–197; and Habermas, *Philosophical Discourse of Modernity*, pp. 238–293.

101. According to MacIntyre, those who criticize inherited group identity and unquestioned religious beliefs cannot replace what they tear down. Emancipation spells uprootedness. Kant and others tried to establish universal moral principles, addressing all rational human beings, regardless of their cultural heritage or social group. But their antilocalism was bound to fail. After the inevitable defeat of universalistic ethics, the average "post-Enlightenment person" was naturally propelled toward skepticism by sheer disappointment. Universalism breeds nihilism, which is why Nietzsche followed Kant with such unseemly haste (MacIntyre, *Whose Justice? Which Rationality?*, p. 353).

102. Nietzsche challenges the antiliberal orthodoxy here too, plausibly claiming that skepticism, far from disturbing, sedates ("Jenseits von Gut und Böse," *Werke*, sec. 208, p. 670).

103. Judith Shklar, "Injustice, Injury, and Inequality: An Introduction," in Frank Lucash, ed., *Justice and Equality Here and Now* (Ithaca, N.Y.: Cornell University Press, 1986), pp. 13–33.

104. Antonym substitution is a social process, not merely an intellectual fallacy. Its plausibility can be historically explained. For example, the opposition of markets to barbarism, of commercialism to rudeness and lack of civilization, while almost universally accepted in the seventeenth and eighteenth centuries, lost its original self-evidence through the upheavals accompanying the industrial revolution. The Enlightenment commonplace that commerce replaces war and tyranny was rudely undermined by subsequent experience. Although the nineteenth century misinterpreted the eighteenth, its misinterpretation can be understood as a natural response to shifting events. Even when convincingly explained, however, historiographical distortions remain distortions.

105. Albert Hirschman, *The Passions and the Interests: Political Arguments for Capitalism before its Triumph* (Princeton: Princeton University Press, 1977).

106. See Stephen Holmes, "The Secret History of Self-Interest," in Jane Mansbridge, ed., *Against Self-Interest* (Chicago: University of Chicago Press, 1989).

107. Wolin, *Politics and Vision*, p. 324; Will, *Statecraft as Soulcraft*, p. 45.

Acknowledgments

In 1988 the Conference for the Study of Political Thought sponsored a conference on the subject "Liberalism and the Moral Life." This was CSPT's twentieth international meeting, and the occasion for the presentation of many of the papers published here. As program organizer, I was supported by the hard work of Melvin Richter, chairman of CSPT, in obtaining funding and making local arrangements. His help was indispensable. I am grateful to him, and to Susan Tenenbaum, Young Kun Kim, and Mitchell Cohen for their contributions to the conference's success. The meeting was held at City University of New York, and thanks are due to Joseph S. Murphy, Chancellor; Dr. Steven Cahn, Provost, Graduate School CUNY; Dr. Donna Shalala, former President, Hunter College; and the Hunter College Faculty Delegate Assembly for their generous support.

Finally, I am grateful to Harvard University Press editors Aida Donald and Elizabeth Suttell for their persistence and patience in the difficult job of synchronizing the work of twelve authors, and to Ann Louise McLaughlin for her excellent work editing the manuscript.

N.L.R.

Contributors

Richard Ashcraft, Professor of Political Science, University of California at Los Angeles

Benjamin R. Barber, Walt Whitman Professor of Political Science, Rutgers University

Seyla Benhabib, Associate Professor of Philosophy and Women's Studies, State University of New York at Stony Brook

William Galston, Professor, School of Public Affairs, and Senior Research Scholar, Institute for Philosophy and Public Policy, University of Maryland

Amy Gutmann, Andrew W. Mellon Professor of Politics, Princeton University

Stephen Holmes, Professor of Political Science, University of Chicago

George Kateb, Professor of Politics, Princeton University

Steven Lukes, Professor of Political and Social Theory, European University Institute, Florence

Susan Moller Okin, Professor of Politics, Brandeis University

Nancy L. Rosenblum, Professor of Political Science, Brown University

Judith N. Shklar, John Cowles Professor of Government, Harvard University

Charles Taylor, Professor of Philosophy, Political Science, McGill University

Index